THE
NORTHERN
CHINESE
COOKBOOK

By the same authors

AN ENCYCLOPEDIA OF CHINESE FOOD AND COOKING

THE
NORTHERN
CHINESE
COOKBOOK

including specialities from

Peking,

Shanghai,

and Szechuan

Wonona W. and Irving B. Chang
Lillian G. and Austin H. Kutscher

CROWN PUBLISHERS, INC., NEW YORK

THIS BOOK IS DEDICATED WITH LOVE
TO THE MEMORY OF
Helene Wald Kutscher

ACKNOWLEDGMENTS

The authors wish to acknowledge with gratitude the assistance given in the preparation of this book by Mrs. Margot C. Wei and Mr. and Mrs. Carl Chou; and the many generous efforts of General and Mrs. H. H. Li and Mr. Jimmy Lee of the China Garden Restaurant, White Plains, New York.

*Printed in the United States of America
Published simultaneously in Canada by
General Publishing Company Limited*

Contents

Preface

Among the many legacies of ancient culture, the Chinese cuisine—fabulously endowed with the pleasures of taste, sight, texture, and aroma—has endured and been enhanced for centuries. The cuisine of China clearly ranks as one of the two great culinary traditions of the civilized world, not only because of its great variety of ingredients but because of the skill with which its chefs have blended and improvised with these ingredients. (The other great cuisine is that of France.)

Western culture has always assimilated Oriental influences into its own artistic forms and endeavors. Chinese designs decorate some of the most admired and beautiful European dinnerware, furniture, and fabrics—all objects that add to the pleasures of living. Certain food substances from China have also been accepted and have assumed importance as staples in the Western kitchen: tea, rice, noodles (and spaghetti), and spices, to name but a few. Yet the essential nature of the Chinese culinary art has not been fully integrated into Western—or "American"—cooking. A large number of ingredients still remain unfamiliar to us. Because of the difficulty encountered in obtaining them and because of the special skills necessary for the preparation of these ingredients prior to cooking, as well as the distinctive techniques involved in cooking them, we have often been slow in appreciating the remarkable qualities of the Chinese cuisine.

The Chinese chef was always prepared to face the challenge of each cooking technique and style, each flavoring spice or herb, each vegetable, fruit or meat. Forever creating new combinations and enlarging his basic repertoire, he became a true Tai See Foo, or master chef. Yet many of his outstanding dishes are unknown in this country.

Before World War II, the American public had been exposed exclusively to Cantonese food. Cantonese-style restaurants were popular then simply because more Chinese immigrants came to this country from Canton Province than from any other area of China. Because of its access to all types of ingredients, including seafood, Cantonese cooking was considered to be the ultimate in Southern Chinese cooking. But since the 1960s, with the arrival of chefs from the Northern, Western and Eastern Chinese provinces, many Chinese restaurants have begun adding to their menus dishes cooked in the tradition of these provinces. The American gourmet has now begun to enjoy newly introduced ingredients with their startling flavors; and he has begun to appreciate the variety of cooking styles and techniques of Chinese culinary art.

This cookbook offers to the "cooking American" Chinese recipes from the Northern, Western and Eastern provinces of China, as well as from its principal cities. Since China does not have an equivalent of our Mason-Dixon line, the points of demarcation between its north and south are represented mainly by centers of population concentration. The Northern region encompasses the general area of Peking, Tientsin, Tsingtao, Shantung, Kaifeng, and Loyang; the Western region includes Szechuan, Hunan, Hupeh, Chungking, Chentu, and Ichang; and the Eastern section encompasses Shanghai, Nanking, Hangchow, Suchow, Wusih, Ninpo, and Yangchow. Those recipes grouped under the heading, General, were prepared throughout China, and although some were originally derived from specific regions, all can be commonly considered Chinese.

The authors have tried to anticipate the problems of preparing a meal from an assortment of esoteric recipes. To this end many practical details have been included in this book, such as a uniform romanization of the Chinese names, Chinese characters and their English equivalents (to facilitate marketing in a Chinese grocery store or direct ordering menus from restaurants).

Each recipe, unless otherwise noted, serves four persons. A satisfying meal would include a soup and four entrees. If a larger quantity of food is needed, the recipes may be doubled. If more than double quantity is required, it is better to repeat the cooking procedure than to augment the quantity of the ingredients used in the preparation of one dish. Or, if the neophyte chef finds it too difficult to prepare and serve four different entrees, it is suggested that only two entrees be cooked in double quantity *or* that steamed, roasted, and cold dishes be served together with one or two stir-fried dishes to make a complete and delicious meal.

From the recipes in this book it should be possible for the Westerner to enjoy exciting new adventures in eating and cooking and to integrate into his cuisine some of the most exquisite elements of Chinese cooking.

THE AUTHORS

Utensils
for Cooking, Serving,
and Eating

IT IS POSSIBLE TO COOK CHINESE DISHES WITH READILY AVAILABLE American utensils, however desirable the authentic Chinese variety. Particularly useful are the American thermostatically regulated electric frying pans. These come in a wide range of sizes, shapes, and depths, and maintain heat at constant temperatures not possible with Chinese utensils. These electric pans achieve heat that rivals the better Chinese cooking utensils, as well as high-heat ranges, and are preferable to ordinary American utensils used on an electric range; quite possibly, many will find them preferable to the Chinese sort. They are capable of producing dishes equal to those of the traditional methods when slow, even cooking is required. The same results also can be achieved by a heavy aluminum pot on a gas range. Ranges in American and Chinese kitchens and restaurants differ markedly. American kitchen ranges are divided between gas and electric types; the former are far preferable for cooking Chinese food. With electric ranges, if the pot is not removed after the heating element is turned off, further cooking, perhaps overcooking, occurs.

Required for best cooking results are twelve tools, three being primary: a large sharp knife (often a cleaver), a hardwood cutting board (or chopping block), and a heavy smooth skillet (often the *wok*) or electric frying pan. The knife and cutting board are essential because knives are not set on the table; hence, practically all foods are served bite-size whether meat or vegetable, cooked sufficiently tender to be grasped by the chopsticks and eaten without further ado. Exceptions are the special dishes, such as whole fish, duck, or chicken, favored at banquets. These are cut in small portions at the table, and served. The other implements are as follows:

Cleaver

The blade of the cleaver is rectangular, approximately 3⅓ inches wide and 8 inches long; its back tapers from a thickness of ⅛ inch to a thinner, sharper, cutting edge; a cylindrically shaped wooden or bamboo handle about 4 inches long is attached at the end along the back. It handles easily, is well balanced, and should be kept extremely sharp. Once the cleaver's versatility and safety are discovered, one can understand why it is employed constantly by chefs.

It is used for chopping through bones (using powerful strokes, as when splitting poultry into halves, quarters, or smaller segments); chopping through the shells of lobsters and crabs; mincing all kinds of meats; scaling large whole fish and chopping the bones; pounding foods flat; tenderizing abalone or beef steaks; crushing, peeling, and pounding garlic, ginger, or onion; mashing; slicing vegetables; crushing Chinese condiments, such as black beans and garlic, into a paste; tearing and slicing ingredients, then scooping and transferring them from the chopping block to a pan or storage utensil. A thin-bladed cleaver is used for light-duty cutting; a heavier one for heavy-duty cutting.

The weight of the blade should be permitted to do the work—it is comparatively infrequent that any sawing back and forth is necessary if the blade cuts cleanly and sharply.

Because it is made of carbon steel, a highly rustable metal, it should not be left wet after washing but should be dried immediately and stored. Carbon steel is preferable to stainless steel because it takes an edge readily and consequently is sharpened easily.

Chopping Block

Actually, this is a smooth-surfaced tree cross section, 12 to 15 inches in diameter and 6 to 8 inches thick. It is used for heavy chopping, mincing, and boning, and gets constant use. Often a small auxiliary block is useful. A chopping block should never be soaked in water. It should be wiped clean with a wet sponge or rubbed with steel wool. When foods must be minced to a pulp or light slicing is to be performed, an ordinary cutting board similar to a breadboard may be used.

Rolling Pin

This is no more than a simple wooden roller, about 1½ inches in diameter and anywhere from 8 to 30 inches long. It is used for rolling dough thin or crushing nuts, and is very popular in China. A roller should never be soaked in water. It should be wiped clean with a moist sponge.

Pastry Board

This smooth-surfaced board is a rectangle about 22 by 28 inches, usually with two projections: a "stop" at each end, one to keep the board steady while dough is being formed into noodles, won-ton, etc., and another to prevent any flour from spilling out over the table and floor. It is also popular in China.

Wok

This is an iron pot that is much like a French frying pan. Its round bottom usually requires a metal ring to hold it steady on modern ranges. The ring sits on or straddles the top-of-the-range burner, permitting the heat to radiate over the wok's entire bottom surface. The ring is perforated with air holes all around to feed the flame and is an essential piece of equipment to be purchased with the wok.

Some woks are made of aluminum or copper. The round bottom provides flexibility in exposing portions to be cooked; also, the sauce and oil drain to the center where the heat is concentrated.

The wok's combined thinness and rounded bottom permit the quick cooking and concentrated heat employed in most Chinese recipes. Stirring is extremely simple. Heat is radiated quickly and is evenly distributed, and the wok's large cooking area is convenient for toss-cooking (in which ingredients are actually tossed), or cooking odd-shaped foods (a whole fish with head).

The wok's size depends upon the amount of food to be cooked (sizes range for from one to ten servings). Diameters range from 10 to 24 inches (the latter commonly used in restaurants). A 14-inch wok most often is recommended for the American kitchen. The 12-incher features an innovation—a frying-pan-type handle, and is handier and less cumbersome. Woks are available at Chinese groceries and at American hardware stores. Attachments include a cover (usually aluminum) and a deep cup for steaming or long cooking. It is one of the most practical utensils devised by man. It is an all-purpose cooking pan, with which many foods can be easily prepared —from stir-frying to braising, stewing, deep frying, steaming, smother-cooking, red-cooking, casserole steaming, poaching, toss-cooking, boiling, and light frying.

When purchased, the wok should be seasoned before it is used. Otherwise the food content will stick to it. It should be washed with hot water and soap, greased over the entire inside surface with peanut oil or any other kind of cooking oil, placed on its special ring over a high heat for about a minute, then rinsed with hot water, and the process repeated several times. Seasoning the wok with peanut oil seals the pores of the metal. This prevents the ingredients from sticking and avoids a metallic flavor in the food. After seasoning it should be washed carefully with hot water only. Any excess oil on the inside should be scraped or scoured, without soap. Scouring here is defined as rubbing with salt on a paper towel. Most often, residual gravy is scraped with a stiff brush and washed away in hot water. Gradually, as it becomes seasoned, the appearance of the wok changes from that of a shiny metal to black. It is then ready for use, after which, because it is made of iron, it should be dried immediately over heat, after rinsing, to prevent rusting.

Though for authenticity a wok is as desirable as a cleaver and chopsticks, the kitchen knife, fork, and electric skillet can replace these quite satisfactorily. The electric frying pan, thermostatically controlled, can for the most part do the work of the wok, especially large woks (their cooking temperatures may be difficult to control on the home burner). A cast-iron wok is preferable to any other. A skillet with a copper-lined bottom, though it is a rapid conductor, does not distribute heat evenly, and, hence, is inferior to the cast-iron wok—whose counterpart in American kitchens is the heavy frying pan. Some people might consider the wok an impractical luxury but doing without one means a considerable diminution of pleasure, if not a decrease in cooking effectiveness.

Ladle and Turner

The ladle is curved and the turner is flat. These are especially useful for stirring and turning quickly to prevent ingredients from burning. The ladle is held in the left hand and the turner in the right as the food is stirred with a circular motion, lifting and dropping it as in a tossed salad, but with care to avoid bruising the ingredients. A large metal spoon and a pancake turner are good substitutes.

Steaming Utensils

Improvised: An inverted flat-bottomed strainer is frequently used, or a small pan or pot perforated with many holes and inverted over a larger pot of boiling water—the water level kept to about three-fourths of the height of the perforated pan or pot. A round rack with legs about 3 inches high is also available, on which the steaming platter (able to withstand steam heat) may be placed.

The platter containing the ingredients to be steamed should be placed upon the inverted pot or strainer and the lid of the steamer placed tightly over. There must be adequate room for steam to circulate freely between food and cover. Additional boiling water may be added during prolonged steaming to avoid total evaporation (and burning of the pot). At the conclusion of steaming, the heat is turned off, and after a wait of a moment for the hot steam to dissipate itself the cover should be removed gently (with a kitchen glove to avoid scalding the hand). The pyrex or aluminum pan (or the food itself, such as a bun) is then removed, using a kitchen glove or a special three-pronged holder.

An electric frying pan may be substituted if it is deep enough to permit the placement of a rack, with two to three inches of boiling water coming up almost to the top level. A flat dish or bowl containing the ingredients to be cooked is placed on top of the rack.

Chinese steam racks, bamboo or aluminum: These are layers or tiers of bamboo mesh or aluminum, perforated trays—porous in construction—designed to permit full steam penetration from a large pot underneath. Water is boiled in the pot. The trays rest on the pot of boiling water and are covered with a large metal lid during the steaming process. The trays can also be stacked on a wok.

The dish containing the food for steaming should be placed on the steam tray. When the water is reboiled, the heat is turned down since rapid boiling does not provide more heat than slow boiling. The cautions and other comments on the improvised methods apply here as well.

As for the bamboo steamers, they are cumbersome and present a storage problem. Also, they have no handles for hanging. Steamers commonly found in this country are aluminum.

Strainers

These are flatter than the standard American variety and consequently better for maneuvering large objects in and out of a vessel of cooking fat. They are not essential.

Fire Pot or Mongolian Stove

This stove is made of brass or aluminum. It is about 15 inches or more in diameter, and features a metal "chimney" in its center in which charcoal is placed and burned. These central coals heat soup and other ingredients that are placed in the bowl surrounding the chimney.

A central stove is used much like a charcoal broiler, employing about six chunks of charcoal (lighter fluid may be used to help start the fire). When the coals are red hot, ingredients are added to the hot soup in the surrounding bowl or container. A cover fits around the chimney and over the bowl. Ingredients to be cooked should be placed on separate dishes around the firepot; also soup bowls, plates, and spoons. Everyone helps himself by picking up with chopsticks a slice of meat or vegetable, placing it in the boiling broth until cooked, and then extracting and eating it. Because the soup is boiling hot and the meat and vegetables are sliced thin, it takes no more than a few seconds' to a few minutes' cooking time; later the soup is served in the bowls, its flavor enhanced by the foods cooked in it.

This stove is essential for all fire-pot cooking, and, of course, it must be kept clean. It derives from the ancient Asian steppes, where nomadic tribes, gathered around a fire, cooked their food in a primitive cauldron by immersing chunks of meat on skewers. Today gourmets use the Mongolian stove in authentic festive fashions. A convenient substitute would be a deep thermostatically controlled electric frying pan.

Pressure Cooker

For red-cooking and other dishes requiring long cooking time and the tenderizing of tougher meat cuts, we have the pressure cooker. The general rules for its use are the same as those for American cooking. Fifteen pounds of pressure and about 20 minutes' cooking time are necessary.

Chopsticks

Gold, silver, ivory, coral, wood, and even twentieth-century plastics are available, but plain bamboo chopsticks are cheapest and perhaps best. Generally the top half is squared, the bottom half rounded and slightly tapered; average length is about 10 inches, with a 1/4-inch thickness at the top. Most chopsticks are durable and rarely break in use. Bamboo and wooden types are used in the kitchen since they can withstand high temperatures and do not alter the taste of the food. They are used as eggbeaters, cooking forks, mixing spoons, draining spoons, etc. Ivory chopsticks are equivalent to sterling silver. They must not become overheated or they will warp and turn yellow or brown. They should be washed in sudsy, lukewarm water and dried thoroughly.

To be eaten with chopsticks, food must be fragile enough to be easily broken into dainty pieces by these instruments or precut or presliced into segments that can be picked up easily. Noodles and rice in particular are eaten with chopsticks. Of the two, the rice is more readily picked up or, more properly, gently shoved into the mouth directly from the bowl.

Chopsticks are not difficult to manage. They are grasped a little below their midpoint, with the smaller ends toward the plate, or bowl. The upper chopstick is held between the pads of the thumb, index, and middle fingers. The lower chopstick remains stationary between the middle of the thumb and index finger and on the pad of the third finger, which supports it. Food is manipulated by the spreading movement of the upper chopstick to encompass the food and then the food is grasped with the aid of the lower chopstick. Firm and steady pressure will hold the food between the tips until it reaches the mouth. Too firm a pressure will cause the food-laden ends of the chopsticks to slip past each other, scattering the food on the plate.

A learner should not attempt to pick up everything without first discriminating between dull-surfaced objects, elusive, slippery objects, or indefinite loose particles. Dull-surfaced objects can be picked up directly with the chopsticks, whereas loose objects must be lifted by sliding the chopsticks under them and more or less scooping them up. The bowl should be held in the fingers or palm. This shortens the distance the food travels from bowl to mouth. To master the skill takes only a little practice and perseverance; an early clumsiness should not discourage one. As with any manual skill, it takes time to learn.

When a diner has finished eating, the chopsticks should be placed together—pointing away from him—on his bowl, thus indicating that, although he has finished eating, other guests should continue enjoying their food.

Eating with chopsticks is the best way to enjoy Chinese food since it permits just the right amount of sauce on a morsel.

Cooking
Preparations

ALTHOUGH NATIVE-BORN CHINESE IN AMERICA WOULD PREFER TO FOL-
low the methods of food preparation in just the same way as their
forefathers did, even to using the authentic utensils, it is totally impractical. Even the orthodox Chinese compromise with traditional
techniques, techniques that are laborious and cumbersome here.

Cutting

However, most Chinese still insist that their foods be brought to
the table cut to uniform size and shape, preferably bite-size, which
of course derives from Chinese cooking techniques. Several methods
are used to achieve this end: straight cutting, diagonal cutting, mincing, dicing, shredding, and strip-and-roll diagonal cutting.

In straight cutting, the knife should enter the meat or vegetable
at right angles to the board. The middle fingers of the left hand act
as a protective surface and guide; they are at right angles to the
food. Slices should be approximately 1 inch long and ⅛ inch thick.
Meats that are slightly frozen are easiest to cut. All are straight cut
against the grain.

In diagonal cutting, the knife enters at a 45° angle. This method
reduces cooking time because more surface is exposed to the heat,
ensuring tenderness and an attractive shape. The left hand (the
guiding, protective surface) should be relaxed and assume a 45°

angle. The cutting motion is a smooth, backward draw of a very sharp knife followed by a roll of the wrist to prevent slices from sticking together. Tender, fleshy vegetables (celery cabbage) or cylindrical or stalky vegetables (celery) are sliced diagonally—or French cut—to avoid a stringy texture.

In mincing, a previously sliced ingredient is cut into very fine pieces with a chopping motion. This is tedious but the Chinese believe it to be so superior that they prefer it to grinding. If ground meat is to be used, it should be ground only once at the coarsest setting.

Dicing produces the same effect as coarse mincing by cutting first in one direction and crosshatching in the other. Shredding cuts thinly sliced food into fine slivers. To shred meat, it should be straight sliced first then cut lengthwise into $\frac{1}{8}$- to $\frac{1}{4}$-inch shreds. To shred a fibrous vegetable (Chinese celery cabbage or celery), the stalk should be straight sliced (with the fibers) into 1- to $1\frac{1}{2}$-inch pieces, about $\frac{1}{8}$ inch wide. To shred a cylindrical vegetable (cucumber) it should be diagonally sliced, then shredded into $\frac{1}{4}$-inch slivers. To shred a firm vegetable, only the back end of the knife should be lifted; the tip remains on the board.

Stripping cuts a cylindrical vegetable (asparagus, carrot) diagonally as the left hand, after each slice, rolls the vegetable toward the cutter in such a way that the knife slices through part of the surface exposed by the previous cut. Stripping produces variously faceted shapes, which may not be as attractive as diagonal slicing.

As for fowl, the Chinese usually cut it into 2-inch pieces, without boning, which facilitates its handling by chopsticks. An advantage of the 2-inch size (at least) is that it makes for an easy cut and the juices and flavor are retained much better. Cuts can be made with a cleaver or poultry shears. Slicers, grinders, and blenders are frequently worth the time and effort saved by their use. However, Chinese chefs insist that there is a difference in the texture of foods prepared with such mechanical devices and do not favor these new conveniences for preparing meats.

Preparing Vegetables

After vegetables are cut, they are washed and drained and set aside for cooking. Frozen vegetables should be thawed completely before using, the pieces separated, and all excess moisture drained off. The Chinese housewife does not wash vegetables until the time of cooking because it is believed that once washed and put into the refrigerator, they may soften. Vegetables should not be left at room temperature for any length of time but should be kept in the refrigerator, preferably in the crisper compartment where light, water, air, and heat cannot reach them and affect their nutritional value. If it is necessary to wash vegetables long before using them, they should be placed in a plastic bag with holes. Vegetables with loose leaves that are washed too soon in advance tend to wilt and rot. Vegetables, especially nonleafy ones, are frequently parboiled beforehand to save time and to avoid overcooking the other ingredients in the recipe. Green vegetables are boiled in water only until they turn bright green, at which time they are removed and plunged briefly into cold water to retain their color, then set aside, ready to be cooked with the other ingredients. Salads consist of fresh, crisp, brightly colored and well-chilled vegetables tossed in a light oil (especially sesame oil in Mandarin foods because of its delicate flavor and fragrance); but any pure vegetable oil, including peanut oil, will do. Often, cold cooked meats or seafoods are added to make a more complete, filling dish. Ingredients should be washed well, dried, tossed lightly in the sauce, and then chilled in the refrigerator. Care must be taken not to leave the ingredients in the sauce too long or it may change their texture. General cooking-time rules are: lettuce, watercress, and bean sprouts require only 2 to 3 minutes; asparagus, bamboo shoots, celery, onions, snow peas, and string beans are stir-fried for about 3 to 5 minutes; Chinese cabbage and other leafy vegetables are stir-fried for 5 to 7 minutes; cucumbers, okra, tomatoes, yellow squash, and zucchini are stir-fried for about 5 minutes; eggplant and turnips, after being properly cut, the former into slices or cubes, the latter into slivers, are stir-fried for approximately 5 minutes; broccoli, brussels sprouts, cabbage, carrots, cauliflower, and corn are stir-fried for about 5 minutes.

When cooking green vegetables, whether stir-fried or boiled, never lift the lid more than once, to prevent deterioration of the green color. The lid is not required when reheating, and should never be used after cooking is complete to prevent the loss of natural colors and crispness.

Dried Ingredients

Dried ingredients (mushrooms, shrimp) should be soaked in hot water until soft. Certain varieties will require cleaning and resoaking in hot water until very soft. They can then be removed, drained, and cut as desired. The liquid often is used for making soup, or as a substitute for water or soup stock. The use of this water enhances rather than dilutes the flavor. Dry ingredients may be soaked in cold or lukewarm water until sufficiently expanded for thorough washing, while any unwanted parts (the tough stems of mushrooms) can be cut away. Occasionally squeezing and drying the ingredients following their removal from the water is necessary when only the flavor itself is desired in the final cooked dish.

Cornstarch

Meat is coated with cornstarch to give the surface a smooth texture and to prevent the loss of juices. The pan and oil must be sizzling hot (at which point the ingredients are added and must be turned constantly with a suitable instrument, with care not to break up the contents and cause a mushy consistency) to sear the meat and seal in its juices. Cornstarch is used also to thicken sauces: a mixture is prepared with stock in advance (½ cup of soup stock to 1 tablespoon of cornstarch) and mixed thoroughly just before introducing it into the cooking sauce so as to avoid lumpiness and to judge the amount needed. Boiling water should be available for diluting an overthick sauce. A high heat should be maintained when adding the cornstarch mixture, which is introduced slowly but continuously for about 30 seconds or until all the cornstarch is thoroughly incorporated. Cornstarch not only thickens sauce and ensures that all the ingredients are evenly coated but also gives the entire dish a bright, piping hot, glistening appearance.

Fats and Oils

The Chinese choose lard over butter in cooking since lard provides a rich flavor and a clear color. Also, butter is scarce because of the paucity of China's dairy products. However, in the United States, animal fat is not considered as healthful as vegetable oils; among vegetable oils most commonly employed for cooking are peanut oil, soybean oil, and sesame oil.

Peanut oil is a favorite of the Chinese. Sesame oil is used as a flavoring oil. Crisco and such fats are not suitable in Chinese cooking as they tend to gel when cold, thus spoiling the food's appearance and consistency. Soybean oil is widely used in China with results almost equal to those obtained with the more expensive peanut oil. Occasionally, sesame oil is used, which imparts an extremely distinctive flavor to any dish.

Peanut oil complements best the flavor of the foods cooked in it. When a high-heat recipe is to be followed, as in stir-fry or tossed cooking, peanut oil is especially useful since it can withstand a high temperature without smoking and is not likely to burn. When, in fact, it does smoke, it imparts a distinctive and desirable aroma and flavor. All these vegetable oils absorb little food odor and can be used over again for deep-fry cooking, whereas fats and oil that have a low-smoke temperature impart unpleasant flavors and odors retained from previous use.

Some *Tai See Foo*s, or master chefs, purify peanut oil before use. This entails pouring 5 cups of peanut oil into a pan, adding about 5 slices of ginger and I leek cut into several sections, and heating the oil until both the ginger and leek turn brown. These are then removed, and the oil is considered improved and ready for use. This practice also gives the oil an excellent aroma and imparts a unique flavor to the dishes in which it is used. One should be aware though that when cold the oil may turn cloudy without, however, any change in its properties or flavor.

Garlic

It is important to know just how long and at what heat garlic can be cooked without burning it, and also when to add ingredients. Generally, garlic is cooked until it stops sizzling in the oil. Ingredients are then added at once. This lowers the temperature, and the garlic does not burn, provided that all the ingredients are stirred at once, and constantly thereafter. To leave garlic in the pan (if it has been used in a large piece) or not is the cook's prerogative. It is usually preferable to use the minced form—which leaves the cook no choice.

Seasoning

Seasoning and condiments are used extensively in Chinese cooking to bring out the flavor inherent in food, as well as to induce the important chemical reaction between food and seasoning that occurs at high temperatures. Seasonings and soy sauce (light or heavy, which are not interchangeable) should be added after the meat or fish has been partially cooked, and applied gradually throughout the remaining cooking process. If added too early, they may cause a toughening of the meat. Salt, however, is nearly always added in full to the oil or water at the very outset, which tends to preserve the brightness of green vegetables. Marinating sauces and seasonings, popular with meats and vegetables, are often added hours or days before cooking for proper penetration or curing.

Most Chinese chefs add sugar to many of their dishes, and some add it to all dishes. These master chefs know that, like salt, sugar should be used to enhance food flavor. Almost any dish, Chinese or American, is improved by the addition of a half teaspoonful of granulated sugar.

Cooking Time

A cooking time is given for each recipe, but it is the degree of heat that is the controlling factor, and attention must be given to the appearance of the food. Timing and temperature can be approximate only because the type and quality of utensil and heating unit affect the required cooking time drastically.

Generally the cooking sequence is as follows. When meat and vegetables are to be combined in a single dish, often they are first cooked separately, since they usually require different cooking conditions, and are later combined in the wok. Vegetables should be cooked first because a waiting period generally will not impair their quality, though some chefs do not see any difference and cook the meat first. The pan should be oiled, preferably with peanut oil, and brought to intense heat, the vegetable sautéed (perhaps parboiled first) for a minute until it turns bright green. Short exposure to intense heat is the key to stir-frying vegetables for color appeal and crispness. Then the vegetable usually is removed from the pan and set aside while the pan, with peanut oil added, reheats to the same degree for the stir-frying of the meat. The meat is sautéed until it is about three-quarters done; if beef, the center should still be slightly red, and if pork, because a concern for health is more important than additional succulence, *it must always be completely cooked* (even in China) until all traces of pink disappear, and then it should be over-cooked slightly as additional ingredients are added. Stir-frying beef may take as little as thirty seconds before seasonings are added— the final addition usually is a sugar, stock, and cornstarch solution. Additional oil may be poured, but around the side of the pan so that it will be hot by the time it reaches the food. As for stock, meat and vegetables release their own juices so that its addition becomes a matter of personal preference. This practice of stretching a meal, although common in American kitchens, is frowned upon by the Chinese chef, who insists that every dish reaching the table be at its peak of taste perfection. However, if the preference is for stock, or water, unless otherwise specified, it should be added hot.

When the seasonings are added, the meat slices should be half-done. And when they are mixed with the meat, they, too, should be piping hot through having been added at the side of the pan. Pepper and certain other seasonings are added just before the dish is ready to be served, after the sugar has been added, in very small quantities. However, these are general rules, and are subject to change, depending on the recipe.

We all make mistakes, but it is the mark of a *Tai See Foo* to remedy them in time. If too much vinegar has been added, a pinch of salt will improve the taste. Conversely, if the dish is too salty, a little vinegar or sugar may help. When too cloying a taste is apparent, salt is the remedy; if too bland, a garnish may be added.

If, in the course of cooking, as in stir-fry, any ingredient shows signs of sticking or burning, a small amount of water should be added, and the stirring increased. The heat should not be lowered. There is nothing more distasteful to the Chinese gourmet than an overcooked vegetable, which is considered done when it is crisp and the flavor is at its height. But the taste should not be raw. Correct timing will come only through experience and training. Much depends on the nature and size of the vegetable, the heat, and the cooking utensil. Young, tender vegetables require less time. Color is an important guide to peak flavor. Remember that vegetables at their brightest color are at their pinnacle of taste and eye appeal.

Initially, it is wise not to attempt more than one stir-fry dish per meal and to depend instead upon steamed and boiled or other types of dishes that can be brought to the serving point and held at the proper temperature in a low oven (200°) or, if steamed, left in the vessel.

Generally, prepared dishes can await the completion of others if set in an oven at the lowest reading so as not to dehydrate or overcook them.

Organization is vital to success. In Chinese kitchens all dry ingredients and sometimes liquids, especially oil, are left in open containers near the range to be available for instant mixing. Other liquids are kept in containers with perforated tops to facilitate sprinkling or pouring. Ingredients are aligned in the order of use, all readily and instantly accessible. It is important that before cooking, everything be washed, where required, and arranged. Obviously, doing so in the midst of preparing a stir-fry dish will inevitably ruin the meal. But where possible it is wise to clean up along the way. Utensils and hands should be washed between handling different ingredients to avoid transmitting an alien flavor to any dishes prepared thereafter.

Whenever possible, groups of ingredients should be mixed beforehand, as indicated in the recipes; thus ingredients A, B, C are mixed and set aside, the D, E, F, G mixture prepared and set aside, and so on. Also, stock should be measured and set aside. This will save time and avoid confusion later. A considerable number of seasonings are frequently incorporated into the final cornstarch-and-water mixture. This is particularly true of the heavier soy sauce— a coloring and seasoning agent. Small mixing bowls or soup bowls that can be stacked are especially useful for holding cut ingredients such as meat or vegetables, as well as sauce mixtures. These bowls can then be stacked in the order of ingredients to be added to the stir-fry pan.

Proper planning should allow for all the elements of a meal to be served together and on time. For four persons having four entrees, 2 to 3 hours of preparation and cooking are usual.

Cooking Techniques

THE CHINESE EMPLOY WELL OVER A DOZEN COOKING METHODS, SOME uniquely Chinese, which will be described in detail.

Each technique is chosen carefully. The nature of the ingredients, the degree of heat, and timing are considered; certain techniques seal in juices, others importantly affect flavor, and so on.

Stir-Frying (Chao)

Ingredients are fried in a small amount of oil over very high heat with constant stirring until cooking is complete, usually within a few minutes. The only oil (peanut oil) needed is that required to cover completely the bottom of the frying pan. Stir-frying resembles sautéeing and is one of the most common methods of Chinese cooking. Stir-frying is best done in a wok.

All ingredients should be on hand before stir-frying is begun. Meat and vegetables should be thinly sliced or cut into small cubes. Before the oil is introduced the pan should be heated sufficiently so that the oil is free-flowing, and then the ingredients added, and stirred vigorously and continuously during the entire cooking period. The highest heat obtainable must be used, while constantly stirring, since stir-fried dishes can be ruined in a matter of seconds. Burned spots in the pan should be wiped with a paper towel and the pan reoiled for further use. This rapid form of cooking leaves comparatively little sauce.

Since stir-frying requires only a few minutes, such dishes are usually the last to be prepared; obviously, they are at their best when served immediately from the pan. Recommended cooking times are only approximate. Stir-frying preserves color, texture, and taste as well as nutritional values.

Steaming or Wet Steaming

Here the food is prepared in a chamber of steam comprised of a large pot filled one-third with water and separated into two compartments either by a perforated metal sheet or a rack. Ingredients are placed above the water level so that they will not be touched, but steamed, by the water, which of course is boiling vigorously before the ingredients are inserted. This method is not to be confused with the Western-style double boiler. Steaming is extremely popular because it is simple and does not require constant attention. The steaming utensil should have a tight-fitting lid but one which permits a slow escape of steam to prevent too much pressure building up inside. After a high heat has brought the water to a boil, and the ingredients inserted, the heat is lowered as the steaming process begins (to avoid vibrations and a burned pot). If the food has been placed initially on a serving platter, there will be no need to transfer it to another platter for serving at the table. Once cooked, food should not be left in the steamer unless the heat has been turned off before cooking is complete, after which the cooking process continues for a few minutes. Thus overcooking is avoided.

Steaming preserves flavors and food nutrients through the use of steam temperature rather than higher temperatures that destroy or leach these values in discarded boiling water. Several tiers can be used in the steamer to cook different foods simultaneously. Cooking time usually varies between 15 to 30 minutes for meat patties but can range from 20 minutes to 5 hours (which may require more water), depending upon the type of food to be steamed. However, meats cooked in this fashion must be of top quality. While steaming is often the best method for reheating leftover steamed meats, steamed fish and seafoods often become tough and lose flavor upon reheating.

Steaming is especially useful for persons recovering from gastrointestinal ailments, as well as for infants, because such dishes are easily digestible and are rich in natural flavor. Steamed Pork with Water Chestnuts; Steamed Pork Patties; Steamed Eggs with Minced Meat; Minced Pork (a smooth dish like a custard is obtained, but with meat interspersed); Dem Sem (wrapped meat balls), all require the steaming method. Sometimes a bowl with the ingredients is immersed partially in the boiling water, and a lid is placed over the entire steaming utensil but none over the bowl, so that the cooking action is performed both by the boiling water on the outside of the bowl and the steam directly on the food.

Red Stewing or Red Cooking

Red stewing is uniquely Chinese, similar to ordinary stewing, but here the food is cooked in large quantities of soy sauce and water rather than in water alone. It is the soy sauce that makes the dish rich, tasty, and reddish brown. It is usually made of pork, beef, ham, chicken, duck, or carp. When these are prepared without soy sauce, but by the same technique, the color will always be light.

The technique is essentially that employed for making American beef stew. It is often necessary to brown the meat first. The laden pot is brought to a boil over high heat, which is progressively reduced until quite low. Red stewing is used primarily for cooking meats, and if vegetables are to be included, they should be fresh and added just before the dish is served, and only in relation to the quantity of stew being served; reheating leftover vegetables overcooks them. Various condiments are added to red-stewed dishes: sherry, ginger, scallions, and so on.

An exact cooking time is not critical. Meat may stew one to six hours, depending on the cut of meat, and may even be cooked a day ahead and rewarmed. In fact, with some dishes the flavor may be enhanced if the stew is refrigerated. It may be kept so for a week and sometimes reheated a number of times without harm. When served cold, vegetables should *not* be added. *Hung-shu* bean cake, squab, and chicken are commonly served cold. Cooked stew can also be poured into a mold and chilled, so that the sauce will become a rich aspic.

Boiling

In parboiling, ingredients are cut and washed first, then put in a large pot in which they can float freely, over high heat. Vegetables to be eaten crisp, like broccoli, are removed from the water just before they come to a full boil; those that cannot be eaten raw or take a long time to cook should remain in the pot for whatever time is required after boiling starts. Slow and prolonged boiling destroys flavor to some degree and certainly much nutritional value is lost in the boiling water that is discarded. Parboiled ingredients are poured with the water into a colander, rinsed or soaked in cold water until thoroughly cooled, and used as the recipe directs, or in salads. Parboiled vegetables are often used in banquet dishes where time may be limited. For full boiling, as in preparing soups, the Chinese employ a slow simmering process. As soon as the water boils, the heat is turned low and the soup allowed to simmer for whatever period of time is necessary. However, preparing soups by rapid boiling in which intense heat is used will result in the same preservation of color, texture, shape, and nutrition as in tossed cooking.

Deep Frying

Ingredients are introduced into 2 inches (or more for conventional-type fryers) of very hot oil, generally 350° to 375° F. (The oil may be saved for future use except when fish has been fried in it.) To avoid spattering, foods should be dried first. Only foods that require a few minutes' cooking time, like shrimp, can be cooked in this fashion. Many meat or poultry dishes cannot be prepared this way because either they will be raw on the inside or burned on the outside, or they will break into little pieces. (Squab, duck, and pheasant often are precooked by steaming before they can be deep fried.)

Deep frying is very similar to what is done in making French-fried potatoes. Peanut oil is heated to 375°. A deep electric frying pan best maintains the oil at the proper temperature but an oil thermometer can be used. Ingredients usually are marinated in a sauce and then coated with cornstarch, flour, or breading before being slipped into the deep oil gently and deep fried until they become tender and deep golden brown. The marinade usually consists of soy sauce, sherry, and other seasonings, in which the ingredients are soaked for about half an hour. Adding water-chestnut flour to batter assures a crispy, crunchy texture to the outside portion of fried foods.

Meat should be cut into medium-sized pieces. If fish is to be served whole, deep gashes should be cut on either side of the fish so that the salt that is rubbed on can penetrate the skin. This type of frying must be done quickly. Coating will preserve the flavor and moisture.

Though the food is ready when it turns a golden brown (depending upon its density and size), some cooks use as an indicator the time at which the batter-coated food floats to the surface of the oil.

Shallow Frying

Shallow frying requires medium heat and a longer cooking time than deep frying. After heating sufficient oil to cover the entire bottom of the pan, ingredients are spread evenly in the pan and allowed to fry slowly for a few minutes, turned over once or twice, browning both sides. This technique seals in juices in meats and is particularly useful for the final cooking of prefried or preboiled foods.

Barbecuing

Barbecuing is done over charcoal on a spit or grill, or on a rotisserie.

Roasting

The Chinese do their roasting in ovens over a charcoal fire, with frequent basting. In this country, the roasting of many Chinese foods (a whole side of pig, etc.) is usually left to the large shop-keepers who specialize in it. However, Chinese roast dishes may be prepared in Western stoves according to directions indicated, with excellent results.

Cold Mixing

Scalded or parboiled ingredients are mixed in salads and chilled before serving. Once used for hygienic reasons, parboiling is now used to tenderize vegetables.

Poaching

This method is similar to that of American-style poached eggs, that is, cooked in liquid just below the boiling point. A whole chicken can be prepared in this manner. Poaching is especially good for cooking delicate fish or boned fowl in a clear soup, slowly simmering until the meat is tender.

Recipes

APPETIZERS

Dien sing (dem sem), which means "pointing to your heart's desire," is the literal translation for Chinese appetizers. They are generally not the sweet kind and are often fried, steamed, or sometimes boiled. They can be served at cocktail hour, with afternoon tea, or as a midnight snack. They also make a good businessman's lunch.

JAO TZE (CHINESE RAVIOLI)
Jao Tze: Peking   餃 子

A. 2 slices ginger, chopped
B. 2 scallions, chopped
C. 1 lb. ground pork (or beef)
D. 1 cup chopped Chinese celery cabbage
E. 1 tablespoon light soy sauce
F. ½ teaspoon salt
G. 1 teaspoon sherry
H. 1 teaspoon cornstarch
I. 1 teaspoon sesame oil
J. 30 jao tze wrappings (see Wrapping for Jao Tze)

PREPARATION:

I. Mix A, B, C, D, E, F, G, H, I thoroughly.
II. Fill each J with A–I meat mixture. Fold over and shape in half moon. Press edge tight.

COOKING:

1. Put jao tze into 3 qts. boiling water. When it boils again, add 1 cup cold water. Repeat once. On final boil, remove jao tze and serve with vinegar and soy sauce.

WRAPPING FOR JAO TZE (CHINESE RAVIOLI)
Jao Tze Pei: Peking   餃 子 皮

A. 2 cups flour
B. ¼ teaspoon salt
C. ½ cup water

PREPARATION:

I. Sift A, B together.
II. Add C, mix well, and cover with cloth 25 minutes.
III. Knead thoroughly on floured board; shape A–C into several long strips. Cut each into several chestnut-size pieces, about 30 altogether. Shape each into a ball and roll into thin 3-inch-round patties.
IV. If jao tze is to be fried, use hot water.

1

FRIED JAO TZE
Go Te: Peking

鍋 貼

A.   2 tablespoons peanut oil
B.   ¼ lb. ground pork
C.   ½ lb. shrimp
D.   2 cups chopped Chinese celery cabbage*
E.   3 slices ginger, chopped
F.   2 tablespoons chopped scallion
G.   1½ tablespoons light soy sauce
H.   ½ teaspoon salt
I.   1 teaspoon sherry
J.   1 teaspoon cornstarch
K.   1 teaspoon sesame oil
L.   jao tze wrappings (see Wrapping for Jao Tze)
M.   ⅓ cup soup stock

PREPARATION:

I.   Shell, devein, and mince C.
II.   Parboil D in boiling water for 1 minute and drain.
III.   Mix B, C, D, E, F, G, H, I, J, K thoroughly.
IV.   Fill center of each L with 1 teaspoon B–K mixture. Fold over and shape in half moon. Press edge tight.

COOKING:

1. Heat frying pan until very hot. Add A. Turn off heat.
2. Arrange jao tze in single layer in frying pan. Cover and brown over low heat 5 minutes. Sprinkle in half of M, cover and cook 5 minutes.
3. Sprinkle in the rest of M, cover and cook for another minute. It is not necessary to turn the jao tze.
4. Serve with vinegar and soy sauce or hot sauce.

   * Frozen chopped spinach may be substituted for Chinese celery cabbage. Defrost and squeeze out water before mixing with other ingredients.

GOLDEN PUFF WITH SWEET BEAN PASTE
Gow Li Dow Sa: Peking

高 力 豆 沙

A.   2 cups peanut oil for deep frying
B.   2 egg whites
C.   1 tablespoon flour
D.   1 tablespoon cornstarch
E.   ½ cup sweet bean paste (filling)

PREPARATION:

I.   Beat B until fluffy.
II.   Add C, D, continue to beat until B forms stiff peaks.
III.   With teaspoon, scoop up E; use another spoon to form into about 10 little balls.
IV.   Roll over B–D, so that each is well coated.

COOKING:

1. Heat A 325°, deep fry B–E for 1 to 2 minutes or until golden brown. Drain on paper towel.

CHICKEN CONGEE
Gee Tso: Peking

雞 粥

A. 1 qt. chicken soup
B. ½ cup rice
C. 2 qts. water
D. 2 tablespoons light soy sauce
E. 3 slices ginger, shredded

F. 1 tablespoon sesame oil
G. 3 scallions
H. salt to taste
I. black pepper to taste
J. 8 fried puffs (see Index)

PREPARATION:

I. Wash B.
II. Combine D, E, F, G.

III. Cut J into ½-inch segments.

COOKING:

1. Place A, B, C in a large, heavy cooking utensil. Bring to boil. Lower heat and simmer 60 minutes. Stir every 10 minutes to avoid scorching bottom of congee.

2. Add additional water when congee becomes too thick. Cook 30 minutes more.
3. Add D–G mixture and adjust with H, I. Serve in individual bowls, sprinkle with J.

DUCK CONGEE*
Ya Tso: Shanghai

鴨 粥

A. 4 Chinese mushrooms
B. ¼ cup chopped Virginia ham
C. ½ cup raw, skinless peanuts
D. ½ cup glutinous rice

E. 13¾-oz. can chicken broth
F. 1 duck breast
G. 2 teaspoons sherry
H. ½ teaspoon salt

PREPARATION:

I. Bone F and cut into cubes, drop into boiling water, let stand 30 seconds, drain.
II. Mix F, G, H, steam over boiling water 1 hour. Save liquid.

III. Wash A, soak in warm water 15 minutes. Drain, saving water. Add water to E to make 2 qts. liquid. Quarter each A.
IV. Wash C, D; drain.

COOKING:

1. Combine A, B, C, D, E, add liquid from steamed F, and bring to boil. Reduce heat, simmer 1 hour.

2. Add F pieces, serve hot, and garnish with Chinese parsley.

* This dish is generally served as a late-night snack.

FRIED WALNUTS
Tza Heh Tao: Hunan

A. 2 cups peanut oil
B. 2 cups shelled walnuts

C. 1 cup sugar
D. ⅔ cup water

PREPARATION:

I. Pour boiling water over B. Let stand 1 to 2 minutes. Peel off skin and dry on paper towels.

II. Mix C, D. Add to B, stir until B is well coated.
III. Remove to plate and let cool.

COOKING:

1. Heat A to 300°. Add B–D mixture, stir-fry until golden brown (about ½ to 1 minute).

2. Drain on paper towels, let cool, and serve.

SHRIMP TOAST
Sha Tze Mein Bao: Shanghai　　蝦 子 麵 包

A. peanut oil to fill deep-fat fryer
B. ½ lb. small shrimp
C. 12 water chestnuts, minced
D. 1 egg white
E. 1 tablespoon light soy sauce

F. ½ teaspoon salt
G. 1 teaspoon sherry
H. 1 tablespoon cornstarch
I. 6 slices white bread

PREPARATION:

I. Shell, devein, wash, and mince B.
II. Mix B, C, D, E, F, G, H.
III. Remove crust from I and cut into 1-inch squares.
IV. Liberally spread each square of I with B-H mixture.

COOKING:

1. Heat A in deep fryer.
2. Deep fry B–I face down in A at 300° until light brown. After 2 to 3 minutes, turn over and fry ½ minute more.
3. Remove; drain well; serve with duck sauce.

RINGING BELL
Shang Ling: Hangchow　　響 鈴

A. 2 cups peanut oil
B. 2 tablespoons hoisin sauce
C. anise pepper salt to taste
D. ½ lb. ground pork
E. 1 egg

F. 2 teaspoons sherry
G. 1 teaspoon salt
H. 8 pieces fresh bean curd skin
I. 1 tablespoon scallion, chopped

PREPARATION:

I. Mix D, E, F, G well.
II. Place ⅛ of D–G mixture across each piece of H, about 2 inches below top, spread out 1½ inches wide.
III. Fold over, press down on D–G mixture, then roll.
IV. Cut each roll into 4 to 5 pieces about 1½ inches long.

COOKING:

1. Heat A to 350°. Deep fry rolls until golden brown, about 2 to 3 minutes.
2. Serve with B, C, mixed. Garnish with I. (Dish becomes so crispy that when chewed it is said to sound like the ringing of a bell.)

STEAMED LITTLE BAO TZE WITH BEEF
Niu Ro Tong Bao: Shanghai　　牛 肉 湯 包

A. 2 cups flour
B. ¾ cup water
C. 1 cup ground beef chuck
D. 1 cup chopped water chestnuts
E. 2 tablespoons Chinese parsley
F. 1 teaspoon light soy sauce
G. ½ teaspoon sesame oil
H. ½ teaspoon sugar
I. ½ to 1 teaspoon salt (to taste)

PREPARATION:

I. Combine A, B, mix well. Knead into a soft dough. Cover, let stand at room temperature 30 to 60 minutes, while preparing filling, as follows:
II. Combine C, D, E, F, G, H, I; mix.
III. Knead dough, then divide into 24 parts. Roll as thin as possible. Place 1 to 2 teaspoons of filling in center of each piece; then wrap each.

COOKING: 1. Steam 15 to 20 minutes. Serve hot.

STEAMED LITTLE BAO TZE WITH PORK
Tsu Ro Tong Bao: Shanghai   豬 肉 湯 包

A. 2 cups flour
B. ¾ cup water
C. 1 cup ground pork
D. ½ cup chopped frozen shrimp
E. ½ cup chopped bamboo shoots
F. 1 tablespoon chopped scallion

G. 1 teaspoon chopped ginger
H. 1 teaspoon salt
I. ½ teaspoon sugar
J. ½ teaspoon sesame oil
K. 2 teaspoons light soy sauce

PREPARATION:

I. Combine A, B, mix well. Knead into a soft dough. Cover, let stand at room temperature 30 to 60 minutes, while preparing filling, as follows:

II. Combine C, D, E, F, G, H, I, J, K; mix thoroughly.

III. Knead dough, then divide into 24 parts. Roll as thin as possible. Place 1 to 2 teaspoons of filling in center of each piece; then wrap each.

COOKING:

1. Steam 20 to 25 minutes. Serve hot.

CHICKEN BAO
Gee Bao: General   雞 包

A. 4 tablespoons peanut oil
B. 1 tablespoon chopped scallion
C. 1 teaspoon chopped ginger
D. 10 black mushrooms
E. 1 cup chopped bamboo shoots
F. ½ lb. chicken (white meat)

G. ½ tablespoon light soy sauce
H. 2½ tablespoons oyster sauce
I. 1 teaspoon sugar
J. 3 teaspoons cornstarch
K. ¼ cup mushroom water
L. 1 to 1½ teaspoons salt to taste

PREPARATION:

I. Soak D in hot water 15 to 30 minutes or until soft. Drain and save water. Chop D.

II. Chop F.

III. Mix G–L.

COOKING:

1. Heat A. Add B, C. Stir-fry 15 seconds.
2. Add D, E and stir 1 minute.
3. Add F, mix well, and cook 1 to 2 more minutes.
4. Add G–L to thicken.
5. Cool thoroughly and use as filling for Snow-White Steamed Bread (see Index).

DRIED SHRIMPBURGERS
Sha Tze Ro Bing: General   蝦 米 肉 餅

A. 10 dried shrimp
B. 1 large onion, chopped
C. 1½ lbs. ground chuck

D. 1 egg
E. 1½ tablespoons light soy sauce
F. 1 teaspoon salt

PREPARATION:

I. Soak A in warm water 10 minutes; shred A fine.

II. Mix A, B, C, D, E, F and make 8 to 10 patties.

COOKING:

1. Grease pan and cook A–F as hamburgers.

EGG ROLLS (SPRING ROLLS)
Chwin Guen: General

春 捲

A. 2 tablespoons peanut oil
B. ½ cup ground pork
C. ¼ cup minced raw shrimp
D. ½ cup shredded Chinese cabbage
E. 1 small onion, chopped
F. ½ cup chopped water chestnuts

G. ½ teaspoon salt
H. ¼ teaspoon pepper
I. ⅛ cup light soy sauce
J. 1-lb. pkg. egg roll skins, fresh
K. 1 egg white
L. 3 cups peanut oil

PREPARATION:

I. Beat K until stiff.

II. Mix D, E, F, G, H, I. Set aside.

COOKING:

1. Put A in very hot skillet and bring to high heat.
2. Add B. Stir-fry 2 minutes.
3. Add C. Stir-fry 3 minutes.
4. Add D–I mixture. Stir-fry 3 minutes.
5. Remove from heat. Cool and drain.
6. Place 2 to 3 tablespoons of cooked B–I mixture in center of each J in shape of an oblong mound.
7. Fold one long side of J skin over stuffing; then both short ends; fold over remaining long side.
8. Seal with K.
9. Heat L in deep-fat fryer to 375°. Fry egg rolls in deep-fat fryer to deep gold color and crisp texture.
10. Remove and drain on paper towels.
11. Serve with duck sauce and mustard, or soy sauce and vinegar.

WON TONS
Won Ton: General

雲 吞

A. 1 egg
B. ½ lb. ground pork
C. 1 tablespoon chopped scallion
D. 8 water chestnuts, chopped
E. 1 teaspoon salt
F. ⅛ teaspoon pepper and a dash of MSG (optional)

G. ½ teaspoon sesame oil to taste
H. 1 teaspoon soy sauce
I. 12 won ton skins (see following recipe for Wrapping Skin for Won Tons)

PREPARATION:

I. Beat A.
II. Mix A, B, C, D, E, F, G, H well.
III. Cut each I into quarters.

COOKING:

1. Fill each I with ½ to 1 teaspoon A–H mixture. Shape each into a cap to make won tons by drawing the four corners together and seal by pressing gently at juncture.
2. Boil 4 qts. water, add won tons, bring to boil, and cook 5 minutes. Drain won tons in colander, run cold water over won tons to cool. Cooked won tons can be frozen or left in refrigerator for a few days.

WRAPPING SKIN FOR WON TONS
Won Ton Pi: General　　雲 吞 皮

A. 2 cups flour
B. 1 teaspoon salt
C. 2 large eggs

PREPARATION:

I. Sift A, B together.
II. Beat C, then blend thoroughly with A–B mixture. Knead until dough is smooth. Cover with a wet paper towel and let stand 15 minutes.
III. Knead once more, then roll dough on floured board until it is paper-thin, making sure that board is well dusted with flour.
IV. Cut into 5 to 6 dozen 3½-inch-square won ton wrappings. If these are not to be used immediately, they may be stacked together with each piece being well floured. Wrap stack in aluminum foil and place in refrigerator. This can be kept for about a week. If the squares become hard or dry, remoisten by wrapping them in a damp towel.

Won ton skins can also be purchased in most Chinese grocery stores. These can be frozen and thus stored for months.

FRIED SWEET WON TONS
Tza Sue Won Ton: Shanghai　　炸 素 雲 吞

A. vegetable oil for deep frying
B. 4 teaspoons sesame seeds
C. ½ cup peanut butter
D. ½ cup packed brown sugar
E. 40 won ton skins

PREPARATION:

I. In small frying pan, heat and brown B; shake so that they do not scorch. Remove from heat when golden.
II. Mix B, C, D thoroughly.
III. Lay out E. Moisten outside to ½ inch from edge; place about ½ to 1 teaspoon B–D filling in centers; fold over, press, and seal edges. Then fold like a nurse's cap.

COOKING:

1. Heat A to 375°; fry won tons 1 to 2 minutes until golden; drain on paper towel.

SWEET WON TONS WITH TANGERINES
Jing Jiu Sue Won Ton: Shanghai　　金 橘 素 雲 吞

A. ½ cup chunky style peanut butter
B. ½ cup packed brown sugar
C. 40 won ton skins (see Wrapping Skin for Egg Rolls and Won Tons)
D. 3 large tangerines or oranges
E. ¼ cup sugar
F. 2 to 4 teaspoons sherry

PREPARATION:

I. Mix A, B thoroughly.
II. Lay out C one at a time. Moisten outside to ½ inch from edge. Put ½ to 1 teaspoon filling A–B in center of each; fold over, press, and seal edges. Then fold like a nurse's cap.
III. Peel D; remove white rind and seeds; place tender meat in 4 to 6 serving bowls.

COOKING:

1. Boil 1 qt. water, add E and filled C. Allow C to boil 1 to 2 minutes; scoop out C.
2. Just before serving, add ½ to 1 teaspoon F to bowls; add hot C and serve.

NEW YEAR'S DUMPLINGS I
Hwa Sun Jiang Tong Yuen: General
花 生 醬 湯 圓

A. 2 cups glutinous rice flour
B. 1 cup water
C. ¼ cup peanut butter (chunk style)
D. ¼ cup brown sugar, packed
E. 1 teaspoon sesame seed
F. 6 teaspoons brown sugar for serving

PREPARATION:

I. Mix A, B into smooth dough; roll into about 30 1-inch balls.
II. Mix C, D, E well.
III. Flatten dough balls by hand into 2-inch discs. In center of each disc, place 1 teaspoon C–E mixture. Fold dough over, seal edges, and roll back into balls.

COOKING:

1. Boil 1½ qts. water in large saucepan. Add dumplings, stirring to prevent sticking. When dumplings float, simmer 7 more minutes.
2. For each serving, place 1 teaspoon F in a bowl, add hot water and 5 dumplings.

NEW YEAR'S DUMPLINGS II
Ro Tong Yuen: General
肉 湯 圓

A. 2 cups glutinous rice flour
B. 1 cup water
C. 4 oz. ground pork
D. ¼ cup chopped celery cabbage
E. 1 slice ginger, minced
F. ¼ teaspoon cornstarch
G. 7 drops sesame oil
H. ½ teaspoon light soy sauce
I. ¼ teaspoon sherry
J. 2 tablespoons minced scallion
K. 1 qt. chicken broth
L. ⅛ teaspoon MSG (optional)

PREPARATION:

I. Mix A, B into smooth dough; roll into about 30 1-inch balls.
II. Mix C, D, E, F, G, H, L and half of J well.
III. Flatten dough balls by hand into 2-inch discs. In center of each disc, place 1 teaspoon C–J mixture. Fold dough over, seal edges, and roll back into balls. Cook 10 at a time.

COOKING:

1. Boil 1½ qts. water in large saucepan. Add 10 dumplings, stirring to prevent sticking. When dumplings float, simmer 10 more minutes.
2. Bring K to a boil, add rest of J. Remove from heat, transfer K to 6 small bowls, and add 5 dumplings per serving. Serve hot.

ROAST PEANUTS
Kow Hwa Sun: General
烤 花 生

A. 3 cups shelled skinless raw peanuts
B. 1 teaspoon salt

PREPARATION:

I. Wash and drain A.
II. Add B, mix well.
III. Line 12- by 18-inch cooky sheet with aluminum foil.
IV. Spread single layer of A over foil.

COOKING:

1. Preheat oven to 325°.
2. Bake prepared A 25 minutes, turn over gently, bake 5 more minutes.
3. Turn over once more, bake 5 minutes.
4. Wait until peanuts are completely cool before storing in jar.

FRIED PUFFS
Yo Tiao: General   油 條

A. 2 qts. peanut oil
B. 1 envelope yeast
C. ½ cup lukewarm water
D. 1 teaspoon baking soda

E. 1 teaspoon salt
F. 1 teaspoon ammonium alum
G. 1 cup flour plus supply for pastry board

PREPARATION:

I. Dissolve B with C in bowl.
II. Add D, E, F, mix well.
III. Add G, stirring until well blended.
IV. Cover bowl with clean towel or lid; let stand at room temperature for 4 to 6 hours.
V. Sprinkle a little flour on pastry board; roll out one-half of dough into a strip 4 to 5 inches long and ¼ inch thick. (If dough is hard to handle, sprinkle a little more flour over it.) Cut into 10 to 12 strips. Repeat procedure with remaining half of dough.
VI. Place two strips together, one on top of the other and make lengthwise indentation down the middle with the back of a knife. Make 10 to 12 strips.

COOKING:

1. Heat A in deep-frying pan to 380° to 400°.
2. Holding a strip with two hands, stretch out as long as possible. Twist it around itself one or two times; drop into A.
3. Using chopsticks, tumble strip as it deep fries.
4. When strip is golden brown, remove from oil and drain on paper towel. Serve hot.

PORK MUSHROOM BAO
Dung Gu Ro Bao: General   冬 菇 肉 包

A. 2 tablespoons peanut oil
B. 10 medium Chinese black mushrooms
C. 1 scallion, minced
D. 1 lb. pork, minced
E. 2 tablespoons cornstarch

F. 4 tablespoons mushroom water
G. 1 tablespoon light soy sauce
H. 1 teaspoon salt
I. ½ teaspoon sugar
J. Snow-White Steamed Bread dough

PREPARATION:

I. Wash B, cover with hot water, soak 10 minutes; drain, saving water, and mince.
II. Mix E, F, G, H, I well.

COOKING:

1. Heat A in pot. Add B, C and stir-fry 30 seconds.
2. Add D. Stir-fry 2 minutes.
3. Add E–I, stir until well mixed. Wait until pork mixture is cold before it is used for stuffing.
4. Stuff J.
5. Cool thoroughly and use as filling for Snow-White Steamed Bread. Makes 32 Bao Tzes. Bao Tze can be frozen and resteamed.

LOTUS ROOT CHIPS
Ngo Bing: General   藕 餅

A. 2 fresh lotus root sections
B. 2 cups peanut oil
C. salt to taste

PREPARATION:

I. Peel A with potato peeler. Cut crosswise into thin slices (1/16 inch).
II. Have B heating in deep fryer.

COOKING:

1. Deep fry A in B at 370°F. until slices are deep golden brown.
2. Remove; drain well; sprinkle with C. Serve instead of potato chips.

SOUP

Since the Chinese are not in the habit of drinking water at the table (tea is traditionally served at the end of the meal), soup is usually served, as a beverage, throughout the meal.

Two soups are served at banquets, one in the middle, and one at the end of the feast, when a few heavy courses appear, accompanied by rice.

The Chinese often add soup to their rice, in the bowl. Soups may be classified as light or heavy. Light soups, usually clear and with meat cooked only until done and tender, are often served at dinner when there are a number of other dishes. Certain smooth, velvety soups (avoiding lumps at all costs), such as egg drop soup, are rich in flavor but are actually quite light. Sour pungent soup has an intriguing, unusual, and distinctive flavor but is not filling. However, for family lunches and light dinners, a "meal in a pot" soup is often concocted, which may include any number of ingredients.

Leftover rice may be cooked to make a thick congee, or liquid or semiliquid soup. Noodles may be combined with mushrooms, sliced abalone, chicken, ham, or celery for a satisfying noodle soup. In other instances, a clear chicken stock may be heated with leftover ingredients that have been cut into strips or shredded.

Stock rather than water should be used whenever possible, because of the flavor and nourishment it adds. In making stock, the

Chinese use bones, such as from the neck and back, and meat scraps, as well as the liquid in which the vegetables have been cooked, the liquid from canned products, and water that has been used to soak dried foods. If chicken, duck, or pork bones are available, very good stock can be made from them. Long cooking of these ingredients, however, is no substitute for the quality of ingredients to be used. The American housewife may prefer to use a can of clear chicken broth rather than boil down several pounds of meat or bone to produce a quart of rich stock. The broth can be diluted with an equal part of water to prevent its masking the flavor of the other ingredients with its own strong broth taste.

The quantity of most soups may be increased when unexpected guests arrive by the addition of more water, stock, or canned chicken broth. Most soups can be prepared, at least in part, well in advance of serving. Thus, although won ton soup should be served as soon as the won tons are cooked, the soup itself could have been ready long before so that only the won tons need be added shortly before serving.

Cornstarch is added to a number of soups at the time of serving to thicken their consistency. This is especially true of egg drop soup. Before serving, cellophane noodles may be added but at a point when it is still possible to soak up a considerable amount of the soup. Dried foods, soaked until tender, may always be added to the soup to enrich its flavor.

DUCK BONE SOUP
Ya Gu Tong: Peking
鴨　骨　湯

A. bones from duck (see Peking Duck)
B. 2 qts. water
C. 1 lb. Chinese celery cabbage
D. 2 teaspoons salt

PREPARATION:

I. Disjoint A.
II. Cut C into 1½-inch pieces.

COOKING:

1. Place A in pot, cover with B. Bring to boil, lower heat, and simmer 1 hour.
2. Add C, cook 10 minutes over low heat.
3. Remove A from soup. Add D and serve hot.

DUCK BONE SOUP WITH CELLOPHANE NOODLES
Fun See Ya Gu Tong: Peking
粉　絲　鴨　骨　湯

Reduce C to ½ lb. and add 1-oz. pkg. cellophane noodles. Soak noodles 30 minutes in hot water. After Step 1, drain soup and discard bones. Bring soup to boil. In Step 2, add C and noodles, cook 10 minutes over low heat. Serve hot.

MUSHROOM GO BA SOUP I
Tsao Gu Go Ba Tong: Shanghai　　草 菇 鍋 巴 湯

A. 3 tablespoons vegetable oil
B. ¼ lb. pork, shredded
C. 1 teaspoon cornstarch
D. 2 teaspoons light soy sauce
E. ½ lb. fresh mushrooms
F. 2 teaspoons cornstarch
G. 1 teaspoon light soy sauce
H. 1 tablespoon sherry

I. ½ teaspoon sugar
J. dash black pepper
K. 1 teaspoon sugar
L. 1 tablespoon cornstarch
M. 13¾-oz. can chicken soup
N. fried rice patty (see Rice Patty or Rice Crust II)

PREPARATION:

I. Wash E, cut off ½ inch of stem, then cut into 3 to 4 pieces. Soak in cold water.
II. Mix E with F, G, H, I, J.

III. Mix B, C, D.
IV. Mix K, L, M. Make sure there are no lumps.

COOKING:

1. Heat A in frying pan. Stir-fry B–D mixture 1 to 2 minutes.
2. Add E–J mixture; stir-fry 1 minute, then cover and cook 2 minutes.
3. Add K–M mixture, cover, and bring to boil. Simmer 3 more minutes.
4. Heat oil in deep fryer to 375°. Fry patties until just golden. Do not wait until they are brown. Remove to cake pan and leave in 300° oven until ready to use.
5. When ready to serve, place N in a large bowl, pour soup over it, and serve. A crackling noise should be heard when soup comes in contact with the hot patties.

MUSHROOM GO BA SOUP II
Dung Gu Go Ba Tong: Peking　　冬 菇 鍋 巴 湯

A. 12 Chinese mushrooms
B. 13¾-oz. can chicken soup
C. 1 tablespoon light soy sauce

D. 2 to 4 oz. fried rice patties (see Rice Patty or Rice Crust II)
E. 1 teaspoon sesame oil

PREPARATION:

I. Wash A in warm water and soak 15 minutes; drain; save water. Discard stems and cut each A into 2 or 3 pieces.
II. Cut D into 1-inch squares.

COOKING:

1. Place A, B, C with enough water added to mushroom water to make 1 cup in saucepan, bring to boil, and simmer 5 minutes Add E.
2. When ready to serve, place hot and crispy D in soup bowl, pour A–E mixture over it and serve.

RED-IN-SNOW AND BEAN SOUP
Shieh Tsai Do Ban Tong: Shanghai　　雪 荣 豆 板 湯

A. 1½ qts. soup stock
B. ¼ lb. pork, shredded
C. 10-oz. pkg. frozen Fordhook lima beans

D. ½ cup preserved red-in-snow
E. salt to taste

PREPARATION:
I. Peel skin off C.

COOKING:

1. Bring A to boil, add B, C, D, cook 10 to 15 minutes.
2. Add E; serve hot.

CELERY CABBAGE AND MEATBALL SOUP
Bai Tsai Chuan Yuan Tze Tong: Peking 白 菜 川 圓 子 湯

A. 1 lb. celery cabbage
B. 1 qt. water (or 13¾-oz. can chicken broth plus 1 can water, without I)
C. ½ lb. pork, ground
D. 1 tablespoon chopped scallion (white part only)

E. 1 teaspoon chopped ginger
F. 2 teaspoons cornstarch
G. 2 teaspoons light soy sauce
H. 1 teaspoon sherry
I. 1 teaspoon salt
J. few drops sesame oil (optional)

PREPARATION:

I. Cut A into 2-inch segments and wash.

II. Mix C, D, E, F, G, H well and make into balls 1 inch in diameter.

COOKING:

1. Place A in pot, add B, bring to boil, simmer 25 minutes.

2. Turn heat high, add C–H mixture and cook 5 to 8 minutes or until meatballs are done.

3. Add I, J and serve hot.

MEATBALL SOUP
Ro Yuen Tong: Peking 肉 丸 湯

A. 1 qt. pork broth
B. 6 dried mushrooms
C. ¼ lb. ground pork
D. ¼ lb. ground shrimp
E. 1 egg

F. 7 water chestnuts
G. ¾ lb. Chinese celery cabbage hearts
H. salt to taste
I. ½ teaspoon sherry

PREPARATION:

I. Soak B in hot water 20 minutes. Drain, saving water. Remove and discard stems; chop into very fine pieces.

II. Chop F very fine.
III. Mix C, D, E, and F. Make spoon-size balls.
IV. Chop G into 2-inch pieces.

COOKING:

1. In saucepan bring A and water from B to boil, add B and C–F mixture, cook 5 to 10 minutes.

2. Add G, H, I and simmer 5 minutes. Serve hot.

STUFFED CHICKEN WING SOUP
Lung Chwan Feng Yi Tong: Shanghai 龍 穿 鳳 翼 湯

A. 1 lb. chicken wings
B. 1 oz. Virginia ham
C. ⅓ chunk of canned bamboo shoot
D. 1 tablespoon sherry

E. ½ teaspoon salt
F. 6 to 8 Chinese mushrooms
G. 13¾-oz. can chicken broth

PREPARATION:

I. Wash and disjoint A. Cook in boiling water 10 minutes, remove from liquid, and take out bones. Save water to mix with G.
II. Cut B, C into strips 3 inches long.
III. Stuff A with B, C. Place in soup bowl.

IV. Mix D, E and pour over A mixture.
V. Wash and soak F in warm water 15 minutes (save water), remove F and discard stems, cut each into 2 or 3 pieces and mix with A mixture.

COOKING:

1. Steam A–F mixture in steamer 30–45 minutes.
2. Dilute G with 1 can mushroom water. Bring

to boil and pour onto A, mix well, and serve hot.

BEAN CURD HOT AND SOUR SOUP
Do Fu Swan La Tong: General 豆 腐 酸 辣 湯

A. 1½ qts. pork stock
B. 3 Chinese mushrooms
C. ½ cup shredded pork
D. ½ cup shredded bamboo shoots
E. ½ cup shredded water chestnuts
F. 1½ tablespoons light soy sauce
G. 1 teaspoon salt
H. 3 cakes bean curd, sliced very thin

I. 3 tablespoons vinegar
J. ½ teaspocn pepper
K. 2 tablespoons cornstarch
L. ¼ cup water
M. 1 egg
N. 1 scallion, chopped
O. Sesame oil to taste

PREPARATION:

I. Wash B, soak 15 minutes in warm water. Drain, adding B water to A. Shred B.

II. Mix F, G.
III. Mix I, J, K, L. Beat M.

COOKING:

1. Bring mixture of A and B water to boil. Add B, C, D, E, cook 1 minute.
2. Add F–G mixture.
3. Add H, bring to boil again. Add I–L mixture, stir until thick.
4. Remove from heat, gradually stir in M.

5. Garnish with N and sprinkle O over it. Serve hot.

Note: Substitute 6 cups chicken broth or 6 chicken bouillon cubes in 1½ qts. water for A. This recipe is handy when soup stock is not available.

HOT AND SOUR SOUP
Swan La Tong: Peking 北 京 酸 辣 湯

A. 13¾-oz. can chicken broth
B. 4 wood ears
C. 12 golden needles
D. 2 Chinese mushrooms
E. ¼ cup shredded preserved kohlrabi
F. ½ cup shredded pork
G. 2 cakes bean curd
H. 2 tablespoons vinegar

I. 1 tablespoon light soy sauce
J. 1 teaspoon sugar
K. ½ to 1 teaspoon pepper
L. 2 tablespoons cornstarch mixed with ¼ cup water
M. 1 egg, beaten
N. 2 scallions
O. Sesame oil to taste

PREPARATION:

I. Cover B with hot water and soak 15 to 30 minutes or until soft.
II. Discard water, wash and shred B.
III. Soak C in cold water for 15 to 20 minutes until soft; discard the hard tips, cut each

into 2 or 3 segments.
IV. Wash D in warm water and soak 15 minutes; shred; save water and add it to A.
V. Chop white part of N.
VI. Slice and shred G. Mix H, I, J, K.

COOKING:

1. In saucepan, dilute A with 1 can water plus mushroom water; bring to boil.
2. Add B, C, D, E and cook for 8 minutes.
3. Add F, cook 1 minute.

4. Add G and H–K; cook ½ minute.
5. Thicken with L.
6. Remove from heat; slowly stir in M.
7. Add N and O; serve hot.

HOT AND SOUR SOUP I
Swan La Tong: Szechuan

酸 辣 湯

A. 13¾-oz. can chicken broth
B. ¼ cup shredded preserved kohlrabi
C. ½ cup shredded roast or fresh pork
D. ½ cup shredded bamboo shoots
E. 2 dried Chinese mushrooms

F. 2 soybean cakes
G. 2 tablespoons cider vinegar
H. 1 teaspoon light soy sauce
I. 2 tablespoons cornstarch

PREPARATION:

I. Wash red powder off B before shredding.
II. Soak E in warm water 20 minutes, remove and discard stems, shred.

III. Slice F very thin.
IV. Mix G, H, I until there are no lumps.

COOKING:

1. Dilute A with 1 can water, boil, add B, and cook 5 minutes.
2. Add C, D, E and boil 1 minute.

3. Add F.
4. When soup boils again, thicken with G–I.

HOT AND SOUR SOUP II
Swan La Tong: Szechuan

酸 辣 湯

A. 3 cups soup stock
B. ⅛ cup dried cloud ears
C. 3 sheets dried bean curd
D. 8 small dried black mushrooms
E. ¼ cup water chestnuts
F. 2 tablespoons cornstarch

G. ½ cup water
H. 1 tablespoon light soy sauce
I. 1 teaspoon Chinese hot sauce
J. 1½ tablespoons vinegar
K. 1 egg
L. 1 teaspoon water

PREPARATION:

I. Separately soak B, C, D in 1 cup hot water each.
II. When soft, cut each sheet of C into eight pieces.
III. When soft, slice D into several slivers.

IV. Slice E. Mix with B, C, D.
V. Mix F, G. Set aside. Stir well before using.
VI. Mix H, I, J. Set aside.
VII. Beat K lightly and then mix with L. Set aside.

COOKING:

1. Heat A over high heat.
2. Add B–E mixture and continue to heat until soup boils.
3. Add F–G slowly, stirring constantly as soup thickens.

4. Add H–J mixture. Stir well.
5. When soup is again boiling vigorously, turn off heat and pour in K–L mixture slowly so as to obtain egg drop consistency.
6. Serve.

PIGS' FEET BEANSPROUT SOUP
Tsu Jio Do Ya Tong: Shanghai

豬 腳 豆 芽 湯

A. 2 to 3 pigs' feet
B. 3 slices ginger
C. ½ lb. soybean sprouts

D. 1½ teaspoons salt
E. 1 tablespoon sherry

COOKING:

1. Wash and clean A thoroughly, cut into 1- to 2-inch pieces. Cover with 3 qts. water, bring to boil.

2. Add B, lower heat and simmer 2 hours.
3. Add C and cook for another half hour.
4. Add D, E, and serve hot.

BEEF TOMATO SOUP
Fan Cheh Niu Gu Tong: Shanghai   蕃 茄 牛 骨 湯

A. 2 to 3 lbs. beef neck bones
B. 1½ lbs. fresh or canned tomatoes
C. 4 stalks celery, with leaves
D. 1 medium onion, sliced
E. 5 slices ginger
F. ½ teaspoon sugar
G. salt to taste

PREPARATION:

I. Wash C, cut across grain, into ½-inch pieces (save leaves for soup).
II. If B are fresh, quarter them.
III. Peel skin off E.

COOKING:

1. Using 5-qt. Dutch oven at high heat, brown A. Add 2 qts. water, and E, cover and simmer 2 hours. Add boiling water occasionally to replace water that evaporates.
2. Add B, C, D, cook 5 to 10 minutes. If canned tomatoes are used, add liquid to soup. Adjust taste with F and G. Makes 1 qt. of soup.

PORK SOUP
Ro Si Tong: Shanghai   肉 絲 湯

A. 1 can chicken broth
B. 6 Chinese mushrooms
C. 12 golden needles
D. ¼ lb. lean pork, shredded
E. 2 teaspoons light soy sauce
F. ½ cup shredded bamboo shoots
G. 1 scallion
H. 1 teaspoon sherry

PREPARATION:

I. Mix D with E.
II. Wash B, C, soak 15 minutes in warm water. Drain, save water, and add to A.
III. Discard tip (hard part) of C. Cut each into 1-inch pieces.
IV. Shred B.
V. Cut G into 1-inch pieces.

COOKING:

1. Empty A into saucepan, dilute with 1½ cans water and water from B, C. Bring to boil.
2. Add B, C, D–E, G, stir well, cook 2 to 3 minutes. Stir in H; serve hot.

WATERCRESS PORK SOUP
Si Yang Tsai Tsu Ro Tong: Shanghai   西 洋 荣 豬 肉 湯

A. 4 cups soup stock
B. ¼ lb. pork loin, shredded
C. 3 slices ginger, minced
D. 1 bunch watercress
E. 1 teaspoon light soy sauce
F. 3 drops sesame oil (optional)
G. ½ teaspoon salt
H. 2 eggs

PREPARATION:

I. Cut D into 2-in. segments.
II. Mix E, F, G. Set aside.

COOKING:

1. Bring A to rapid boil in large saucepot.
2. Add B, C. Cook 5 minutes.
3. Add D. Cook 3 minutes without cover.
4. Add E–G mixture. Stir well. Turn off heat.
5. Drop H one by one into soup. Let stand 3 minutes.
6. Serve hot in large soup tureen.

PORK AND TURNIP SOUP
Ro Pien Lo Bo Tong: Shanghai 肉 片 蘿 蔔 湯

A. 1 lb. white turnip
B. ¼ lb. pork tenderloin
   (or boneless lamb)
C. 1 scallion, chopped
D. 2 slices ginger, chopped

E. 2 teaspoons light soy sauce
F. ½ teaspoon sugar
G. 2 teaspoons wine vinegar
H. ¼ teaspoon sesame oil
I. salt, pepper to taste

PREPARATION:

I. Slice B thin, mix with C, D, E, F, G, let stand several minutes.

II. Peel A, cut into bite-size pieces.

COOKING:

1. Place A in cooking pot, add 1 qt. water. Bring to boil, lower heat, and cook 30 minutes, or until tender.

2. Add B–G mixture, bring to boil, cook 1 to 2 minutes.
3. Add H, I. Serve hot.

TOMATO, MEAT AND SHRIMP SOUP
Fan Chieh Ro Pien Sha Tze Tong: Shanghai 蕃 茄 肉 片 蝦 子 湯

A. 13¾-oz. can chicken broth
B. ¼ lb. pork
C. 1 teaspoon cornstarch
D. 1 tablespoon sherry
E. ¼ lb. shrimp

F. 2 teaspoons light soy sauce
G. ½ lb. tomatoes
H. few drops sesame oil (optional)
I. 1 to 2 tablespoons chopped scallion

PREPARATION:

I. Cut B into thin slices and mix with C, D.
II. Shell, devein, and wash E. Mince.

III. Pour boiling water over G, let stand for a few seconds. Remove G, peel off skin and cut G into thin slices.

COOKING:

1. Empty A into saucepan, add 1 can of water, bring to a boil.
2. Add B–D mixture, stir well, cook 3 to 5 minutes.

3. Add E, F, stir well and cook 1 minute.
4. Add G and H, turn off heat. Pour into serving bowl.
5. Garnish with I and serve hot.

TURNIP AND SPARERIB SOUP
Lo Bo Pai Gu Tong: General 蘿 蔔 排 骨 湯

A. 1 lb. spareribs
B. 1 medium turnip (about 1 lb.)

C. 1 tablespoon chopped scallion
D. 1 to 1½ teaspoons salt

PREPARATION:

I. Cut A into 1-inch pieces.

II. Peel B, cut into bite-size pieces.

COOKING:

1. Put A and 2 qts. water into a cooking pot, bring to boil. Lower heat, simmer 1 to 1½ hours.

2. Add B, cook another 30 to 45 minutes.
3. Add C, D.

WINTER MELON BOWL
Dung Gwa Tsung: General

冬 瓜 盅

A. 1 whole winter melon (about 8 lbs.)
B. ¼ cup lotus seeds
C. 3 to 4 dried scallops
D. 5 diced black mushrooms
E. 2 slices of ginger
F. ¼ cup diced Virginia ham
G. 1 chicken breast
H. ¼ cup diced fresh shrimp
I. ¾ cup diced bamboo shoots
J. ¾ cup diced water chestnuts
K. about 7 cups of chicken broth (or enough so that when all ingredients fill the melon, the soup comes to 2 inches below edge of melon)
L. 1 tablespoon sherry

PREPARATION:

I. Wash A; cut a zigzag pattern 1 to 2 inches below the stem and remove this part of the shell. Remove seeds and clean the inside of the melon to remove fibrous material. Place A in a bowl in an upright position.
II. Soak B in hot water with a little salt; remove skin; rinse.
III. Rinse C; cover with water and L, soak ½ hour.
IV. Rinse D and soak in hot water 15 minutes or until soft; dice.
V. Bone and dice G.

COOKING:

1. Place B, C, E in boiling water; cook 10 to 15 minutes.
2. Place B, C, D, E, F, G, H, I, J inside A. Place A in bowl for steaming.
3. Add K.
4. Place A in a large pot and cover. Steam over boiling water 2 hours or until melon is soft.
5. Just before serving, remove bowl from steamer and wipe outside of A with a piece of greased paper towel so that it will look shiny.

WINTER MELON SOUP WITH CHICKEN
Dung Gwa Gee Tong: General

冬 瓜 雞 湯

A. 6 cups soup stock
B. 1-lb. slice of winter melon
C. 4 dried black mushrooms
D. 1 slice ginger, minced
E. 1 chicken breast
F. ⅛ teaspoon garlic powder
G. 1 teaspoon sherry
H. 1 teaspoon sugar
I. ½ teaspoon light soy sauce
J. ½ teaspoon salt
K. 1½ teaspoons light soy sauce
L. 2 teaspoons peanut oil

PREPARATION:

I. Soak C in warm water 15 minutes. Discard water. Slice C.
II. Cut B into ¼-inch slices. Skin may be left intact or cut off. Set aside.
III. Bone E. Cut into bite-sized pieces.
IV. Mix E, F, G, H, I thoroughly and set aside to stand 15 minutes.
V. Mix J, K, L. Set aside.

COOKING:

1. Heat A to boiling.
2. Add B, C, D and simmer for 25 minutes.
3. Add E–I mixture. Stir well.
4. Add J–L mixture.
5. Cook until chicken is tender and done.
    Note: Even though B skin may be left intact, it is *not* eaten.

TRIPLE SOUP
San Sien Tong: Shanghai

三 鮮 湯

A. 13¾-oz. can chicken broth
B. ½ cup shredded abalone
C. ½ cup shredded Smithfield ham

D. ½ cup shredded white meat chicken
E. salt to taste
F. few drops sesame oil

COOKING:

1. Empty A into a pot, add 1 can water, and bring to boil.
2. Add B, C, D, mix well, cover, and bring back to boil.

3. Cook 1 to 2 minutes. Remove fatty foam from top, and discard.
4. Add E, F, and serve hot.

YANGCHOW TRIPLE SOUP
San Si Tong: Yang Chow

三 絲 湯

A. ½ lb. lean pork
B. 1 scallion
C. 2 slices ginger
D. 13¾-oz. can chicken broth diluted with pork broth from I below

E. 1 egg
F. 3 Chinese mushrooms
G. ¼ cup shredded cooked ham
H. ¼ cup shredded chicken meat
I. 1 tablespoon sherry

PREPARATION:

I. Shred A, and dip in boiling water; remove immediately.
II. Beat E well, pour into hot greased pan, and spread as evenly as possible by tipping pan. When set, remove and shred.
III. Soak F in warm water 15 minutes, drain, and remove stems.
IV. Cut B into 2-inch pieces.
V. Place F in bottom of small bowl, arrange E, G, H, along edge of bowl and place A in center.
VI. Spread B, C, I and 2 tablespoons D on top.

COOKING:

1. Steam A mixture in steamer over boiling water 35 minutes, discard B, C.
2. Bring D to boil.

3. Just before serving invert small bowl containing A mixture into large soup bowl. Add boiling D.

VEGETARIAN TRIPLE SOUP
Sue San Sien Tong: Shanghai

素 三 鮮 湯

A. ½ cup sliced bamboo shoots
B. 1 cup fresh mushrooms
C. ¼ cup chopped preserved red-in-snow

D. 1 qt. water
E. 1 teaspoon salt

PREPARATION:

I. Wash B, cut each into 3 to 4 pieces.

COOKING:

1. Place A, B, C in a pot, cover with D, and bring to boil.

2. Cover, cook over low heat 10 minutes.
3. Add E and serve.

RICE PATTY OR RICE CRUST I
Go Ba: General　　　　　鍋 巴

A. 2 cups rice

B. 3 cups water

COOKING:

1. Place A in cooking pot. Wash and drain.
2. Add B to drained, wet rice. Bring to boil. Lower heat and cook until very little water is left. Cover and allow to simmer. Rice is generally cooked in 15 minutes; however, in order to form crust, allow to simmer for a longer period, until a thick brown crust forms on bottom of pot. Take care not to char crust.

3. Scoop out all the soft rice. The remaining crust may be dried by maintaining low heat while turning crust a few times (crust must be hard and crispy) or by removing crust from pot and placing it in the oven at a very low heat until it is crispy.
4. Cut crispy crust into 2- to 3-inch squares. Crust in this form may keep in tightly covered jar 1 to 2 months.

RICE PATTY OR RICE CRUST II
Go Ba: General　　　　　鍋 巴

A. 2 cups cooked rice

PREPARATION:

I. Hand pat A into a 10-inch flat-bottom pan until it contains rice (moisten hand so that rice does not stick) approximately two grains thick.

COOKING:

1. Heat under low heat in oven 30 minutes or until a rice crust forms. Then turn over patty and brown on other side 20 minutes. If not to be used immediately, patty can be stored in a tightly covered jar 2 to 3 months.

PRESERVED KOHLRABI SOUP WITH PORK
Tza Tsoi Ro Si Tong: General　　榨 菜 肉 絲 湯

A. 2 tablespoons peanut oil

B. 3 slices ginger, chopped

C. 1 small scallion, chopped

D. ¼ lb. pork

E. ¼ cup preserved kohlrabi, cut as in Preparation I.

F. 2 oz. cellophane noodles

G. 2 teaspoons light soy sauce

H. 1 qt. water or pork stock

PREPARATION:

I. Slice D, E, then cut into pieces 1 inch to 1½ inches long.

II. Soak F in hot water 30 minutes.

COOKING:

1. Heat A, add B, C, stir-fry a few seconds.
2. Add D, continue stir-frying 1 to 2 minutes. Add E, F, G, mix well.

3. Add 1 qt. boiling H. Bring to boil. Cook over low heat 5 minutes. Salt to taste, serve hot.

CLAMS WITH PICKLED VEGETABLE SOUP
Ga Li Swan Tsai Tong: Shanghai
蛤 蜊 酸 荣 湯

A. 2 tablespoons vegetable oil
B. 1 large pork chop
C. 1 teaspoon light soy sauce
D. 1 tablespoon cornstarch
E. 3 slices ginger
F. ½ cup pickled mustard greens

G. 1 qt. chicken soup
H. 10½-oz. can clams
I. 1 tablespoon sherry
J. dash pepper
K. salt to taste

PREPARATION:

I. Bone and shred B, mix with C and D.
II. Shred E.

III. Rinse F and slice into bite-size pieces.
IV. Mix H, I, J.

COOKING:

1. Heat A in frying pan.
2. Add B–D, stir-fry 1 to 2 minutes.
3. Add E, F, stir-fry 1 to 2 minutes.

4. Add G, bring to boil.
5. Add H–J. Boil 5 to 10 minutes.
6. Adjust with K.

RED-IN-SNOW FISH SOUP
Shieh Tsai Yu Tong: Ninpo
雪 荣 魚 湯

A. ¼ cup peanut oil
B. 1 scallion
C. 2 slices ginger
D. 1 porgy (about 1 lb.)

E. 1 tablespoon sherry
F. ¼ cup preserved red-in-snow
G. ½ cup sliced bamboo shoots
H. 1 teaspoon salt

PREPARATION:

I. Clean and wash D, dry between paper towels. Make 2 diagonal slashes on each side.

II. Tie B into a knot.

COOKING:

1. Heat A, add B, C, stir-fry 1 to 2 minutes.
2. Add D, brown on both sides; discard B, C; add E and cover for a few seconds.
3. Add 1 qt. cold water, bring to boil, cook 1 minute.

4. Spread F, G over fish, add salt, cover and simmer 15 minutes or until fish is done.
5. Turn heat high and cook 1 more minute. Remove oil that floats to top of soup.
6. Serve hot.

WON TON SEA CUCUMBER SOUP
Won Ton Hai Sun: Szechuan
雲 吞 海 參 湯

A. ¼ cup refined dried sea cucumbers
B. 1 cup sliced bamboo shoots
C. 8 Chinese mushrooms
D. 2 qts. chicken soup
E. 1 scallion, chopped

F. 3 slices ginger, chopped
G. 24 won tons (see Index)
H. dash salt, pepper
I. 2 slices ginger
J. 1 scallion

PREPARATION:

I. Soak A in water at room temperature for two days. Discard water, boil in fresh water with I and J 45 minutes or until A is soft. Drain; wash and cut A into 2- by ½- by ¼-inch pieces.

II. Soak C in warm water 20 minutes. Remove and discard stems; cut each in half.

COOKING:

1. Place A, B, C, D, E, F in large heavy pot. Bring to boil.

2. Add G, simmer for 3 minutes. Adjust with H. Serve hot.

SQUID IN HOT AND SOUR SOUP
Swan La Yo Yu Tong: Szechuan　　酸 辣 魷 魚 湯

A. 13¾-oz. can chicken broth
B. 1 dried squid
C. ¼ cup shredded preserved kohlrabi
D. ½ cup shredded roast pork
E. ½ cup shredded bamboo shoots
F. 2 cakes bean curd
G. 2 tablespoons cider vinegar

H. 1 teaspoon light soy sauce
I. 2 scallions
J. salt to taste
K. 2 tablespoons cornstarch mixed with ¼ cup cold water
L. ½ teaspoon baking soda

PREPARATION:

I. Soak B overnight, remove soft bones and membrane. Change water. Add L, cover, and boil 30 minutes. Then soak ½ hour, drain and rinse. Shred B.
II. Mix C, D, E.
III. Slice F into thin pieces.

COOKING:

1. Mix A with 1 can water. Bring to boil. Add B and C–E, cook 1 minute.
2. Add F, G, H, I, boil again.
3. Adjust with J and then, stirring gradually, add K. When soup has thickened, it is ready to serve.

GINGER BEEF TEA
Jiang Tze Niu Ro Tong: General　　薑 汁 牛 肉 湯

A. ½ lb. boneless chuck
B. 1 tablespoon sherry
C. 6 slices ginger

D. dash black pepper (optional)
E. salt to taste

PREPARATION:

I. Cut A into 1½ inch cubes.

COOKING:

1. Place A, B in a heated, thick, 3-qt. saucepan. Brown A, stirring continuously to avoid scorching.
2. When A is browned, add C, D and 1 qt. water.
3. Simmer 1 to 1½ hours, adjust with E. Serve hot.

SIMPLE EGG DROP SOUP
Dan Hwa Tong: General　　蛋 花 湯

A. 13¾-oz. can chicken broth
B. 2 tablespoons cornstarch mixed with ¼ cup water

C. 1 egg
D. 1 tablespoon chopped scallion

PREPARATION:

I. Dilute A with 1 can water.
II. Beat C.

COOKING:

1. Bring diluted A to boil.
2. Thicken with B.
3. Turn off heat, slowly stir in C.
4. Garnish with D.

BIRD'S NEST SOUP
Yen Wuo Tong: General

燕 窩 湯

A. 2-oz. bird's nest
B. 1 qt. chicken soup
C. ⅛ teaspoon sherry
D. 1 boned chicken breast, chopped very fine
E. ¼ cup diced meat crumbs from Chinese grocery

F. 2 teaspoons cornstarch
G. 1 egg white
H. 5 drops sesame oil (optional)
I. several drops peanut oil

PREPARATION:

I. Soak A in water overnight. Next day, sprinkle several drops I on A, wash with warm, clear water. Feathers should float to surface, making removal easier. Repeat oil-and-wash treatment until A is clean.

II. Mix F with ¼ cup water.

COOKING:

1. Place A and 2 cups B in large bowl. Add C, D. Place in steamer, steam 1 hour.

2. Transfer A mixture to 3-qt. saucepan. Add D, E, rest of B, boil 2 minutes.

3. Add F mixture to soup, boil, then turn off heat.

4. Beat in G. Sprinkle with H. Serve hot.

CHICKEN WITH CUCUMBER SOUP
Huang Gwa Gee Pien Tong: General

黃 瓜 雞 片 湯

A. 13¾-oz. can chicken broth
B. 2 slices ginger (optional)

C. 1 chicken breast
D. 1 teaspoon cornstarch

E. ½ teaspoon salt
F. 1 cucumber

PREPARATION:

I. Bone C, slice thin.
II. Mix C with D, E.

III. Peel F, cut in half lengthwise. Discard seeds, then cut into ¼-inch slices.

COOKING:

1. Empty A into saucepan, add B, dilute with 1 can water. (If desired, enrich stock by adding breastbone.) Bring to boil.

2. Add C–E mixture, stir well, cook 2 minutes.

3. Add F, bring to boil again, cook 2 to 3 more minutes. Serve hot.

SPARERIBS CUCUMBER SOUP
Pai Gu Hwang Gwa Tong: General

排 骨 黃 瓜 湯

A. 1 lb. spareribs
B. 3 slices ginger

C. 10 dried shrimp
D. 3 black dried mushrooms

E. salt to taste
F. 1 cucumber
G. 1 scallion, minced

PREPARATION:

I. Cut A into 1½-inch pieces.
II. Soak C in cold water 20 minutes.
III. Peel F and slice.

IV. Soak D in hot water 20 minutes, then slice and remove stems.

COOKING:

1. Place 1½ qts. water in saucepan. Bring to boil.

2. Add A, B, C, D. Simmer 1 hour or until A is done.

3. Add E.

4. Add F, G, simmer 10 minutes. Serve.

CHICKEN SOUP WITH CELERY CABBAGE
Gee Ro Bai Tsai Tong: General　　　雞 肉 白 菜 湯

A. 3-lb. roasting chicken
B. 4 dried mushrooms
C. 2 scallions
D. 3 slices ginger
E. 2 tablespoons sherry

F. 1- to 2-lb. celery cabbage
G. salt to taste
H. 2 tablespoons light soy sauce
I. 1 teaspoon sesame oil

PREPARATION:

I. Soak B in hot water 20 minutes. Drain, reserving water.
II. Clean F well. Split tender center piece in half. Then cut each into 2 to 3 parts.

III. Fold C 3 times. Take green end, tie into bundle.

COOKING:

1. Place cleaned whole A in Dutch oven. Add B water, 1 additional qt. water, bring to boil. Add B, C, D, E. Simmer covered 35 to 40 minutes.
2. Add F, boil 5 minutes. Remove and discard C. Add G.

3. If desired, dipping sauce can be prepared by combining H, I, and 1 tablespoon minced scallion.
4. Serve whole and carve at table.

CHICKEN SOUP WITH ASPARAGUS SHOOTS AND BEAN CURD
Lu Shun Dow Fu Tong: General　　　蘆 筍 豆 腐 湯

A. 1 qt. clear chicken broth and 2 cups water
B. 4 black dried mushrooms
C. 10 dried shrimp
D. 1 chicken breast
E. 1 tablespoon sherry

F. 3 slices ginger
G. ½ lb. asparagus shoots
H. 2 cakes bean curd
I. salt to taste

PREPARATION:

I. Clean tips of G, discard hard stems. French-cut tips into thin pieces.
II. Soak B in hot water 20 minutes.

III. Soak C in cold water 20 minutes.
IV. Cut H into thin ½- by 1-inch pieces.
V. Bone D and slice meat into thin pieces.

COOKING:

1. Place A in 3-qt. saucepan. Add B, C, D, E, F and cook 10 minutes.

2. Add G, H and cook 5 minutes. Add I. Serve hot.

CALF BRAIN SOUP
Niu Nao Tong: General　　　牛 腦 湯

A. 13¾-oz. can chicken broth and ½ can water
B. 1 calf brain
C. 2 teaspoons dry sherry

D. 1 egg white
E. 1 teaspoon minced ginger
F. 1 teaspoon lard

PREPARATION:

I. Place B in cold water; remove blood vessels with a toothpick, rinse and drain. Mince B.

II. Mix B with C.

COOKING:

1. Bring A to boil in saucepan.
2. Add B mixture, stir well.
3. Stir in D gradually.

4. When mixture boils again, add E, F; serve hot.

SEA OF TRANQUILLITY SOUP
Ping On Dun Rieh Tong: General   平 安 登 月 湯

A. 1 large Chinese mushroom
B. ¾ cup shredded baked Virginia ham
C. ½ cup shredded bamboo shoots
D. ¼ cup shredded abalone

E. ¾ cup shredded cooked chicken meat
F. 3 to 4 cups chicken broth
G. salt to taste
H. 1 tablespoon chopped scallion

PREPARATION AND COOKING:

I. Wash A and soak in warm water 15 minutes or until soft; save the water and mix with F.
II. Place A, topside down, in center of shallow bowl; arrange B in 3 strips like the spokes of a wheel.
III. In two sections place C and in the third place D. Mushroom forms a hub, B forms the 3 spokes and C and D the background.
IV. Spread E over the top.
V. Steam over boiling water 10 minutes.
VI. Place a large soup bowl over the bowl with A mixture; invert.
VII. Just before serving, pour boiling F over mixture, add G and garnish with H.

SEAWEED SOUP
Tze Tsai Tong: General   紫 荣 湯

A. 2 cups soup stock
B. 3 thin sheets purple seaweed
C. 1 tablespoon sherry
D. 1 slice ginger, minced

E. 1 egg
F. 1 tablespoon water
G. 2 scallions, sliced

PREPARATION:

I. Cut B into ½-inch slivers with kitchen shears or scissors.
II. Mix C, D. Set aside.
III. Mix E, F. Beat lightly.

COOKING:

1. Heat A to boiling.
2. Add B. Stir 15 seconds.
3. Add C–D mixture. Stir well.
4. Bring to boil again. Remove from heat and slowly pour in E–F mixture, stirring constantly.
5. Serve in soup tureen with garnish of G.

SLICED FISH WITH VEGETABLE SOUP
Yu Pien Tong: General   魚 片 湯

A. 13¾-oz. can chicken broth
B. 2 slices ginger
C. 4 Chinese mushrooms
D. ½ cup sliced bamboo shoots
E. Chinese cabbage heart (few stalks)
F. ½ lb. flounder fillet
G. 1 tablespoon chopped scallion

H. 1 teaspoon ginger juice (see Index)
I. ½ teaspoon salt
J. ½ teaspoon sugar
K. 2 teaspoons sherry
L. 1 tablespoon cornstarch
M. 1 tablespoon water
N. few drops sesame oil

PREPARATION:

I. Slice F into thin pieces, mix well with H, I, J, K, L, M, N.
II. Dilute A with 1 can water.
III. Wash C in warm water and soak 15 minutes; drain and cut each in half.
IV. Cut E into 1-inch-long pieces.

COOKING:

1. Bring A to boil, add B, C, D, cook 3 minutes.
2. Add E and cook 1 minute.
3. Add F mixture and G; boil ½ to 1 minute.
4. Serve hot.

SPECIAL SHARK FIN SOUP
Song Gwan Yu Chi Gung: General
上 官 魚 翅 湯

A. 1½ qts. chicken broth
B. 1 oz. shark fins
C. 2 tablespoons Smithfield ham, shredded
D. ⅛ teaspoon pepper
E. ½ teaspoon salt
F. 6 Chinese mushrooms
G. ⅓ cup shredded bamboo shoots

H. ½ chicken breast (½ cup shredded chicken white meat)
I. 1 teaspoon cornstarch
J. 1 teaspoon light soy sauce
K. 3 tablespoons water chestnut flour mixed with ¼ cup water
L. 1 egg, beaten
M. 3 slices ginger

PREPARATION:

I. Soak B in cold water overnight; wash and clean well. Put B, M into 3 cups boiling water; bring to boil; simmer covered 30 minutes. Remove from heat and cook with cover on until water is cooled. Drain; rinse in cold water.
II. Mix H, I, J.
III. Rinse F, soak in warm water for 15 minutes; shred.

COOKING:

1. Bring A to boil; add B, C, D, E; lower heat and cook 1 hour.
2. Add F, G; cook 10 more minutes.
3. Turn up heat; add H–J mixture, stir 1 minute. Thicken with K so shark fins will float.
4. Add L gradually, stirring at the same time. Serve hot.

ABALONE SOUP WITH BLACK MUSHROOMS
Bao Yu Dung Gu Tong: General
鮑 魚 冬 菇 湯

A. ½ cup abalone liquid
B. 5 cups soup stock
C. 4 large dried black mushrooms
D. 1 cup thinly sliced pork loin

E. ½ can (8 oz.) abalone
F. 1 tablespoon light soy sauce
G. ½ teaspoon salt
H. 3 drops sesame oil (optional)

PREPARATION:

I. Soak C in hot water 15 minutes. Squeeze dry, and cut into strips.
II. Cut E into slices. Save liquid for A above (and for other recipes). Mix E, F, G.

COOKING:

1. Pour A into a pot and add B. Heat to boiling.
2. Add C, D. Cook over low heat 10 minutes.
3. Add E–G. Continue to cook 2 minutes only.
4. Add H. Serve.

EGGS

Eggs are seldom served alone (soft-boiled or fried), as in the West. Because when they are raw they mix easily with other ingredients and yet solidify upon cooking, they are often used by the Chinese to give body to certain soft foods and to bind other ingredients—as with foo yong, or omelet dishes.

Omelets require only small amounts of expensive foods such as meat, fish, shellfish, or poultry, and yet create a dish high in protein content. Sometimes omelets are shredded into strips to be used as a garnish for main dishes and soups, largely because of their color rather than for their nutritional or taste value.

Many Chinese egg dishes are steamed, mixed with a variety of seasonings and flavorings, including many additional substantial ingredients. Often such dishes are very salty or highly seasoned, and these relatively solid but easily mixable concoctions are served over a bowl of rice.

PEKING CUSTARD
Kao Don: Peking
烤 蛋

A. 4 eggs
B. 4-oz. can mushrooms (drained)
C. ¼ cup chopped frozen shrimp
D. ¼ cup ground pork

E. 1 teaspoon salt
F. ⅛ teaspoon sherry
G. 1 cup chicken broth
H. 1 teaspoon sesame oil

PREPARATION:

I. Beat A.
II. Chop B into small pieces.
III. Combine A, B, C, D, E, F, G; mix well.

IV. Pour A–G mixture into well-greased baking dish.

COOKING:

1. Preheat oven to 375°.
2. Bake A–G mixture until golden brown (about 35 minutes).

3. Sprinkle with H and serve.

STIR-FRIED EGGS WITH PORK, BLACK MUSHROOMS, AND CLOUD EARS
Mo Shu Ro: Peking
木 須 肉

A. 2 tablespoons peanut oil
B. ½ lb. ground pork
C. ½ teaspoon salt
D. ½ teaspoon minced ginger
E. 6 dried black mushrooms
F. 2 tablespoons cloud ears

G. ½ cup sliced bamboo shoots
H. 2 teaspoons light soy sauce
I. 2 teaspoons heavy soy sauce
J. 3 tablespoons peanut oil
K. 8 eggs
L. 3 scallions, sliced

PREPARATION:

I. Soak E in warm water 15 minutes. Discard water. Slice E in thin slivers.
II. Soak F in warm water 15 minutes. Discard water. Shred.

III. Beat K lightly. Set aside.
IV. Mix C, D. Set aside.
V. Mix E, F, G. Set aside.
VI. Mix H. I. Set aside.

COOKING:

1. Put A in very hot skillet and bring to high heat.
2. Add B and C–D. Stir-fry until pork is well done.
3. Add E–G mixture. Stir-fry 1 minute.
4. Add H–I mixture. Stir-fry 1 minute.

5. Remove B–I mixture from pan. Set aside.
6. Put J in very hot skillet and bring to high heat.
7. Add K. Stir-fry until set firmly. Place K on platter; pour B–J mixture over it.
8. Serve with garnish of L.

PRESERVED 100-YEAR-OLD EGGS
Pi Don: Shanghai
皮 蛋

A. 2 preserved eggs
B. 1 tablespoon light soy sauce

C. ½ teaspoon sugar

PREPARATION:

I. Crack, peel A, rinse in water; cut each into eighths.

II. Pour B over A; sprinkle with C.
Note: Serve with congee or noodles. Sugar is used in Shanghai preparation.

PRESERVED 100-YEAR-OLD EGGS
Pi Don: General

皮 蛋

A. 4 preserved eggs
B. 2 tablespoons vinegar

C. 3 slices ginger, minced
D. 1 tablespoon light soy sauce

PREPARATION:

I. Remove shells from A. Whites will appear gray but translucent.
II. Cut each egg into 6 lengthwise pieces. Yolk will appear gray-green-black.

III. Arrange sections of A on serving dish.
IV. Mix B, C, D.
V. Pour over A. Serve.

FRIED 100-YEAR-OLD EGGS
Tza Pi Don: General

炸 皮 蛋

A. 1 cup peanut oil
B. 3 100-year-old eggs
C. 1 salted egg
D. 3 tablespoons flour

E. ½ teaspoon sugar
F. 2 teaspoons wine vinegar
G. ½ teaspoon salt
H. 2 tomatoes

PREPARATION:

I. Scrape ashes from B with a knife, wash. Cover B with water, bring to a boil and cook 3 minutes (so that B is firmed). Drain, cover with cold water a few seconds. Shell; quarter each B.

II. Break up yolk of C with fork and beat C until fluffy.
III. Mix in D gradually; add E, F, G, mix well.
IV. Dip H in boiling water a few seconds; remove skin and cut H into slices.

COOKING:

1. Heat A to 375°.
2. Dip each B in C–G until well coated. Deep-fry until all sides are golden brown.

3. Place in the middle of dish, garnish with H. Serve hot or cold.

TEA EGGS
Tsa Yieh Don: Peking

茶 葉 蛋

A. 6 eggs
B. 2 tablespoons red tea leaves

C. 1½ tablespoons salt

COOKING:

I. Boil A 5 to 10 minutes. Discard boiling water, let A stand in cold water until cool. Then crack, but do not shell.
II. Fill saucepan with 3 cups water, add B, C,

bring to boil. Add A, cook over low heat 1 hour.
III. Remove from heat. Leave A in B–C mixture; remove when ready to eat.

SWEET TEA EGGS
Bing Tang Tsa Yieh Don: Peking

冰 糖 茶 葉 蛋

Substitute 2 tea bags for B and 3 tablespoons rock sugar for C.

SMOKED EGGS
Shuin Don: Peking   燻 蛋

A. 10 hard-cooked eggs
B. ¼ cup light soy sauce
C. ½ teaspoon pepper
D. 1½ teaspoons sugar

E. ⅓ cup dark brown sugar
F. ⅓ cup red tea leaves
G. ⅓ cup rice
H. ¼ teaspoon sesame oil

PREPARATION:

I. Shell A. Slash each in 4 places, touching yolk.
II. Mix B, C, D thoroughly.
III. Soak A in B–D mixture at least 2 hours, turning A over after 1 hour.
IV. Mix E, F, G.

V. Line a heavy iron pot with aluminum foil. Spread E–G mixture on foil. Top with a rack.
VI. Arrange A on rack, cover tightly. (Reserve B–D sauce.)

COOKING:

1. Place prepared A on low heat. After several minutes, smoke will appear. Smoke A for 3 to 5 minutes, turn over, and smoke for 3 more minutes.

2. Remove A, place back in B–D sauce, discard E–G, add H, and let cool.
3. When completely cold, quarter each A, and serve.

SCRAMBLED EGGS WITH SCALLIONS
Tsung Hwa Don: General   葱 花 蛋

A. 4 tablespoons peanut oil
B. 8 eggs
C. 4 scallions, sliced
D. 1 teaspoon light soy sauce

E. ¾ teaspoon salt
F. 1 teaspoon heavy soy sauce
G. 1 scallion, sliced

PREPARATION:

I. Beat B slightly. Add C.

II. Mix D, E, F. Set aside.

COOKING:

1. Put A in very hot skillet and bring to high heat.
2. Add B, C. Scramble well.

3. Add D–F mixture. Stir well 15 seconds.
4. Remove from skillet at once; serve with garnish of G.

CRAB OMELET
Shia Ro Tsao Don: Shanghai   蟹 肉 炒 蛋

A. ¼ cup peanut oil
B. 7-oz. can crab meat (or lobster)
C. 6 eggs

D. 2 slices ginger
E. 1 scallion
F. 1 teaspoon salt
G. few drops hot sauce

PREPARATION:

I. Chop D, E very fine.

II. Beat C, mix with B, D–F.

COOKING:

1. Heat A in frying pan. Add B–F mixture, pan-fry both sides until golden brown (about 2 minutes). Serve hot or cold and add G.

FANCY OMELET
Gee Don Jiao: General　　　雞　蛋　餃

A.　¼ cup vegetable oil
B.　4 oz. pork (or leftover chicken or white turkey meat), shredded
C.　2 teaspoons light soy sauce
D.　2 slices ginger, shredded
E.　6 dried Chinese mushrooms
F.　10-oz. pkg. frozen peas
G.　6 eggs
H.　1 teaspoon salt

PREPARATION:

I.　Defrost F.
II.　Soak E in hot water 20 minutes, drain, save water. Slice each E into 3 pieces.
III.　Break G into bowl, beat, and add H.
IV.　Marinate B with C, D.

COOKING:

1.　Using high heat, add 1 tablespoon A to hot skillet. Add B–D mixture, stir-fry 1 minute. If water is needed, add some from soaking mushrooms. Add E, F, continue stir-frying 1 to 2 minutes. Remove to bowl.

2.　Add remaining A to cleaned skillet. Use high heat. Add G–H mixture to pan without stirring. Allow skin to form. Lower heat when skin thickens.

3.　Add A–F mixture to half of pan. Fold over G–H skin so that it forms a pouch. Serve hot.

FANCY OMELET
Yang Tsung Ro Si Don Jiao: General　　洋　葱　肉　絲　餃

Substitute 1 medium onion for F. Omit E. In Step 1, wash and skin onion, slice into rings, and cook onion and B together 3 to 5 minutes. Add small amount of water when needed. Remove to bowl.

FANCY OMELET
Ching Do Sha Ding Don: General　　青　豆　肉　絲　蛋　餃

Substitute fresh shrimp for B. In Step IV, shell, devein, and dice shrimp. Marinate with C, D and 1 teaspoon sherry.

SCRAMBLED EGGS WITH DRIED SHRIMP
Sha Mi Tsao Don: General　　蝦　米　炒

A.　¼ cup peanut oil
B.　12 dried shrimp
C.　6 eggs
D.　2 teaspoons dry sherry
E.　1 teaspoon salt
F.　½ teaspoon sugar

PREPARATION:

I.　Wash B well, soak 5 minutes in hot water. Drain, and chop very fine. Save water.
II.　Beat C; add B and its water, and D, E, F, and mix well.

COOKING:

1.　Heat A until very hot.
2.　Add B–F mixture, scramble, and serve hot.

GOLDEN COIN EGG
Jing Tsen Don Bing: Hunan

金 錢 蛋 餅

A. 2 tablespoons peanut oil
B. 6 hard-cooked eggs
C. 1 hot green chili pepper
D. 2 slices ginger
E. 1 tablespoon chopped scallion
F. 2 tablespoons light soy sauce
G. 1 tablespoon vinegar

H. 1 teaspoon sugar
I. 2 teaspoons sherry
J. ½ teaspoon sesame oil
K. 1 teaspoon cornstarch mixed with
   1 tablespoon water
L. a few lettuce leaves
M. 1 to 2 tablespoons cornstarch

PREPARATION:

I. Slice each B into 5 pieces; sprinkle both sides with M until well coated.
II. Discard seeds and stem of C, then chop.

(Two tablespoons chopped sweet green pepper may be substituted for C.)
III. Mix C, D, E, F, G, H, I, J, K.

COOKING:

1. Heat A, brown B on both sides.
2. Add C–K mixture, mix well.

3. Place on top of L and serve.

PLAIN EGG FU YONG
Ru Ee Fu Yong Don: General

如 意 芙 蓉 蛋

A. 4 tablespoons peanut oil
B. 2 scallions, minced
C. 6 Chinese black mushrooms
D. 2 cups bean sprouts
E. ¼ cup shredded canned water chestnuts

F. 6 eggs
G. ½ teaspoon salt
H. ¼ teaspoon pepper
I. 2 teaspoons light soy sauce

PREPARATION:

I. Wash and soak C 15 minutes in warm water, drain, and slice into long, thin strips.

II. Wash D thoroughly. Drain.
III. Beat F, mix with G, H, I thoroughly.

COOKING:

1. Heat 1 tablespoon A, stir-fry B, C about a minute.
2. Add D, E, stir constantly 1 to 2 minutes.
3. Add cooked B–E mixture to F–I mixture, emptying frying pan contents.
4. Heat remaining A in frying pan. Cook egg-vegetable mixture over medium heat until one

side is brown. Turn over, press, and fry until second side is brown. Serve hot.
Note: To serve as pancake (Fu Yong Don Bang) with oyster sauce, combine ¼ cup oyster sauce, ½ cup water, and 1 teaspoon cornstarch in a saucepan. Cook until thickened. Pour sauce over egg fu yong pancake and serve hot.

FISH

Much of the fish eaten in China is similar to Western types: carp, porgy, sea bass, catfish, cod, herring, trout, mullet, smelt, sea perch, salmon, shad, tuna, snapper, sole, sturgeon, turbot. Shellfish, too, include familiar varieties: shrimp, prawn, crab, lobster, clams, oysters, and scallops.

Fish in China often are bought alive and kept in large vats of water until ready to be cooked. This retains their freshness; also it combats the lack of commercial refrigeration. Preserving, salting, or cooking techniques, too, are widely used at the time of the catch. Some Chinese are so fond of salted fish that they eat it at almost every meal; it is soaked, seasoned with fresh ginger, and steam-cooked over rice.

ABALONE WITH CHINESE CABBAGE HEARTS
Bao Yu Bai Tsai Shing: Shanghai　鮑 魚 白 菜 心

A. 2 tablespoons peanut oil
B. 1 or 2 cloves garlic
C. 2 teaspoons sherry
D. ½ cup liquid from H
E. 2 tablespoons oyster sauce
F. 1 teaspoon sugar
G. ½ teaspoon sesame oil
H. 1-lb. can abalone
I. 2 teaspoons cornstarch mixed with 2 tablespoons water
J. 1 lb. Chinese cabbage heart
K. ½ teaspoon salt

PREPARATION:

I. Cut H into ¼-inch by 2½-inch slices.
II. Pound B with side of cleaver, discard skin.
III. Mix C, D, E, F, G.
IV. Clean and wash J, cut into 4- or 5-inch-long pieces, parboil 1½ minutes. Bring water to boil, add K and J, bring back to boil and cook for a few seconds. Drain J and arrange on plate.

COOKING:

1. Heat A, add B, stir-fry until light brown, add C–G mixture, bring to boil.
2. Add H, cook 2 to 3 minutes.
3. Thicken with I, place on top of J, and serve.

33

ABALONE WITH ASPARAGUS AND TURKEY
Lu Shun Bao Pien: Shanghai
蘆 筍 鮑 片

A. ¼ cup vegetable oil
B. ½ can (8 oz.) abalone
C. ½ lb. asparagus
D. 1 cup shredded cooked turkey breast
E. 4 oz. canned or fresh button mushrooms

F. 3 slices ginger
G. ¾ cup chicken or meat stock
H. 1 tablespoon cornstarch
I. 1 tablespoon light soy sauce

PREPARATION:

I. Slice B into thin pieces. Save juice as substitute for water later.

II. French-cut tender C tips; discard tough stems.
III. If fresh E are used, slice each into thirds.

COOKING:

1. Place A in hot skillet. Add B, C, stir-fry 2 minutes.
2. Add D, E, F, stir-fry 2 more minutes. If liquid is needed, add ¼ cup B juice.

3. Mix G, H, I, then add to skillet. Salt to taste. Serve hot.

BRAISED SLICED ABALONE
Hung Sao Bao Pien: General
紅 燒 鮑 片

A. 2 tablespoons peanut oil
B. 1 scallion (white part only), chopped
C. 2 tablespoons light soy sauce
D. 2 teaspoons sherry
E. ½ cup chicken broth
F. ½ teaspoon ground pepper

G. 1 teaspoon sugar
H. 1-lb. can abalone
I. 2 teaspoons cornstarch mixed with 2 tablespoons water
J. few drops sesame oil (to taste)

PREPARATION:

I. Slice H into thin pieces.

II. Mix C, D, E, F, G.

COOKING:

1. Heat A, add B, stir-fry a few seconds.
2. Add C–G mixture, bring to a boil.
3. Add H and cook 3 minutes.

4. Thicken with I.
5. Add J and serve.

RED-IN-SNOW CARP
Shwe Tsai Li Yu: Shanghai
雪 菜 鯉 魚

A. 2 tablespoons peanut oil
B. 1 scallion
C. 4 slices ginger, chopped
D. 1 carp (1 to 1½ lbs.), sea bass, or porgy
E. 1 tablespoon sherry

F. ½ cup sliced bamboo shoots
G. 1 cup chicken broth
H. ½ cup red-in-snow
I. salt to taste

PREPARATION:

I. Clean and wash D.

II. Cut B into 2-inch-long pieces.

COOKING:

1. Heat A, add B, C, stir-fry a few seconds.
2. Add D, E, F, G and bring to boil; cover and cook 5 minutes.

3. Add H, I, and cook 2 to 3 more minutes, or until fish is done.

BASS, TURNIPS, AND SPARERIBS
Pai Gu Mun Yu: Peking

排 骨 燜 魚

A. 1 lb. spareribs
B. 1½-lb. sea bass or porgy
C. 1 teaspoon salt
D. 1 lb. turnips
E. dash black pepper
F. 1 teaspoon sherry

G. Chinese parsley (optional)
H. 4 slices ginger, minced
I. 2 scallions, minced
J. 1 tablespoon light soy sauce
K. 2 teaspoons cider vinegar
L. 1 teaspoon sesame oil

PREPARATION:

I. Clean and scale B. Slit skin diagonally every 2 inches. Rub with C.

II. Cut A into pieces 2 inches long.
III. Peel and shred D.

COOKING:

1. Wash A and simmer 1 hour in 1 qt. water.
2. Add B–C, D, E, salt to taste, and boil 20 minutes. Add F. Serve in long dish; add G.

3. Prepare sauce by mixing H, I, J, K, L.
4. Fish is dipped in H–L sauce for eating.

FIVE WILLOW SWEET AND SOUR SEA BASS
Wu Liu Yu: Hangchow

五 柳 魚

A. 1- to 2-pound sea bass (or pike, carp, haddock, halibut, mackerel, bluefish)
B. 1 teaspoon salt

C. 2 tablespoons peanut oil
D. sweet and sour sauce (see Index)

PREPARATION:

I. Eviscerate, clean, and wash A.   II. Rub with B.   III. Place on deep serving platter.

COOKING:

1. Place platter with A–B in steamer containing boiling water.
2. Steam 20 minutes (or until fish is done).

3. Remove platter and set aside.
4. Heat C to smoking; pour over A.
5. Pour D over A and serve at once.

CRISPY BASS
Chui Pi Yu: Szechuan

脆 皮 魚

A. 2 cups peanut oil
B. 1½-lb. sea bass
C. 1 tablespoon chopped scallion
D. 1 teaspoon chopped ginger
E. 2 tablespoons catsup
F. 2 tablespoons sugar
G. 2 tablespoons vinegar

H. salt to taste
I. 2 teaspoons cornstarch mixed with 2 tablespoons water
J. 1 tablespoon cornstarch
K. 1¼ teaspoons salt
L. ¼ teaspoon pepper
M. 1 tablespoon white or yellow wine

PREPARATION:

I. Clean and wash B, dry between paper towels.
II. Mix K, L, M and rub all over B.

III. Rub B with I, then coat with J.

COOKING:

1. Heat A to 325°, deep-fry B until it is golden brown, about 5 minutes, turn over once or twice during frying; remove to a dish.

2. Heat 1 tablespoon A, add C, D, stir-fry ½ minute; add E, F, G, H, and cook 1 to 2 minutes; place in small dish and serve with B.

SWEET AND SOUR FISH
Tang Tsu Yu: Shanghai

糖 醋 魚

A. 3 cups peanut oil
B. 1- to 1½-lb. porgy or bass
C. ½ cup shrimp, diced
D. ½ cup peas
E. 1 tablespoon light soy sauce
F. 1 tablespoon sherry
G. 3 tablespoons catsup
H. 1 tablespoon sugar

I. 1½ tablespoons vinegar
J. 2 tablespoons cornstarch
K. 1 tomato
L. 1 teaspoon cornstarch mixed with
   2 tablespoons water
M. 1 teaspoon salt
N. dash pepper

PREPARATION:

I. Mix L, M, N thoroughly.
II. Mix E, F, G, H, I, and 1 teaspoon J.
III. Slash both sides of B diagonally at 2-inch intervals, rub with L–N mixture. Roll in J so that B is coated with a thin layer.
IV. Mix C with remaining J and dash of salt.
V. Place K in boiling water for a few seconds, remove, peel, and cut into cubes.

COOKING:

1. Heat A to 325°; deep fry B until golden brown (about 5 minutes). Remove to dish.
2. Heat additional 1 tablespoon oil, stir-fry C 1 to 2 minutes, add D, stir for 1 minute.
3. Add K and E–J mixture, stir until thickened.
4. Pour over B and serve.

WEST LAKE BOILED SWEET AND SOUR FISH
Si Wu Tsu Liu Yu: Shanghai

西 湖 醋 柳 魚

A. 1½-lb. bass or trout
B. 1½ teaspoons salt
C. 1 tablespoon sherry
D. 1 scallion cut into 2- to 3-inch pieces
E. 2 slices ginger
F. 3 tablespoons peanut oil
G. 1 or 2 cloves garlic, chopped
H. 1 cup fish soup
I. 3 tablespoons sugar

J. 2 tablespoons light soy sauce
K. 2 teaspoons sesame oil
L. 3 tablespoons wine vinegar
M. 1 tablespoon cornstarch mixed with
   ⅓ cup water
N. 2 scallions
O. ½ teaspoon pepper
P. 1 tablespoon shredded ginger

PREPARATION:

I. Clean and wash A, dry between paper towels. Split A open through stomach up to backbone, so that fish becomes one flat piece.
II. Add B, C, D, E to a pan of water (enough to cover fish), boil ½ minute.
III. Shred N diagonally into long strips.
IV. Mix I, J, K, L.

COOKING:

1. Add A to boiling B–E water mixture. Cover and cook 3 minutes; Remove pan from heat, but leave A in water 10 to 12 minutes more; place A on plate, being careful not to break A.
2. Sprinkle O over A and arrange N, P over top of A.
3. Heat F, add G and stir-fry a few seconds.
4. Add H, bring to a boil.
5. Add I–L, stir well and thicken with M.
6. Pour over A and serve hot.

SHAD ROE CAKES
Jien Yu Tze: Shanghai

煎 魚 子

A. peanut oil for deep frying
B. ½ lb. shad roe
C. 1 egg, beaten
D. 1 scallion, minced

E. 2 tablespoons cornstarch
F. ¾ teaspoon salt
G. dash black pepper or paprika
H. ¼ teaspoon MSG (optional)

PREPARATION:

I. Wash B and remove membrane.

II. Mix B, C, D, E, F, G, H until smooth.

COOKING:

1. Heat A in deep fryer.

2. Add 1 tablespoon B–H mixture at a time and fry until golden brown. Serve hot.

STEAMED SHAD
Tsen Sih Yu: Shanghai

蒸 鰣 魚

A. 3-lb. shad, cleaned
B. 1½ teaspoons salt
C. 2 scallions
D. ¼ cup shredded Virginia ham
E. 5 slices ginger, shredded

F. 1 tablespoon sherry
G. 2 teaspoons shredded ginger
H. 3 tablespoons cider vinegar
I. 1 to 2 tablespoons light soy sauce

PREPARATION:

I. Scale and clean A, rub with B.

II. Cut each C into 4 sections.

COOKING:

1. Place A–B in large bowl. Place bowl in steamer.
2. Place C inside fish cavity.
3. Spread D, E and F over A–B.

4. Steam for 1½ hours or until meat separates easily from bones.
5. Mix G, H, I and serve as sauce for dipping.

RED-COOKED MANDARIN FISH
Hung Sao Yu: Peking

紅 燒 魚

A. 6 tablespoons peanut oil
B. 1 2-lb. sea bass
C. ¼ cup sliced bamboo shoots
D. 8 Chinese mushrooms
E. 1 scallion
F. 2 slices ginger, chopped

G. 1 clove garlic, chopped
H. ¼ cup light soy sauce
I. 1 tablespoon sherry
J. 1 teaspoon sugar
K. 2 teaspoons cornstarch
L. ½ cup chicken broth

PREPARATION:

I. Wash B well, dry with paper towels, and diagonally slash on each side about 2 inches apart.

II. Wash D, soak in warm water 15 minutes, drain. Cut each into 4- to 5-inch pieces.
III. Cut E into pieces 1½ inches long.
IV. Mix H, I, J, K, L.

COOKING:

1. Heat A. Brown B on both sides. Discard A, reserving 1 to 2 tablespoons.
2. Add C, D, E, F, G, H–L mixture to B. Bring

to boil, cover, and cook over low heat about 30 minutes. During this time, baste B two or three times with sauce. Serve hot.

STUFFED RED SNAPPER
Yu Riong Ro Bing: Shanghai

魚 釀 肉 餅

A. 2-lb. red snapper
B. 1 teaspoon salt
C. 4 oz. ground pork
D. 2 slices ginger, minced
E. 2 scallions, minced
F. 2 teaspoons sherry
G. 2 teaspoons light soy sauce
H. 1 teaspoon cornstarch

I. ½ tablespoon brown sugar
J. 3 slices ginger
K. 2 scallions
L. 1 tablespoon cornstarch
M. 1½ cups water
N. 2 tablespoons light soy sauce
O. 5 stalks Chinese parsley (optional)

PREPARATION:

I. Clean A. Make diagonal slashes in skin, one inch apart. Rub B over skin.

II. Mix C, D, E, F, G, H and stuff A with mixture.

III. Mix I, J, K, L, M, N for sauce.

COOKING:

1. Fry A–H in skillet with ½ cup hot oil, until browned on both sides. Pour off excess oil.
2. Add I–N sauce to skillet; cover tightly. Simmer A 15 to 20 minutes on each side. Add small amount of water, if needed. Serve hot. O may be sprinkled on top, if desired.

SHANGHAI SMOKED FISH *
Shwin Yu: Shanghai

上 海 燻 魚

A. 2 to 3 scallions, chopped
B. 5 slices ginger, chopped
C. ⅓ cup sherry
D. ½ teaspoon five spices powder
E. 1 tablespoon sugar

F. ¼ cup light soy sauce
G. ½ teaspoon salt
H. 1 pt. peanut oil
I. 1- to 2-lb. carp

PREPARATION:

I. Wash I thoroughly. Dry well with paper towels.
II. Cut I into ½-inch pieces (cross section). Leave in cool, drafty place for air-drying 30 minutes.

III. Mix A, B well with C, D, E, F, G.
IV. Marinate I in A–G mixture. Refrigerate at least ½ day.
V. Drain I thoroughly before frying, saving sauce mixture in small cooking pot.

COOKING:

1. Heat A–G in pot, bring to boil. Turn off heat and add few drops sesame oil.
2. Heat H in 2-qt. pot. Deep fry I at 350° until brown and crisp (about 3 minutes).

3. Dip each piece of fried I in cooked sauce for a few seconds. Remove from sauce, and place in container. Fish will be tastier if left in refrigerator overnight and eaten cold.

* This fish is not really smoked but dipped in a spice sauce to give it a mellow flavor. The proper frying time gives it fragrance without making it dried out.

RED-COOKED CARP WITH BEAN CURD SKIN
Fu Pi Hung Sao Yu: Shanghai   腐 皮 紅 燒 魚

A. bean curd skin to cover H.
B. 2 scallions, minced
C. 7 slices ginger, minced
D. 2 tablespoons sherry
E. 1 tablespoon light soy sauce
F. 1 clove garlic, chopped

G. 2 teaspoons brown sugar
H. 3-lb. carp, cleaned and scaled
I. 1 teaspoon salt
J. 2 teaspoons cornstarch
K. ½ cup broth
L. 3 tablespoons peanut oil

PREPARATION:

I. Soak A in hot water 20 minutes.
II. Mix B, C, D, E, F, G.
III. Slit skin of H diagonally every ¾ inch and rub I over it. Take a piece of heavy-duty aluminum foil longer than H and place it in large cooky pan. Place H in foil.
IV. Drape A over H. Pour B–G, K, over H. Sprinkle with L. Fold foil over to seal A in steam.

COOKING:

1. Preheat oven to 350°.
2. Place foil-wrapped A–I in oven. Cook 1 hour.
3. Add ¼ cup water to J. Mix until smooth. Add to A–I as needed to thicken gravy. Check fish; if it comes off bone easily dish is ready to serve.

CARP WITH BEAN CURD CAKE
Do Fu Mun Li Yu: Shanghai   豆 腐 燜 鯉 魚

A. 6 oz. frozen broccoli tips
B. 6 black dried Chinese mushrooms
C. 2- to 3-lb. carp, whole, cleaned, scaled
D. 2 tablespoons sherry
E. 4 slices ginger
F. 4 scallions
G. ⅓ cup peanut or salad oil

H. 2 tablespoons light soy sauce
I. 1 teaspoon salt
J. 3 tablespoons salad oil
K. 4 cakes bean curd
L. ½ cup shredded fresh pork
M. 2 teaspoons cornstarch mixed with 2 tablespoons water

PREPARATION:

I. Cut A into pieces 2 inches long.
II. Soak B in hot water ½ hour; discard stems; slice each B into 3 to 5 pieces.
III. Slit skin of C diagonally every ¾ inch and rub I over it. Take a piece of heavy-duty aluminum foil longer than C and place it in large cooky pan. Place C in foil.
IV. Mix D, E, F, G, H. Pour over C.
V. Add J to hot skillet. Add A, L. Stir-fry 3 minutes. Remove and place in dish.
VI. Dice K into squares and spread, with B, over C.

COOKING:

1. Preheat oven to 350°.
2. Place foil-wrapped fish in oven. Cook 50 minutes. Remove from oven; open foil. Put A, L over B–K. Seal foil, leave in oven 10 more minutes.
3. Add M to sauce in foil. Serve C with sauce poured over.

PEKING FRIED FISH
Gahn Jien Yu: Peking

乾 煎 魚

A. ¼ cup peanut oil
B. 1½-lb. porgy
C. 2 teaspoons chopped scallion
D. 1 teaspoon sesame oil
E. 1 teaspoon chopped ginger
F. 1 tablespoon vinegar

G. 1 scallion tied into a knot
H. 4 slices ginger
I. 2 teaspoons salt
J. 1 to 2 tablespoons flour
K. 1 egg, beaten

PREPARATION:

I. Clean and wash B, dry between paper towels. Make 2 or 3 slashes on each side.
II. Place G, H in B cavity and rub outside with

I. Let stand 15 minutes.
III. Coat B with J and roll in K.
IV. Mix E, F.

COOKING:

1. Heat A and in it brown B on each side for ½ to 1 minute.
2. Over medium heat, brown each side 3 to 5 minutes longer; turn B over once or twice or until it is done.

3. Remove B to plate.
4. Pour off excess oil, in same pan stir-fry C, D ½ minute, pour over B.
5. Serve with E–F mixture or Chinese hot sauce.

FRIED FISH CAKES
Yu Bing: Shanghai

魚 餅

A. 4 tablespoons peanut oil
B. ½ lb. fillet of flounder, bass, or haddock, minced
C. 1 cup thinly sliced bamboo shoots
D. 6 Chinese dried mushrooms
E. ½ cup thinly sliced Smithfield ham
F. 1 scallion
G. 1 teaspoon sugar

H. 1 tablespoon light soy sauce
I. 1 teaspoon cornstarch
J. dash salt, pepper
K. 3 tablespoons mushroom water
L. 1 teaspoon cornstarch
M. 10 dried shrimp, chopped
N. 2 teaspoons sherry
O. salt to taste

PREPARATION:

I. Mix B with I, J.
II. Wash M. Marinate M in N.
III. Mix B mixture and M, N and shape into 12 cakes.

IV. Wash D and soak in water 15 minutes; drain, saving 3 tablespoons (K); cut each D in half.
V. Slice F into 1-inch pieces.
VI. Mix K, L.

COOKING:

1. Heat A in frying pan; brown B cakes lightly on both sides (from Preparation Step III); remove to dish.
2. Add C, D, E, F to same pan, stir-fry 1 minute.

3. Replace B cakes in pan, mix well with other ingredients. Add G, H; cover and cook over low heat 2 minutes.
4. Add O and thicken with K, L; serve.

SCALLION FISH
Tsung Shang Yu: Shanghai　　葱 香 魚

A. 1½-lb. sea bass, porgy, or red snapper
B. 1 teaspoon salt
C. 4 scallions
D. 5 slices ginger, minced
E. 1 clove garlic, minced
F. 3 tablespoons vegetable oil
G. 1 teaspoon sugar
H. 2 tablespoons light soy sauce
I. 1 tablespoon cornstarch
J. ⅓ cup water

PREPARATION:

I. Clean and scale A. Slash skin diagonally at 1- to 1½-inch intervals. Rub on B inside and out.
II. Slit C. Place aluminum foil in flat pan and spread C on it. Place A on top.
III. Mix D, E, F, G, H.
IV. Preheat broiler.
V. Mix I, J and stir into D–H.

COOKING:

1. Broil A–C in pan 20 minutes, then turn over for another 20 minutes.
2. Pour D–J in pot. Stir and heat. Pour over A–C.
3. Lower broiling pan. Cover A–C with additional foil and cook 10 minutes.

STIR-FRIED HADDOCK FLAKES
Tsao Yu Pien: General　　炒 魚 片

A. 6 tablespoons vegetable oil
B. 1 lb. fillet of haddock
C. 2 heaping tablespoons cloud ears
D. 6 dried mushrooms
E. 2 stems celery
F. 1 package (10 oz.) frozen peas
G. 5 slices ginger
H. 2 to 3 scallions, minced
I. dash black pepper (optional)
J. 1 teaspoon salt
K. 3 tablespoons sherry
L. 3 tablespoons cornstarch

PREPARATION:

I. Slice B into strips ⅝ inch by 2 inches by ⅝ inch. Marinate in J, K. Then mix, and coat with L.
II. Soak D in hot water 20 minutes. Cut off stems, cut into 3 pieces each. Reserve water.
III. Cut E into pieces ⅛ inch thick, across grain.
IV. Defrost F.
V. Soak C in hot water 20 minutes, drain, and wash.

COOKING:

1. Place 5 tablespoons A in large frying pan. Stir-fry B 5 minutes, remove from pan.
2. Place remaining A in pan. Add C, D, E; cook 5 minutes. Add F, G, H, cook 1 minute more.
3. Add B, I. Stir a few times. Serve hot.

STIR-FRIED FILLET OF SOLE, FLOUNDER, OR SEA BASS FLAKES
Tsao Yu Pien: General　　炒 魚 片

Substitute fillet of sole, flounder, or sea bass for B. Cook 2 minutes in Step 1.

FISH MAW IN CRAB SAUCE
Sha Hwang Yu Du: Shanghai 蟹 黃 魚 肚

A. 4 tablespoons vegetable oil
B. 4 slices ginger, chopped
C. 2 scallions, chopped
D. 2 cups chicken soup
E. ½ teaspoon salt
F. 6 Chinese mushrooms
G. 4 oz. fish maw

H. 4 oz. crab meat
I. 1 teaspoon sugar
J. 1 tablespoon cornstarch
K. 3 tablespoons sherry
L. 1 tablespoon light soy sauce
M. ½ cup mushroom water

PREPARATION:

I. Wash G in cold water and soak overnight. Squeeze out water. Cook in boiling water with 4 slices B and 2 tablespoons K for 10 minutes. Drain; rinse with cold water; squeeze out water. Cut into bite-size pieces.

II. Soak F in warm water 20 minutes. Discard stems and cut each into three pieces.

III. Mix I, J, 1 tablespoon K, L, M until smooth.

COOKING:

1. Put 2 tablespoons A into deep frying pan (or wok). Add B, C. Stir-fry ½ minute; add D, E, F. Bring to boil.
2. Add G and simmer 15 minutes. Place in serving bowl.

3. Into same frying pan put rest of A and heat. Add H, stir-fry ½ minute.
4. Add I, J, K, L, M to make crab sauce.
5. Pour sauce into fish maw soup and serve.

CAUL FAT STEAMED FISH
Wong Yo Tsen Yu: Szechuan 網 油 蒸 魚

A. 1½-lb. bass
B. 1½ teaspoons salt
C. 1 tablespoon sherry
D. 2 cloves garlic, chopped
E. 1 red-hot pepper

F. 3 tablespoons salted black beans
G. 1½ teaspoons sugar
H. 1 tablespoon light soy sauce
I. 1 piece caul fat 8 by 12 inches
J. 1 tablespoon cornstarch

PREPARATION:

I. Clean and wash A, dry between paper towels. Make 2 slashes diagonally on both sides. Rub inside and outside with B.
II. Sprinkle A with C and marinate 10 minutes.
III. Discard stem and seeds of E, chop.
IV. Soak F in a cup of water 1 minute so that any sand will settle on bottom; remove F, wash, drain, and mash.

V. Mix D, E, F, G, H well with 1 tablespoon water. Stuff A with 1 tablespoon of D–H mixture.
VI. Wash I in warm water, dry between paper towels, sprinkle lightly with J.
VII. Spread ½ of D–H mixture over I, J.
VIII. Place A on top of D–H mixture and place the other half of D–H mixture over A.
IX. Wrap I over fish and place in a dish.

COOKING:

1. Steam in a steamer 15 minutes or until fish is done.

STEAMED FISH
Ching Tsen Yu: Szechuan

清 蒸 魚

A. 1- to 1½-lb. bass or trout
B. 1½ teaspoons salt
C. 1 tablespoon white wine
D. ¼ to ½ teaspoon pepper or to taste
E. 4 Chinese mushrooms

F. 1 scallion
G. 4 to 6 slices Virginia ham
H. 4 slices ginger
I. few slices pork fat
J. ⅓ cup chicken broth

PREPARATION:

I. Clean and wash A; make 2 or 3 slashes on each side.
II. Mix B, C, D, rub over A; place A on a dish.
III. Wash E and soak in warm water 15 minutes, drain, cut each into 4 or 5 pieces.

IV. Cut F into 1½-inch pieces.
V. Spread G on top of A.
VI. Spread E on top of G.
VII. Put F, H over E.
VIII. Arrange I on top of all.

COOKING:

1. Steam in steamer over boiling water 15 minutes or until fish is done, discard pork fat and fish juice.
2. Boil J, add to steamed fish and serve.

BOILED FISH WITH SZECHUAN SAUCE
Sao Yu: Szechuan

燒 魚

A. 1- to 1½-lb. sea bass
B. 2 tablespoons peanut oil
C. ¼ cup shredded bamboo shoots
D. 4 Chinese mushrooms
E. 1 tablespoon chopped scallion
F. 1 teaspoon chopped ginger
G. 1 clove garlic, minced
H. 2 teaspoons light soy sauce

I. 2 teaspoons brown bean sauce
J. ½ teaspoon salt
K. 2 teaspoons sherry
L. 2 teaspoons vinegar
M. 1 teaspoon sugar
N. 2 teaspoons cornstarch mixed with ½ cup mushroom water

PREPARATION:

I. Wash A, make 3 or 4 diagonal slashes on each side.

II. Wash and soak D in warm water 15 minutes. Drain (save water for N) and shred.
III. Mix H, I, J, K, L, M, N.

COOKING:

1. Place A in frying pan, cover with boiling water and cook over low heat 3 minutes. Remove from heat but leave in water 12 to 15 minutes, remove to plate.

2. Heat B, add C, D, E, F, G, stir-fry 1 minute, add H–N mixture, stir until gravy is thickened; pour over fish and serve.

SZECHUAN STEAMED FISH
Do Jiang Tsen Yu: Szechuan

豆 醬 蒸 魚

A. 1½- to 2-lb. carp
B. ¼ cup peanut oil
C. 1 clove garlic, minced
D. 2 slices ginger, chopped
E. 1 tablespoon brown bean sauce
F. ½ cup water
G. 2 teaspoons sherry
H. 1 tablespoon light soy sauce

I. 1 teaspoon sugar
J. 1 teaspoon salt
K. 1 tablespoon chopped scallions
L. 1 tablespoon cornstarch mixed with
   ¼ cup water
M. anise pepper to taste
N. ½ teaspoon salt
O. ¼ to ½ teaspoon ginger juice (see Index)

PREPARATION:

I. Scale, clean, and wash A, dry with paper towel, rub with N, O.
II. Mix C, D, E.
III. Mix G, H, I, J, K.

COOKING:

1. Place A in dish, steam in a steamer over boiling water 15 minutes or until done. Pour all the juice from A into another dish (may be added to H to make ½ cup).
2. Heat B to smoking, pour over A, return B to pot, heat; when it is hot, add C–E, stir-fry ½ minute, add F, bring to boil.
3. Add G–K mixture, cook for 1 minute.
4. Thicken with L. Pour over fish, add M to taste and serve hot.

BRAISED FROGS' LEGS WITH VEGETARIAN STEAK
Tien Gee Mun Kow Fu: Shanghai

田 雞 燜 烤 麩

A. ½ cup vegetable oil
B. 5 oz. vegetarian steak
C. 2 scallions
D. 1 lb. frogs' legs
E. 2 tablespoons cornstarch
F. 3 tablespoons sherry
G. ½ teaspoon salt

H. 1½ tablespoons light soy sauce
I. 5 slices ginger
J. 1 teaspoon sugar
K. 1 cup chicken soup
L. ½ tablespoon cornstarch mixed with
   2 tablespoons water
M. 1 teaspoon sesame oil (optional)

PREPARATION:

I. Wash and clean D, then drain.
II. Mix E, F, G, H, and M; separate into 2 portions.
III. Mix ⅔ of E–H with D; add I, J; let stand.
IV. Cut B into ½-inch by 1½-inch pieces, mix with ⅓ E–H mixture.
V. Cut C into 1½-inch pieces.

COOKING:

1. Heat A in frying pan.
2. Add B mixture, C and stir-fry 1 to 2 minutes.
3. Add D–J mixture and stir-fry 2 minutes. Add small amount of soup if pan dries out.
4. Add ¼ to ½ cup K and simmer 2 minutes. Thicken with L and serve.

STIR-FRIED FROGS' LEGS
Tsao Tien Gee Twei: Shanghai 炒 田 雞 腿

A. ⅓ cup peanut oil
B. ½ teaspoon sesame oil
C. ¼ cup sherry
D. 1 teaspoon salt
E. 2 teaspoons vinegar
F. 2 teaspoons sugar

G. 1 tablespoon light soy sauce
H. 1 lb. frogs' legs
I. 2 tablespoons cornstarch
J. 6-oz. can fried vegetable steak
K. 1 scallion, minced
L. 6 slices ginger, minced

PREPARATION:
I. Cut J into ½ inch chunks.
II. Clean H and cut each into 2 to 3 small pieces.
III. Mix B, C, D, E, F, G.

IV. Marinate H in B–G mixture ½ hour.
V. Place I in paper bag, add H and shake.

COOKING:
1. Heat A in skillet until hot.

2. Brown B–I in A. Add J, K, L, and cook additional 3 minutes with small amount of water.

FROGS' LEGS WITH FROZEN PEAS
Tien Gee Tsao Ching Do: Shanghai 田 雞 炒 青 豆

A. ¼ cup vegetable oil
B. 1 lb. tender frogs' legs
C. ½ teaspoon sugar
D. 1 teaspoon sesame oil (optional)
E. 2 teaspoons sherry
F. 1 teaspoon salt

G. ½ teaspoon ginger juice (see Index) or ¼ teaspoon ginger powder
H. 2 teaspoons cornstarch
I. 1 tablespoon light soy sauce
J. 10-oz. pkg. frozen peas
K. 2 scallions, shredded

PREPARATION:
I. Cover J with boiling water 1 minute or until peas are thoroughly thawed out; drain.

II. Wash and clean B, drain and dry.
III. Mix B with C, D, E, F, G, H, I.

COOKING:
1. Heat A, add B–I mixture and stir-fry 2 minutes.

2. Add J and ¼ cup water, if needed; simmer 1 to 2 minutes or until B and J are done.
3. Remove to serving dish and garnish with K.

SPICY FROGS' LEGS
Tsao Tien Gee Twei: Szechuan 炒 田 雞 腿

A. 3 tablespoons vegetable oil
B. 2 large sweet green peppers
C. 2 hot red peppers (optional)
D. 1 clove garlic
E. 1 lb. frogs' legs
F. 2 tablespoons hoisin sauce
G. 1 teaspoon light soy sauce

H. 1 tablespoon sherry
I. ½ teaspoon salt
J. 5 slices ginger
K. ⅓ cup soup stock
L. 2 teaspoons cornstarch mixed with 2 tablespoons water

PREPARATION:
I. Clean and wash E; drain.
II. Split B, C; discard stems and seeds.

III. Mash D, remove skin.
IV. Mix F, G, H, I, J, K.

COOKING:
1. Heat A in frying pan. When smoking, add B, C, D. Stir-fry a few seconds; add E, stir-fry 1 minute.

2. Add F–K, cover and simmer 4 minutes.
3. Thicken with L and serve.

FISH WITH BROWN BEAN PASTE
Do Ban Jiong Yu Pien: General   豆 板 醬 魚 片

A. 4 tablespoons vegetable oil
B. 1½ lbs. haddock, fillet sole, or flounder
C. 1½ tablespoons cornstarch
D. 3 tablespoons brown bean paste
E. 1 tablespoon brown sugar

F. 3 slices ginger
G. 2 scallions, minced
H. 1 tablespoon light soy sauce
I. ¼ teaspoon salt
J. 1 clove garlic, chopped (optional)

PREPARATION:

I. Cut B into slices ¼ inch thick. Rub C over.

II. Mix D, E, F, G, H, I, J with ¼ cup water.

COOKING:

1. Place A in hot skillet. When heated, add B–C and stir-fry 1 to 2 minutes.

2. Add D–J, lower heat, simmer 2 minutes, and serve hot.

BUTTERFISH IN BEER SAUCE
Go Sao Gih Yu: General   鍋 燒 節 魚

A. ¼ cup peanut oil
B. 1½ lbs. butterfish (about 5)
C. ¾ teaspoon salt
D. 3 scallions, shredded
E. 4 slices ginger, shredded
F. 1 teaspoon sugar

G. 1 tablespoon brown bean sauce
H. 1 tablespoon cider vinegar
I. 1 teaspoon light soy sauce
J. 1 tablespoon sherry
K. ¾ cup beer
L. 2 teaspoons cornstarch

PREPARATION:

I. Scale and clean B. Rinse in cold water, then dry with paper towels. Slash skin diagonally 1 inch apart across the width of the fish on both sides. Rub C over B and inside cavity.

II. Mix D, E, F, G, H, I, J.

COOKING:

1. Heat frying pan. When hot, add A.
2. Brown B in A 3 to 4 minutes on each side.
3. Pour off excess A and add D–J.
4. Add ½ cup K, cover and simmer 15 minutes.

5. Mix L with rest of K so that no lumps remain. Add to frying pan to thicken sauce. Mix well and serve hot.

FRIED SMELTS
Jien Sa Tsan Yu: General   煎 沙 昌 魚

A. 1 cup vegetable oil
B. 15 smelts (1 lb.)
C. ¼ cup light soy sauce
D. ¼ teaspoon five spices powder

E. 1 tablespoon sherry
F. 4 slices ginger
G. Chinese parsley (optional)
H. ¼ teaspoon sesame oil (optional)

PREPARATION:

I. Clean and scale B, drip dry in colander, then dry with paper towels.

II. Make sauce by mixing together C, D, E, F.

III. Marinate B in C–F sauce 30 to 60 minutes. Drip dry in colander.

COOKING:

Heat A to 375°. Deep fry B–F 1 to 2 minutes on each side. Sprinkle with G, H. Use toasted salt and anise pepper mixture as dip (see Index for Anise Pepper Salt).

GOLDEN FISH ROLLS
Don Pi Yu Guan: Hupeh

蛋 皮 魚 捲

A. ¼ cup peanut oil
B. 6 eggs
C. ½ teaspoon salt
D. 1 lb. fillet of flounder, minced (or crab meat, freshly cooked; or shrimp, shelled and deveined)
E. 4 scallions, minced

F. 3 slices ginger, minced
G. 2 teaspoons sherry
H. ½ teaspoon salt
I. dash black pepper
J. 1 teaspoon cornstarch
K. ¾ cup soup stock

PREPARATION:

I. Mix D, E with F, G, H, I, J.

II. Break B into bowl, add C, beat mixture lightly.

COOKING:

1. Put 2 tablespoons A in 8-inch skillet, heat and spread. Add a cooking ladleful of B–C mixture to form skin about 8 inches in diameter. Using low heat, make 6 such skins.
2. Divide D–J mixture into 6 equal portions. Place 1 portion in each egg skin, and roll 6 fish rolls.
3. Fry fish rolls over medium heat in remaining A, turning to ensure even cooking. Add K, cover and simmer 10 minutes. To serve, cut rolls crosswise, thereby forming round slices with golden edges.

FISH BALLS
Yu Yuen: General

魚 丸

A. 1 lb. fillet of flounder
B. 3 water chestnuts
C. 1 egg, beaten
D. 3 scallions, chopped

E. 1 slice ginger, minced
F. ½ teaspoon salt
G. 4½ teaspoons cornstarch
H. 1 teaspoon light soy sauce

PREPARATION:

I. Chop or grind A into fine pieces. Place in mixing bowl.
II. Chop B fine.
III. Mix, B, C, D, E, F, G, H and add to A.

Combine thoroughly.
IV. Form A–H mixture into balls, each containing a heaping tablespoon of ingredients.
V. Bring 2 qts. water to a rolling boil.

COOKING:

1. Drop A–H balls into boiling water a few at a time.
2. When they float to surface, remove.
3. Cool. Serve with duck sauce or light soy sauce.

BRAISED FISH BALLS WITH OYSTER SAUCE
Ho Yow Yu Yuen: General   蠔 油 魚 丸

A. 6 tablespoons peanut oil
B. 1 tablespoon chopped scallion
C. 2 slices ginger, chopped
D. 18 to 20 fish balls (see Fish Balls)
E. 6 to 8 Chinese mushrooms
F. 1 cup bite-size pieces bamboo shoots
G. 1 cup frozen peas

H. 1 tablespoon oyster sauce
I. 2 teaspoons cornstarch
J. 2 teaspoons sherry
K. ½ cup water
L. salt to taste
M. 1 teaspoon sugar

PREPARATION:

I. Wash E, soak 15 minutes in warm water. Drain, crosscut each into quarters.

II. Defrost G.

III. Mix H, I, J, K, M.

COOKING:

1. Heat A, stir-fry B, C a few seconds.
2. Add D, E, F, stir-fry 2 minutes.
3. Add G, cook 1 minute.

4. Add H–M mixture, stir well until thickened. Add L; serve hot.

SHRIMP AND OTHER SEAFOOD

Seafoods are considered delicacies and some require long and elaborate preparations prior to cooking. They are often cooked with strong flavoring agents, such as fermented black beans, garlic, ginger, pickled mustard greens, or pickled red-in-snow. They also can be cooked in sweet and sour sauce or cooked in a simple sauce when a delicate balance of flavor is called for, such as Dragon Well Tea Leaves Shrimp.

PHOENIX TAIL SHRIMP
Tza Fung Wei Sha: Peking　　　炸 鳳 尾 蝦

A. peanut oil for deep frying
B. ½ lb. jumbo shrimp (about 8)
C. ¼ teaspoon ginger juice (see Index)
D. 2 teaspoons chopped scallion
E. 1 teaspoon salt
F. 1 teaspoon sherry
G. 2 egg whites
H. 2 tablespoons cornstarch
I. ¼ cup flour
J. ½ cup bread crumbs

PREPARATION:

I. Shell B, leaving tail parts intact. Split backs lengthwise and devein. Wash and drain.
II. Mix B, C, D, E, F thoroughly.
III. Beat G, gradually mix in H, and beat until mixture is stiff.
IV. Coat B–F mixture with I; then cover with G–H mixture.
V. Roll each B (but not tail parts) in J.

COOKING:

1. Heat A to 325°.
2. Deep fry B 3 to 4 minutes.

49

PHOENIX TAIL SHRIMP
Fung Wei Sha: Szechuan

鳳 尾 蝦

A. 2 cups vegetable oil
B. ½ lb. jumbo shrimp (about 8)
C. 2 egg whites
D. 1 tablespoon cornstarch
E. 2 teaspoons flour
F. 1 teaspoon cornstarch

G. 1½ tablespoons vinegar
H. 1½ tablespoons sugar
I. 1 teaspoon light soy sauce
J. 1 tablespoon chopped scallion
K. ½ teaspoon chopped ginger
L. ½ teaspoon salt

PREPARATION:

I. Shell B, leaving tail parts intact. Split backs lengthwise and devein. Wash and drain.
II. Beat C until stiff. Gradually add D, E, beating until mixture is stiff.

III. Coat B with C–E mixture.
IV. Mix F with 1 tablespoon water.
V. Mix G, H, I, J, K, L with F mixture thoroughly.

COOKING:

1. Heat A to 325°.
2. Deep fry B–E 3 to 4 minutes. Drain on paper towel and place on dish.

3. Heat F–L mixture until it thickens, pour over fried shrimp. Serve hot.

SHRIMP BEAN CURD
Sha Tze Go Te Dow Fu: Peking

蝦 子 鍋 貼 豆 腐

A. 1 cup peanut oil for deep frying
B. 4 cakes bean curd
C. ¼ lb. small shrimp
D. 1 to 2 eggs
E. ¼ cup chicken broth
F. few drops sesame oil (optional)
G. Chinese parsley (optional)
H. ½ teaspoon ginger juice (see Index)

I. 1 tablespoon minced scallion
J. 1 tablespoon light soy sauce
K. 1 teaspoon sherry
L. ½ teaspoon sugar
M. ½ teaspoon salt
N. 1 teaspoon peanut oil
O. ⅓ cup flour

PREPARATION:

I. Cut B horizontally and then into halves that make each B into 4 pieces.
II. Mix H, I, J, K, L, M, N well, and pour over B, marinate 15 minutes.

III. Shell, devein, and wash C. Wash, drain, and mix with 1 teaspoon cornstarch and dash of salt.
IV. Beat D.
V. Coat B pieces with O and then D.

COOKING:

1. Heat A to 375°, deep fry B until golden brown. Drain on paper towel. Drain excess oil into a container.
2. In same pan arrange B in single layer, spread C on top.

3. If any D is left from dipping, mix with E and pour over B, C mixture; cover and cook over medium heat 3 minutes; remove lid and cook until liquid is absorbed.
4. Remove B and C to plate in a flat layer.
5. Add F and garnish with G.

FRIED SHRIMP WITH HOISIN SAUCE
Gahn Jien Sha: Peking

乾 煎 蝦

A. 3 tablespoons peanut oil
B. 2 cloves garlic, chopped
C. 1 tablespoon chopped scallion
D. 1 lb. large shrimp

E. 2 tablespoons hoisin sauce
F. 2 teaspoons light soy sauce
G. 1 teaspoon sherry

PREPARATION:

I. Shell, devein, and wash D.

II. Mix E, F, G.

COOKING:

1. Heat A, add B, C and stir-fry a few times.
2. Add D, continue stirring 1 to 2 minutes.

3. Add E–G mixture, mix well, stir until sauce is almost dry (about 4 to 5 minutes).

FRIED PRAWN IN SHELL
Yo Bao Sha: Shanghai

油 爆 蝦

A. ¼ cup peanut oil
B. ½ lb. jumbo shrimp
C. 1 tablespoon chopped scallion
D. 2 slices ginger, chopped

E. 1 tablespoon sherry
F. 2 tablespoons light soy sauce
G. 1 teaspoon sugar
H. several sprigs of Chinese parsley, chopped

PREPARATION:

I. Wash B with shells on, dry with paper towel, halve each, devein.

II. Mix C, D, E, F, G.

COOKING:

1. Heat A until smoking. Add B, stir-fry until shell turns golden red (about 1 minute), remove from heat, pour off excess A.

2. Return B to heat, add C–G, stir 3 more minutes (until sauce is reduced to half). Sprinkle with H. Serve hot or cold as hors d'oeuvres.

BROILED BACON WITH SHRIMP
Yen Ro Sha: Shanghai

煙 肉 蝦

A. 1 lb. frozen shrimp
   (about 24 shrimp), defrosted
B. 1 tablespoon sherry
C. 1 tablespoon light soy sauce
D. ½ teaspoon sugar

E. ½ to 1 teaspoon ginger juice (see Index)
F. salt and pepper to taste
G. 1 teaspoon cornstarch
H. 6 strips bacon

PREPARATION:

I. Mix A, B, C, D, E, F, G and marinate 25 to 30 minutes.
II. Cut each H into 4 pieces.

III. Wrap pieces of A–G with pieces of H; fasten with wooden toothpicks.
IV. Arrange in a single layer in a foil-lined pan.
V. Pour rest of marinade over A.

COOKING:

1. Preheat broiler 15 to 20 minutes.

2. Broil A 3 to 4 minutes on each side or until H is cooked.

DRIED SHRIMP WITH RADISHES
Sha Mi Sao Lo Bo: Shanghai

蝦 米 燒 蘿 蔔

A. 3 tablespoons vegetable oil
B. 15 dried shrimp
C. 2 scallions, minced
D. 2 bunches red whole radishes

(or 1 cup shredded turnips)
E. ¾ cup meat or chicken broth
F. ¼ teaspoon salt
G. 1 teaspoon cornstarch

PREPARATION:

I. Soak B in hot water 20 minutes. Drain, reserving water.

II. Remove and discard green from D; wash D well in cool water; shred.

COOKING:

1. Place A in hot skillet, using high heat. Add B, C, stir-fry 1 minute.
2. Add D, E, F and water from B; cover, simmer

15 minutes.

3. Mix G with a little water; stir this mixture into other ingredients. Serve.

DRIED SCALLOPS WITH TURNIPS
Gahn Bei Lo Bo Si: Shanghai

干 貝 蘿 蔔 絲

Substitute 1 cup shredded turnips for D and 6 dried scallops for B.

STIR-FRIED KIDNEY AND SHRIMP
Tsao Yao Sha : Shanghai

炒 腰 蝦

A. 2 kidneys
B. ¼ lb. snow pea pods or
   1 cup water chestnuts
C. ⅓ cup peanut oil
D. ½ lb. large shrimp
E. 1 teaspoon sherry
F. ½ teaspoon salt
G. 1 teaspoon cornstarch

H. 2 slices ginger
I. 1 scallion
J. 2 teaspoons light soy sauce
K. ½ teaspoon sugar
L. dash pepper, salt
M. 1 teaspoon cornstarch mixed with
   2 tablespoons water

PREPARATION:

I. Wash and remove any outer membrane from A; split lengthwise, remove all the white veins; make tiny crisscross slashes on top, then cut into ¼-inch slices.

II. Shell, devein, and wash D; dry between paper towels, mix with E, F, G.
III. Remove tips of B (or slice water chestnuts).
IV. Shred H and cut I into 1-inch segments.
v. Mix J, K, L, M.

COOKING:

1. Put A slices into 2 cups of boiling water; when water returns to boil, turn off heat, drain.
2. Add B to boiling water, stir, then drain immediately.
3. Heat ½ of C, add D–G mixture, stir-fry 2

minutes; add B, stir-fry ½ minute. Remove to dish.

4. Heat rest of C, add H, I, stir-fry a few seconds; add A and stir-fry 1 minute.
5. Add J–M mixture, mix well.
6. Add D–G mixture, stir well and serve.

STIR-FRIED SHRIMP
Ching Tsao Sha Ren: Peking   清 炒 蝦 仁

A. ⅓ cup peanut oil
B. 1 lb. large shrimp
C. 1 egg white
D. 2 teaspoons sherry
E. 1½ teaspoons salt

F. 1 tablespoon cornstarch
G. 1 teaspoon sherry
H. few drops sesame oil
I. 1 tablespoon chopped scallion

PREPARATION:

I. Wash B, dry between paper towels, then shell and devein. (The outstanding feature of stir-fried Peking shrimp is for the shrimp to be washed first, then shelled and cooked so that

shrimp pieces will be a brighter pink.)
II. Beat C, add D, E, F, mix well.
III. Add B, mix well.

COOKING:

1. Heat A to smoking, add B–F mixture, stir-fry 1 minute.
2. Remove B–F mixture to a dish, drain all the oil away.

3. In same pan, heat 2 more teaspoons peanut oil, add B–F mixture and G, and stir-fry 2 more minutes.
4. Add H and garnish with I.

STIR-FRIED SHRIMP WITH CABBAGE HEARTS
Sha Tsao Bai Tsai Shing: Szechuan   蝦 仁 白 荣 心

A. 2 tablespoons peanut oil
B. 8 to 10 dried shrimp
C. 1 teaspoon sherry
D. 1 to 1½ lbs. Chinese cabbage hearts
E. 1 teaspoon salt

F. ½ teaspoon sugar
G. 2 teaspoons light soy sauce
H. 1 teaspoon sherry
I. 1 tablespoon finely chopped scallion
J. ½ to 1 teaspoon sesame oil (to taste)

PREPARATION:

I. Cut D into pieces 2 to 3 inches long, parboil 1 minute, drain.

II. Clean, wash, and soak B in hot water 15 minutes; drain and mince.
III. Mix E, F, G, H.

COOKING:

1. Heat A, add B, stir-fry a few seconds, add C, continue stirring 1 minute.

2. Add D, stir few times, add E–H mixture; stir until no liquid is left.
3. Add I, J, mix well and serve.

STIR-FRIED SPINACH WITH DRIED SHRIMP
Sha Mi Bo Tsai Nee: Shanghai   蝦 米 菠 荣 泥

A. 3 tablespoons vegetable oil
B. 12 dried shrimp
C. 1 tablespoon minced scallion
D. 10 oz. pkg. fresh spinach

E. ½ teaspoon sugar
F. 1 teaspoon salt
G. ½ teaspoon sesame oil
H. ¼ teaspoon MSG (optional)

PREPARATION:

I. Wash D, drain.

II. Soak B in hot water 20 minutes. Drain and chop, saving water.

COOKING:

1. Heat A in skillet.
2. Add B, C, stir-fry 30 seconds.
3. Add B water and D; stir continuously 1 to 2

minutes.
4. Add E, F, H; mix well. Remove to bowl.
5. Add G, and mix in bowl. Serve hot.

FRIED SHRIMP
Tza Sha: Shanghai　　　　　　　　炸 蝦

A. 1 lb. large shrimp
B. 2 eggs
C. 1 teaspoon salt
D. dash pepper

E. ½ cup flour
F. peanut oil for deep frying
G. cocktail sauce or Tabasco

PREPARATION:

I. Shell A, except end part. Devein.
II. Cut lengthwise until back is connected slightly.

III. Beat B lightly.
IV. Sprinkle A with C, D; dip first in B, then in E.

COOKING:

1. Put several inches of F in deep fryer or saucepan. Heat.

2. Fry prepared A in hot F until golden brown.
3. Eat with G.

STIR-FRIED SHRIMP IN SHELL
Yo Bao Sha: Shanghai　　　　　　油 爆 蝦

A. 3 tablespoons peanut oil
B. 1 lb. large shrimp
C. 2 tablespoons light soy sauce
D. 2 tablespoons sugar
E. 2 tablespoons sherry
F. 1 tablespoon vinegar

G. 1½ teaspoons minced ginger
H. ⅛ teaspoon garlic powder
I. ½ teaspoon heavy soy sauce
J. ¼ cup water
K. 2 scallions, sliced

PREPARATION:

I. Remove legs from B (use small curved scissors). Wash well.

II. Mix C, D, E, F, G, H, I, J.

COOKING:

1. Put A in very hot skillet and bring to high heat.
2. Add B, stir-fry ½ minute.

3. Add C–J mixture. Cover. Cook over moderately high heat 5 minutes.
4. Serve with garnish of K. May be served cold.

STIR-FRIED SHRIMP WITH BEAN CURD
Do Fu Tsao Sha Ren: Peking　　　豆 腐 炒 蝦 仁

A. 4 tablespoons peanut oil
B. 1 scallion, chopped
C. 2 slices ginger, chopped
D. 1 lb. large shrimp
E. 1 egg white
F. 1 teaspoon salt

G. 3 teaspoons cornstarch
H. 2 cakes bean curd
I. ½ cup frozen peas, defrosted
J. 1 tablespoon sherry
K. 1 tablespoon light soy sauce

PREPARATION:

I. Shell, devein, and wash D. Split each into 2 pieces. Dry with paper towels.
II. Mix D with E, F, and 1 teaspoon G.

III. Cut each H into 16 pieces.
IV. Mix J, K and 2 teaspoons G with ½ cup broth or water.

COOKING:

1. Heat A. Add B, C, stir a few times. Add D–G and sauté over high heat 2 minutes. Add H, I.
2. Mix well, keep stirring a minute or so.

3. Add J–K mixture, and stir until sauce is thickened. Serve hot with rice.

STIR-FRIED SHRIMP WITH CHINESE VEGETABLES
Shia Tze Lo Han Chai: General   青 豆 冬 菇 蝦 仁

A. 3 tablespoons peanut oil
B. 4 slices ginger, shredded
C. 1 pkg. frozen shrimp (about 1 lb.)
D. 10-oz. can Chinese vegetables
E. 4 tablespoons light soy sauce

F. 4 tablespoons heavy soy sauce
G. 4 tablespoons sherry
H. 1 can beef broth
I. 1 tablespoon cornstarch mixed with 2 tablespoons water

PREPARATION:

I. Mix E, F, G, H, I in saucepan; set aside.

COOKING:

1. Heat A to smoking in deep pot; turn off heat, let stand 30 seconds.
2. Add B, turn up heat, stir-fry 1 minute.
3. Add C, stir for 5 to 7 minutes or until cooked.
4. Add D, mix in well, then pour into a bowl.
5. Heat E–I mixture until it thickens.
6. Pour E–I mixture over C mixture. Serve with rice.

Note: Lo Han Chai is a traditional Buddhist vegetarian dish. It adds an unusual flavor to any meat.

STEAMED SCALLOPS WITH CHINESE CABBAGE
Gahn Bei Bai Tsai: Peking   乾 貝 白 菜

A. 6 dried scallops
B. 1 Chinese cabbage or celery cabbage (1 to 2 lbs.)

C. 1 teaspoon salt

PREPARATION:

I. Wash A, soak in ½ cup hot water 30 to 45 minutes until soft. Drain, saving water.
II. Discard few outside tough leaves of B. Wash, clean whole B, then cut into 2-inch cross-section pieces (try not to separate leaves). Put into a bowl.
III. Sprinkle A over B. Add ½ cup A water or chicken broth and C.

COOKING:

1. Steam in steamer over boiling water 30 minutes. Serve hot.

DRIED SCALLOPS WITH TURNIPS
Gahn Bei Sao Lo Bo Si: General   乾 貝 蘿 蔔 絲

A. 3 tablespoons vegetable oil
B. 6 dried scallops
C. 2 scallions, minced
D. 1 cup shredded turnip

E. ¾ cup meat or chicken broth
F. ¼ teaspoon salt
G. 1 teaspoon cornstarch

PREPARATION:

I. Soak B in hot water 20 minutes or until soft. Drain, reserving water.
II. Break B into shreds.

COOKING:

1. Place A in hot skillet, using high heat. Add B, C, stir-fry 1 minute.
2. Add D, E, F, and water from B; cover, simmer 15 minutes.
3. Mix G with a little water; stir this mixture into other ingredients. Serve.

CRAB WITH SWEET AND SOUR SAUCE
Tien Swan Pong Sha: Shanghai　　甜 酸 螃 蟹

A. 1½ cups peanut oil
B. 3 to 4 medium crabs
C. 1 tablespoon minced scallion
D. 2 slices ginger, minced

E. 1 tablespoon sherry
F. ¼ teaspoon salt
G. 2 tablespoons cornstarch
H. 1 egg

PREPARATION:

I. Wash B well; remove claws (crack with back of cleaver), legs, shell. Cut each B into quarters.
II. Mix C, D, E.

III. Marinate B in C–E mixture 10 minutes.
IV. Combine F, G, H to make batter.
V. Coat B with F–H.

COOKING:

1. Heat A to 375°. Deep-fry B–H mixture until golden brown (about 5 minutes). Remove from oil.

SAUCE:

A. 2 tablespoons peanut oil
B. 1 tablespoon chopped scallion
C. 1 teaspoon chopped ginger
D. 1 clove garlic, chopped
E. 2 tablespoons light soy sauce

F. ¼ cup vinegar
G. ¼ cup sugar
H. 2 teaspoons cornstarch
I. ¼ cup water

PREPARATION:

I. Mix E, F, G, H, I thoroughly.

COOKING:

1. Heat A in hot frying pan. Stir-fry B, C, D 1 minute.

2. Add E–I mixture, continue stirring until mixture comes to boil.
3. Add pieces B–D, mix well and serve hot.

CRAB MEAT WITH CELERY CABBAGE
Sha Ro Bai Tsai: Peking　　蟹 肉 白 菜

A. 3 tablespoons vegetable oil
B. 2 scallions
C. 3 slices ginger
D. 1 clove garlic
E. 6 oz. canned crab meat
F. 1 teaspoon sherry
G. ½ teaspoon sugar

H. 2 teaspoons cornstarch
I. 2 tablespoons water
J. 1 cup chicken broth
K. 1½ lbs. celery cabbage
L. ½ cup thinly sliced bamboo shoots
M. salt to taste

PREPARATION:

I. Chop B, C, D and mix.
II. Cut K diagonally into 1-inch segments.

III. Mix F, G, H, I.

COOKING:

1. Heat A in frying pan; add B–D and stir-fry ½ minute.
2. Add E and stir-fry 2 minutes.
3. Add F–I mixture, simmer 2 to 3 minutes.

4. Heat J to boiling in large (11-inch) frying pan.
5. Add K, L; bring to boil; simmer 5 minutes; add M. Place in bowl and top with B–I mixture.

CRAB MEAT WITH CELERY CABBAGE HEARTS
Sha Huang Bai Tsai: Peking

蟹 黃 白 荣

A. 4 medium crabs
B. 1 teaspoon ginger juice (see Index) or
   ½ teaspoon black pepper
C. 1 tablespoon sherry
D. ½ teaspoon salt
E. 1 lb. celery cabbage hearts

F. 2 tablespoons vegetable oil
G. ½ teaspoon salt
H. 2 cups chicken soup
I. 1 tablespoon cornstarch mixed in
   ¼ cup water

PREPARATION AND COOKING:

I. Steam A 20 minutes, cool and shell. Remove triangular sack connected to shell. Also remove black vein and spongy gills. Save crab yellow and meat for making crab sauce.
II. Add B, C, D to A.
III. Cut E into 2-inch pieces.

IV. Put F into frying pan and stir-fry E, G, 1 to 2 minutes.
V. Add H and boil 2 minutes. Remove E, leaving soup in pan. Arrange E neatly on platter.
VI. Add A mixture to soup. Boil 1 to 2 minutes. Then add I to thicken. Pour over E and serve.

BRAISED SOFT-SHELL CRABS
Yo Mun Shiao Sha: Shanghai

油 燜 小 蟹

A. 4 tablespoons peanut oil
B. 8 soft-shelled crabs
C. 1 teaspoon wine vinegar
D. 2 tablespoons minced ginger

E. 1 tablespoon light soy sauce
F. 1 teaspoon heavy soy sauce
G. 2 teaspoons sugar
H. ¼ cup chicken broth

PREPARATION:

I. Wash B well, and cut each in half.
II. Mix C, D; stuff into cut side of crab and

let stand 15 minutes. Drain.
III. Mix E, F, G, H.

COOKING:

1. Heat A, brown both sides of B.
2. Add E–H and bring to boil. Cover and cook

over low heat 3 minutes; turn over and cook another 2 to 3 minutes. Serve hot.

STIR-FRIED CRAB
Tsu Pong Sha: Hunan

煮 螃 蟹

A. ¼ cup peanut oil
B. 3 to 4 live crabs
C. 3 tablespoons light soy sauce
D. 2 tablespoons sherry
E. 1 tablespoon sugar
F. 1½ tablespoons vinegar

G. 1 tablespoon chopped scallion
H. 1 teaspoon chopped ginger
I. 1 teaspoon cornstarch mixed with
   ¼ cup water
J. 1 teaspoon sesame oil
K. 2 tablespoons cornstarch

PREPARATION:

I. Wash B well; using cleaver, cut in quarters; remove claws, discard shell and legs; crack claws with back of cleaver; quarter each B.

II. Coat B with K.
III. Mix C, D, E, F, G, H, I.

COOKING:

1. Heat A, brown B.
2. Add C–I mixture, stir well, cook over low heat 10 minutes.

3. Sprinkle J on top and serve.

STEAMED CRAB
Tsen Pong Sha: Shanghai
蒸　螃　蟹

A. 2 to 4 blue crabs per person
B. 2 large slices fresh ginger root per crab
C. 1 tablespoon cider vinegar per crab
D. 1 tablespoon light soy sauce per crab

PREPARATION:

I. Wash A well.
II. Place A in large steamer.
III. Peel B and chop very fine.
IV. Mix B, C, D for use as a dipping sauce.

COOKING:

1. Boil water in steamer; steam A (with visible steam escaping from steamer) 20 to 25 minutes. Place crabs on large tray and cover to keep hot.
2. Each person should shell his own crab, remove and discard gills, veins, food pouch (triangular-shaped pouch that is attached to the mouth), and shells. The rest of the crab is edible. Dip in sauce and eat hot.

SERVING AND EATING:

1. Place 3 to 4 layers of newspaper or paper towels on table to protect the surface from spattered juice.
2. Serve Ginger Tea (see Index) after eating crab.

CRAB MEAT LION'S HEAD
Sha Hwang Si Tze Tou: Shanghai
蟹　黃　獅　子　頭

A. 3 teaspoons vegetable oil
B. 1 lb. ground pork
C. 6 oz. chopped cooked or canned crab meat picked clean of cartilage
D. 2 eggs
E. 2 teaspoons sherry
F. 1 teaspoon salt
G. 2 tablespoons cornstarch
H. dash black pepper
I. 2 scallions, minced
J. 4 slices ginger, minced
K. 1 tablespoon light soy sauce
L. 2 cups chicken soup
M. 1 lb. celery or Chinese cabbage
N. 1 tablespoon cornstarch mixed with 3 tablespoons water

PREPARATION:

I. Cut M into 2-inch segments.
II. Mix B, C, D, E, F, G, H, I, J, K and form 5 large meatballs.

COOKING:

1. Heat A in heavy frying pan, then fry B–K until brown on all sides (approximately 8 minutes).
2. Add L and cover. Simmer 15 minutes.
3. Add M, cover. When M is cooked but still crisp (approximately 5 minutes), add N to thicken sauce.

SWEET AND SOUR SHRIMP
Tien Swan Sha: Shanghai
甜　酸　蝦

A. 4 to 6 tablespoons salad oil
B. 1 lb. large shrimp
C. ½ cup tomato paste
D. 3 to 4 tablespoons cider vinegar
E. 2 to 3 tablespoons sugar
F. 1 tablespoon chopped fresh ginger
G. 2 tablespoons chopped scallion
H. 1½ teaspoons salt
I. 1 tablespoon cornstarch

PREPARATION:

I. Shell, devein, and wash B.
II. Prepare sauce by mixing C, D, E, F with ¼ cup water, G, H and I.

COOKING:

1. Heat A in frying pan, sauté B 10 minutes, stirring constantly.
2. Add C–I, simmer 5 more minutes.

PRESSED BEAN CURD SHRIMP
Sha Tze Gahn Si: Shanghai
蝦 子 乾 絲

A. ¼ cup peanut oil
B. ½ cup shrimp as in Preparation I
C. 2 teaspoons sherry
D. 2 teaspoons light soy sauce
E. 4 to 6 Chinese mushrooms

F. 3 slices ginger, shredded
G. 4 pieces pressed bean curd
H. 1 cup chicken broth
I. ½ to 1 teaspoon sesame oil (to taste)
J. 1 stalk celery heart, chopped

PREPARATION:

I. Shell, devein, wash, and dice B.
II. Soak B in C 15 minutes.

III. Wash E and soak in warm water 15 minutes or until soft, remove stem, shred; add E water to chicken broth.

COOKING:

1. Heat 2 tablespoons A, add B–C mixture, stir-fry ½ to 1 minute, add D, mix well, remove to dish.
2. Heat 2 tablespoons A until smoking, add E, F, stir a few times, add G, mix well.

3. Add H, bring to boil, simmer until gravy is reduced by half, add B mixture and continue cooking until gravy is completely absorbed.
4. Add I, mix well and garnish with J.

BRAISED SHRIMP
Tsao Da Sha: Shanghai
炒 大 蝦

A. 4 tablespoons vegetable oil
B. 1 tablespoon chopped scallion
C. 2 slices ginger, chopped
D. ½ lb. large shrimp
E. 8 water chestnuts
F. 6 dried Chinese mushrooms
G. ½ cup Smithfield ham cut into small pieces
H. 1 cup peas

I. 2 teaspoons light soy sauce
J. 2 teaspoons sherry
K. ½ cup chicken broth
L. 1½ teaspoons salt
M. 2 teaspoons cornstarch mixed with 2 tablespoons water
N. ½ teaspoon sesame oil
O. 1 teaspoon cornstarch

PREPARATION:

I. Shell, devein D, split each in half. Soak 15 minutes in water to which 1 teaspoon L has been added. Rinse well, drain.
II. Mix D with O.

III. Wash F, soak 15 minutes in warm water. Drain; quarter each.
IV. Cut E into small pieces.

COOKING:

1. Heat A. Stir-fry B, C a few seconds. Add D, stir-fry 1 minute.
2. Add E, F, G, H, mix well.

3. Add I, J, K, and rest of L, stir-fry another 1 to 2 minutes.
4. Thicken with M. Just before serving, mix in N.

STIR-FRIED SHRIMP WITH DRAGON WELL TEA LEAVES
Lung Jing Tsao Sha Ren: Hangchow *
龍 井 炒 蝦 仁

A. ⅓ cup peanut oil
B. 1 lb. medium shrimp
C. 1 tablespoon dragon well tea leaves
D. 1 tablespoon sherry

E. 1 scallion, chopped
F. 1 egg white
G. 1 tablespoon cornstarch
H. 1 teaspoon salt

PREPARATION:

I. Shell, devein, and wash B, dry between paper towels.
II. Mix B with F, G, H.

III. Pour ½ cup boiling water over C, stir as leaves start to open; drain.

COOKING:

1. Heat A, add B mixture, stir-fry 1 minute; pour off excess oil.
2. Add C, stir-fry 1 minute.

3. Add D, mix well.
4. Add E, stir well and serve.

* Hangchow is famous for the Dragon Well Tea. This dish owes its delicate bouquet to the Dragon Well Tea.

During President Nixon's historic trip to China this was included in the menu served to him in Hangchow.

GLAZED SHRIMP
Gahn Tsao Sha: Shanghai
乾 炒 蝦

A. 3 tablespoons vegetable oil
B. 1 lb. medium shrimp
C. 1 egg white
D. 1 tablespoon cornstarch
E. dash baking soda

F. 1 tablespoon sherry
G. 3 slices ginger, chopped
H. 2 tablespoons light soy sauce
I. 2 scallions, minced

PREPARATION:

I. Shell B, devein, and wash in 1 pt. water containing 1 teaspoon salt. Drain, then dry on paper towels.

II. Mix B, C, D, E, F, G, H. Marinate for 30 minutes.

COOKING:

1. Place A in hot skillet. When oil is hot, add B–H mixture and stir continuously 1 minute. Lower heat, simmer 5 more minutes.

2. Add I, cover and cook on low heat for additional 5 minutes.

BRAISED SEA CUCUMBER
Hung Pa Hai Sun: Szechuan
紅 扒 海 參

A. 3 tablespoons peanut oil
B. 2 scallions
C. 4 slices ginger
D. 1 tablespoon light soy sauce
E. 1 tablespoon oyster sauce
F. 2 tablespoons sherry

G. 1 cup chicken broth
H. ⅛ teaspoon pepper
I. 1 cup refined dried sea cucumber
J. 1 tablespoon cornstarch mixed with ¼ cup water

PREPARATION:

I. Soak I in water 2 nights prior to cooking. Discard water; boil 15 minutes in fresh water with ½ B, ½ C. Drain I, wash, and cut into bite-size pieces.

II. Cut remaining B, C into 1-inch pieces.
III. Mix D, E, F, G, H.

COOKING:

1. Heat A, add B, C, brown a little.
2. Add D–H.

3. Add I, bring to boil; lower heat, simmer 30 to 35 minutes or until I is soft. Thicken with J.

RED-COOKED SEA CUCUMBERS
Hung Sao Hai Sun: Peking　　紅 燒 海 參

A. ½ cup bite-size dried sea cucumber
B. 6 chicken gizzards (or pork stomach)
C. 2 oz. Virginia ham, shredded
D. 2 chicken legs (or pork shoulder)
E. 2 teaspoons light soy sauce
F. 1 teaspoon oyster sauce
G. 2 scallions
H. 1 teaspoon sugar

I. 1½ teaspoons sherry
J. salt to taste
K. dash pepper
L. 1 cup chicken soup
M. 3 tablespoons cornstarch
N. 2 slices ginger
O. 1 scallion

PREPARATION:

I. Soak A in water 48 hours. Discard water, then boil A in 2 cups fresh water with N and O 15 minutes; wash, cut into bite-size pieces.

II. Cut each B into 2 pieces, slit each piece.
III. Bone D.

COOKING:

1. Place A, B, C, D, E, F, G, H, I, J, K, L in bowl. Steam 30 to 45 minutes, until A is soft.

2. Mix ⅓ cup water with M. Add to A–L for thickening. Serve.

STIR-FRIED SEA CUCUMBER AND MUSHROOMS
Dung Gu Hai Sun: General　　冬 菇 海 參

A. 3 tablespoons vegetable oil
B. 6 dried Chinese mushrooms
C. 1 bamboo shoot, shredded
D. 3 scallions
E. 2 slices ginger
F. 1 cup chicken soup

G. ½ cup refined dried sea cucumber
H. 4 oz. turkey white meat, shredded
I. 2 teaspoons cornstarch mixed with a little water
J. salt to taste

PREPARATION:

I. Soak G in water 48 hours prior to cooking. Discard water and boil G with 1 D and E 35 minutes, or until tender. Slice G into 1½-by-½-inch pieces and wash.

II. Soak B in hot water 20 minutes. Drain, saving water. Slice B into quarters; discard stems.
III. Mix I with ¼ cup B water.
IV. Cut remaining D into 1½-inch pieces.

COOKING:

1. Place A in hot frying pan. When A is smoking, add B, C, and remaining D. Stir-fry 2 minutes. Add ½ F if needed.

2. Add G and rest of F; stir-fry 5 minutes.
3. Add H. Cook 2 minutes.
4. Thicken with I. Add J. Serve hot.

GOLDEN COIN SHRIMP
Jing Tsien Sha Bing: Yangchow

金 錢 蝦 餅

A. 2 tablespoons peanut oil
B. ½ lb. green leaf vegetable
C. ½ cup chicken broth
D. 1½ teaspoons cornstarch mixed with
1 tablespoon water
E. pepper to taste
F. 1 lb. medium shrimp

G. 2 oz. pork fat
H. 1 egg white
I. 2 teaspoons sherry
J. 2 teaspoons cornstarch
K. 1 tablespoon chopped scallion
L. 1 teaspoon salt

PREPARATION:

I. Shell, devein, and wash F, dry between paper towels.
II. Mix F, G, and mince.

III. Mix F–G and H, I, J, K, L thoroughly; form into 20 to 24 balls.

COOKING:

1. Heat A in frying pan over medium heat.
2. Place shrimp balls in pan and flatten each lightly with ladle.
3. Brown on both sides until they are done; remove to platter.

4. Stir-fry B with a little salt and place around the shrimp balls.
5. In saucepan, heat C and thicken with D; pour over the dish; sprinkle with E and serve.

SQUID WITH GREEN PEPPERS
Ching Jao Yo Yu: Shanghai

清 椒 魷 魚

A. 4 tablespoons vegetable oil
B. 1 medium onion, shredded
C. 1 large pork chop
D. 3 dried squid
E. 1 large green pepper
F. 2 pieces pressed bean curd
G. 1 tablespoon sherry

H. 2 teaspoons light soy sauce
I. 1½ teaspoons cornstarch
J. ½ teaspoon sugar
K. dash pepper
L. ½ teaspoon baking soda
M. salt to taste

PREPARATION:

I. Soak D overnight. Remove soft bones and membranes. Change water. Add L and boil 30 minutes, covered. Then soak ½ hour, drain and rinse. Cut into thin shreds.
II. Bone C and cut into ¼- to ½-inch-wide strips.

III. Remove seeds from E and shred into ¼-inch-wide strips.
IV. Cut F into ¼-inch-wide strips.
V. Mix G, H, I, J, K with D and soak 20 minutes.

COOKING:

1. Heat A in frying pan. Add B, C, stir-fry 1 to 2 minutes.
2. Add E and D mixture, stir-fry 1 to 2 minutes.

3. Add F and a small amount of water or meat stock. Cover for a total cooking time of 6 minutes. Adjust with M.

BRAISED SQUID WITH CHICKEN
Sao Yo Yu Gee: Shanghai

燒 魷 魚 雞

A. 4 tablespoons vegetable oil
B. 3 dried squid
C. 2 chicken legs
D. 3 scallions
E. 5 slices ginger
F. 2 tablespoons light soy sauce
G. 1 teaspoon sugar

H. 2 tablespoons sherry
I. 6 Chinese mushrooms
J. ½ cup diced bamboo shoots
K. salt to taste
L. 1 tablespoon cornstarch mixed with
   ¼ cup water
M. ½ teaspoon baking soda

PREPARATION:

I. Soak B overnight. Remove soft bones and membranes. Change water. Add M, cover, and boil 30 minutes. Leave soaking ½ hour; drain and rinse. Cut into thin strips.

II. Soak I in hot water 30 minutes, save water, remove stems, cut each I into three pieces.
III. Cut C into bite-size pieces.
IV. Mix B, C, D, E, F, G, H.

COOKING:

1. Heat A in large frying pan. Add B–H and stir-fry 1 minute.
2. Add I, J and water from I; cover and sim-

mer 5 minutes or until B and C are tender. Add some soup or water if needed.
3. Adjust with K, L.

SWEET AND SOUR SQUID
Tien Swan Yo Yu: Shanghai

甜 酸 魷 魚

A. 3 tablespoons vegetable oil
B. 2 tablespoons wood ears
C. 1 cup shredded bamboo shoots
D. ½ teaspoon salt
E. 3 dried squid
F. ½ teaspoon baking soda

G. 2 tablespoons light soy sauce
H. 2 tablespoons cider vinegar
I. 2 tablespoons sugar
J. 1 tablespoon sherry
K. 1 tablespoon cornstarch
L. 1 teaspoon salt

PREPARATION:

I. Soak E overnight. Remove soft bone and membrane. Change water. Add F and boil 30 minutes, covered. Then soak ½ hour, drain and rinse. Score E in crisscross fashion then cut into 1-inch-square pieces.

II. Soak B in hot water 40 minutes. Rinse and wash away extraneous material.
III. Mix E with G.
IV. Mix H, I, J, K, L.

COOKING:

1. Put 1 tablespoon A into frying pan, add B, C, stir-fry 1 to 2 minutes, add D. Remove mixture from pan.

2. Put rest of A into frying pan. Stir-fry E–G ½ minute, add B–D, and H–L sauce; cover, add ½ cup water, simmer 3 minutes or until E is tender.

SQUID IN WHITE SAUCE
Bai Tze Yo Yu: Shanghai

白汁魷魚

A. 3 tablespoons vegetable oil
B. 3 dried squid
C. ½ teaspoon baking soda
D. 1 cup meat stock or chicken soup
E. 6 Chinese mushrooms
F. 1 lb. Chinese cabbage hearts

G. 4 oz. cooked ham
H. 1 tablespoon cornstarch
I. 5 slices ginger, chopped
J. 1 teaspoon salt
K. 2 tablespoons sherry

PREPARATION:

I. Soak B overnight. Remove soft bones and membranes. Change water. Add C, cover and boil 30 minutes. Then soak ½ hour, drain and rinse. Score B in crisscross fashion, then cut into 1-inch squares.

II. Soak E in hot water 30 minutes. Discard stems, save water, cut E into strips.
III. Wash F and cut into 1½-inch pieces.
IV. Cut G into same size pieces as B.
v. Mix I, J, K with B.

COOKING:

1. Heat A in frying pan, add B mixture. Stir-fry 1 minute.
2. Add D, cover and simmer 2 minutes.

3. Add E, F, G, simmer 3 minutes.
4. Mix E water with H, and add to thicken sauce.

SQUID WITH PICKLED MUSTARD GREENS
Sien Tsai Tsao Yo Yu: Shanghai

鹹菜炒魷魚

A. 3 tablespoons vegetable oil
B. 3 dried squid
C. ½ teaspoon baking soda
D. 1½ tablespoons sherry
E. 1½ teaspoons cornstarch
F. 1½ teaspoons sugar

G. 1 large pork chop
H. 1 cup chopped bamboo shoots
I. 1 cup pickled mustard greens
J. ½ cup meat stock
K. 4 slices ginger
L. salt to taste

PREPARATION:

I. Soak B overnight. Remove soft bones and membranes. Change water, add C, and boil 30 minutes, covered. Then soak ½ hour, drain and rinse. Cut into ¼-inch shreds.
II. Shred K.

III. Bone G and cut into pieces ¼-inch wide. Discard bone.
IV. Mix D, E, F with ¼ cup water and mix with B.

COOKING:

1. Heat A in frying pan, add B, D–F mixture, stir-fry 1 to 2 minutes.
2. Add G, H, I, J, K, cover, allow to simmer 5 minutes. Stir-fry 1 to 2 minutes.
3. Adjust with L and serve.

STIR-FRIED FRESH SQUID
Tsao Moh Yu: Szechuan　　炒 墨 魚

A. 3 tablespoons peanut oil
B. 1 lb. squid
C. 1 tablespoon dry sherry
D. 1 scallion, cut into pieces 1½ inches long
E. 1 clove garlic, chopped
F. 2 slices ginger, shredded
G. 1 cup sliced bamboo shoots

H. ½ cup sliced preserved kohlrabi
I. 1 teaspoon oyster sauce
J. 2 teaspoons cornstarch
K. ½ cup water
L. ½ teaspoon sugar
N. ½ teaspoon salt
M. ¼ teaspoon MSG (optional)

PREPARATION:

I. Cut B into a flat strip, remove bone and black membrane. Wash B and score in crosswise fashion. Then cut each into 3 to 4 slices. Mix with C, D, E, F. Let stand for 15 minutes.
II. Mix I, J, K, L, M, N.

COOKING:

1. Heat A, add B–F. Stir-fry 1 minute.
2. Add G, H. Mix well and cover. Cook 3 to 4 minutes.
3. Add I–N and stir until thickened. Serve immediately.

SHARK FINS WITH CORNISH HEN AND ABALONE
Bao Yu Ju Gee Mun Yu Tse: General　　鮑 魚 子 雞 魚 翅

A. 1½-lb. Cornish hen (or fryer)
B. ½-lb. can abalone
C. 2 scallions
D. 2 teaspoons sherry
E. 6 dried mushrooms

F. 7 slices ginger
G. 2 teaspoons water chestnut flour
H. 1 egg white
I. ¼ lb. refined, dried shark fins
J. 1 teaspoon salt

PREPARATION:

I. Place I in cold water and soak overnight. Wash clean. Place I in pot with 1 qt. water, cover; simmer for 30 minutes. Remove pot from heat, allow to cool. Rinse and drain.
II. Slice B into thin, flat slices. Save liquid.
III. Clean and wash A. Cut in half and place in large shallow bowl. Add I, J, 2 slices F and half of liquid from B. Steam over boiling water 15 to 20 minutes. Bone A and leave soup in bowl.
IV. Mince 3 slices F.
V. Soak E in hot water 20 minutes, drain, remove stems, and quarter.

COOKING:

1. Put boned A in bowl. Spread B, C, D, E, remaining F, and remaining half of boiling soup from B over A. Steam 20 minutes.
2. Mix G with H and 2 tablespoons B soup. Beat mixture into hot soup. Salt to taste. Serve hot.

SHARK FIN CASSEROLE
Mun Yu Tse: Szechuan

烟 魚 翅

A. ½ roasting chicken
B. ¼ duck
C. 6 oz. ham
D. 1 qt. chicken soup
E. 2 oz. dried, refined shark fins
F. 4 slices ginger

G. 2 scallions
H. 2 tablespoons sherry
I. salt to taste
J. 3 tablespoons water chestnut flour with
⅓ cup water

PREPARATION:

I. Follow shark fin preparation (see Shark Fins with Cornish Hen and Abalone) using H and

2 pieces F with soaking water.
II. Slice C into thin pieces.

COOKING:

1. In a Dutch oven or flameproof casserole place A, B, C, D and simmer until soft. Remove bone.

2. Add prepared E, rest of F, G, and I. Cover and bring to a boil.
3. Add J to casserole for thickening.

SESAME EELS
Tsao San Hu: Shanghai

炒 鳝 糊

A. ⅓ cup vegetable oil
B. 2 cloves garlic
C. 1 to 2 lbs. eel
D. 10 slices ginger, shredded
E. ⅓ cup light soy sauce

F. 2 teaspoons sugar
G. 3 teaspoons sherry
H. 1 tablespoon cornstarch mixed with
¼ cup water
I. 1 tablespoon sesame oil

PREPARATION:

I. Skin, clean C. Cut into 1-inch segments.   II. Mix D, E, F, G.   III. Mash B, remove skin.

COOKING:

1. Heat A in frying pan; brown B.
2. Add C and stir-fry. Maintain high heat, cover, cook 1 minute.
3. Add D–G mixture, stir-fry 1 to 2 minutes; lower heat and simmer, adding water if neces-

sary. After 6 minutes add H, stir and simmer ½ minute.
4. Heat I in small pot until smoking; pour over eels and serve.

DRIED SHRIMP WITH CABBAGE
Jing Go Bai Tsai: General

金 鈎 白 菜

A. 2 tablespoons peanut oil
B. 1 scallion, chopped
C. 2 slices ginger, chopped
D. 12 dried shrimp

E. ½ cabbage, cut into bite-size pieces
(about 4 or 5 cups)
F. 1 teaspoon sugar
G. 1 teaspoon salt
H. 3 tablespoons shrimp water

PREPARATION:

I. Wash D, soak in water for 10 minutes; drain, save water.

COOKING:

1. Heat A in frying pan.
2. Add B, C, stir a few times.
3. Add D, stir-fry 30 seconds.

4. Add E, stir a few times.
5. Add F, G, H. Cook 5 more minutes.

SHRIMP ROLL
Sha Guan: General

蝦 捲

A. 1 lb. large shrimp
B. 1 scallion, minced
C. 1 teaspoon salt
D. 2 slices ginger, minced
E. 2 teaspoons cornstarch
F. 1 teaspoon sesame oil
G. dash black pepper
H. 1 teaspoon sherry
I. 3 eggs
J. vegetable oil for greasing pan
K. 2 cups clear chicken soup
L. ½ cup shredded cooked ham

PREPARATION:

I. Shell, devein and wash A. Then chop or grind.
II. Mix B with half of C and all of D, E, F, G, H.
III. Beat I well. Add remaining C.
IV. Heat J in skillet and add 1 tablespoon I.

Spread as thin as possible by tilting skillet. After formed, egg skins should be about 5 inches in diameter. Remove egg skins when done. Repeat until I is used up.

V. Place A–H mixture in each I. Roll into 1-inch by 4-inch rolls.

COOKING:

1. Place rolls in skillet. Add K. Cover and simmer for 20 minutes.

2. Put rolls in shallow bowl. Spread L over rolls and serve hot.

SHRIMP BALLS
Sha Yuen: General

蝦 圓

A. 1 lb. large shrimp (or fillet of flounder, minced)
B. 8 water chestnuts
C. 1 egg
D. 3 scallions, sliced
E. 1 slice ginger, minced
F. 1 teaspoon salt
G. 4½ teaspoons cornstarch
H. 1 teaspoon light soy sauce

PREPARATION:

I. Shell, devein, and wash A. Drain. Then chop or grind into fine pieces. Place in mixing bowl.
II. Chop B fine.
III. Mix B, C, D, E, F, G, H and add to A. Combine thoroughly.
IV. Form mixture into balls (a heaping tablespoon each).
V. Bring 2 qts. water to a rolling boil.

COOKING:

1. Drop shrimp balls into boiling water one at a time.

2. When shrimp balls float to surface, remove.
3. Cool. Serve with duck sauce.

STEAMED SHRIMP WITH PORK
Sha Tze Ro Chio: General

蝦　子　肉　球

A. ½ lb. medium shrimp
B. ⅛ lb. ground pork
C. 4 water chestnuts, chopped fine
D. 1 slice ginger, minced

E. 1 teaspoon light soy sauce
F. 1 tablespoon gin
G. 1 teaspoon salt
H. 1 scallion, sliced

PREPARATION:

I. Shell, devein, and wash A. Slice lengthwise partway through the back.
II. Mix B, C. Set aside.
III. Mix D, E, F, G. Pour over A and marinate 15 minutes.

IV. Arrange A on serving platter suitable for steaming.
V. Distribute B, C evenly over A. Pour marinade from A over A, B, C.

COOKING:

1. Boil water in steamer.
2. Place serving platter in steamer containing rapidly boiling water.

3. Cover and steam 25 minutes. Remove.
4. Serve with garnish of H.

FRIED FRESH OYSTERS
Tza Sun How: General

炸　生　蠔

A. 2 cups peanut oil
B. ½ pint oysters (about 12)
C. 1 teaspoon salt
D. 1 teaspoon dry sherry
E. 1 teaspoon light soy sauce
F. ¼ teaspoon ground pepper
G. 1 scallion, chopped

H. ½ teaspoon chopped ginger
I. ½ cup flour
J. ½ teaspoon baking powder
K. 1 teaspoon salt
L. 1 egg
M. ¼ cup water

PREPARATION:

I. Rub B lightly with C; place in colander and rinse under cold water ½ minute.
II. Put B into 2 cups boiling water, stir 30 seconds, drain.
III. Mix D, E, F, add B and marinate 10 min-

utes, turning once.
IV. Sift I, J, K together.
V. Beat L.
VI. Mix G, H, I, J, K, L, M well.
VII. Mix B with egg batter.

COOKING:

1. Heat A to 350°, add B–M a tablespoonful at a time; deep fry until golden brown (about

2 to 3 minutes) on each side. Serve with lemon or Szechuan pepper salt.

CHICKEN

In China, chicken is one of the more expensive meats, and is therefore prepared in many fancy manners and styles. For better flavor the fresh killed chicken is preferred, although frozen chicken is more available and convenient.

CHICKEN VELVET AND PEAS
Gee Yung Ching Do: Peking　　　　雞 蓉 青 豆

A.	6 tablespoons vegetable oil	G.	1 teaspoon sherry
B.	6 oz. fresh peas, shelled (or snow peas)	H.	2 teaspoons light soy sauce
C.	3 tablespoons chicken soup	I.	6 egg whites
D.	2 chicken breasts	J.	2 tablespoons cornstarch
E.	3 slices ginger, chopped	K.	dash pepper
F.	3 scallions, chopped	L.	2 oz. cooked ham, minced

PREPARATION:

I. Bone D, mince very fine.

II. Mix E, F.

III. Mix E, F, G, H, I, J, K until any lumps disappear.

COOKING:

1. Heat A in frying pan, add B, stir-fry 2 minutes (1 for snow peas). Add C and stir-fry 1½ minutes.

2. Add D–K, stir-fry vigorously 2 minutes. Break up any large lumps.

3. Place mixture in bowl. Garnish with L and serve.

CHICKEN VELVET
Fu Yung Gee Pien: General

芙 蓉 雞 片

A. 1 chicken breast
B. 3 tablespoons peanut oil
C. 1 scallion, chopped
D. 4 slices ginger, chopped
E. 10 Chinese mushrooms

F. 4 stalks Chinese cabbage
G. ½ teaspoon salt
H. dash sugar
I. ½ cup cornstarch

PREPARATION:

I. Slice A into 2-inch by ¾-inch pieces; roll each piece in I.
II. Wash E and soak in hot water for 15 minutes. Drain (save water); cut each E into halves.
III. Cut F diagonally same size as chicken pieces.

COOKING:

1. Put prepared A in boiling water to cook; stir and cook 2 minutes; remove.
2. Heat B; add C, D. Stir for a few seconds; add E, F; stir well.
3. Add ¼ cup mushroom water, cover and cook five minutes.
4. Add A and G, H. Stir for another two minutes and serve.

PEKING FRIED CHICKEN I
Tza Ba Quai: Peking

炸 八 塊

A. 1 qt. peanut oil for deep frying
B. 2-lb. fryer
C. 1 scallion, cut into 1-inch pieces
D. 1 teaspoon ginger juice (see Index)

E. 3 tablespoons light soy sauce
F. 1 teaspoon sugar
G. 1 tablespoon sherry

PREPARATION:

I. Clean and wash B, cut into 8 pieces.
II. Mix B, C, D, E, F, marinate for 3 to 4 hours.
III. Remove B from sauce and dry between paper towels.

COOKING:

1. Heat A to 350°, deep fry B until golden brown (about 6 minutes) and is done.
2. Serve with anise pepper salt (see Index).

PEKING FRIED CHICKEN II
Yo Tza Gee: Peking

油 炸 雞

A. 6 to 8 chicken drumsticks (about 2 lbs.)
B. 2 to 3 cups peanut oil for deep frying
C. 1½ teaspoons salt

D. 1 tablespoon sherry
E. 1 egg
F. ¼ cup cornstarch

PREPARATION:

I. Mix C, D and rub all over A, marinate 30 minutes.
II. Beat E.
III. Dip A in E and coat lightly with F.

COOKING:

1. Deep fry A in B (350°) until golden brown.
2. Serve with anise pepper salt (see Index).

FRIED SPICY CHICKEN NUGGETS
Tswei Pi Dza Gee: Shantung
脆 皮 炸 雞

A. 4 tablespoons vegetable oil
B. 1 clove garlic, chopped
C. 3 slices ginger, chopped
D. 2 scallions, chopped
E. 2 chicken legs (or 4 pork chops)
F. 1 tablespoon cornstarch
G. 1 egg white
H. 3 to 10 drops hot sauce or ¼ to 1 teaspoon red pepper (optional)

I. 1 teaspoon sherry
J. ½ teaspoon salt
K. ½ cup diced bamboo shoots
L. ¼ cup button mushrooms with liquid
M. 1 teaspoon light soy sauce
N. 1 teaspoon cider vinegar
O. 1 tablespoon catsup
P. 1 teaspoon sugar

PREPARATION:

I. Bone E and cut into 1-inch nuggets.
II. Mix E, F, G, H, I, J.

III. Mix B, C, D.
IV. Mix K, L, M, N, O, P.

COOKING:

1. Heat A in frying pan. When hot add B–D and stir-fry ½ minute.
2. Add E–J mixture, stir-fry 3 minutes (10 minutes for pork) over medium heat until nuggets are brown outside and tender in the center.
3. Add K–P, including liquid from L. Cover and simmer for 5 minutes, stirring occasionally.

SPICY SMOKED CHICKEN
Woo Siang Shwin Gee: Shanghai
五 香 燻 雞

A. 3-lb. roasting chicken
B. 2 tablespoon sherry
C. 2 teaspoons salt
D. ¼ teaspoon cinnamon
E. 2 cloves star anise
F. ½ cup sugar

G. 1 tablespoon molasses
H. 2 scallions
I. 3 tablespoons light soy sauce
J. ¼ teaspoon sesame oil
K. 7 drops tabasco sauce

PREPARATION:

I. Clean A, dry thoroughly with paper towels.
II. Mix B, C; rub on A.

III. Stuff A cavity with H. Refrigerate overnight.
IV. Mix D, E, F, G.

COOKING:

1. Steam prepared A over boiling water 30 minutes. Remove from heat, let A stand in steamer 15 more minutes.
2. Line a Dutch oven with aluminum foil. Spread D–G uniformly over foil. Place a rack above D–G mixture.
3. Place prepared A on rack, cover, and cook over low heat 10 to 15 minutes. Remove from heat.
4. When Dutch oven is cool remove prepared A and cut into bite-size pieces.
5. Mix I, J, K, paint on A. Serve hot or cold.

SPICY CHICKEN
La Tze Gee: Shangtung

辣 子 雞

A. ¼ cup peanut oil
B. 2 chicken breasts
C. 1 tablespoon sherry
D. 1 tablespoon light soy sauce
E. 1 tablespoon cornstarch

F. 8-oz. can bamboo shoots, diced
G. 2 tablespoons hoisin sauce
H. ½ teaspoon crushed red-hot pepper
I. 1 tablespoon chopped scallion
J. 1 teaspoon chopped ginger

PREPARATION:

I. Bone B, cut into cubes.
II. Mix C, D, E.

III. Marinate B in C–E mixture. Let stand a few minutes.

COOKING:

1. Heat A.
2. Add B–E; stir 2 minutes; take out B.
3. Add F, G, H, I, J; stir 2 minutes.

4. Put B back into mixture and stir well.
5. Serve.

SALT-CURED CHICKEN
Yen Fung Gee: Peking

鹽 風 雞

A. 2-lb. fryer
B. 1½ tablespoons salt

C. 1 scallion
D. 3 slices ginger, shredded

PREPARATION:

I. Wash A well, dry with paper towels, rub with B inside and out. Place in bowl, refrigerate at least 1 day (3 days preferably).

II. Cut C in half, cut 2 or 3 times crosswise.
III. Drain excess water from A, split breast open, place on dish. Cover wth C, D.

COOKING:

1. Steam A–B in steamer 30 to 45 minutes. Remove from heat, let cool. Discard C, D.

2. When cold, cut into bite-size pieces. Serve.

SPICY WHITE-CUT CHICKEN
Bai Dzan Gee: Peking

白 割 雞

A. 2 qts. water
B. 2½-lb. frying chicken (or Cornish hen)
C. 1 teaspoon salt

D. 2 to 3 oz. cooked ham
E. 2 to 3 tablespoons oyster sauce
F. 1 tablespoon hot mustard

PREPARATION:

I. Wash B, dry with paper towel. Rub C on B inside and out.

II. Slice D in thin, small pieces.
III. Mix E, F.

COOKING:

1. Place A in Dutch oven, bring to boil, then add prepared B. Cover and lower to medium heat; boil for 10 to 15 minutes.

2. Remove from heat but leave cover on. After 5 minutes, remove B.
3. Cut B into bite-size pieces. Place D over it. Pour over E–F mixture.

STEAMED CHICKEN WITH WINE
Jiu Tsen Gee: Peking

酒 蒸 雞

A. 1½-lb. chicken
B. 1½ teaspoons salt
C. 2 scallions (white part only)

D. 4 slices ginger
E. ½ cup sherry

PREPARATION:

I. Clean and wash A, dry between paper towels, rub with B inside and outside.
II. Cut C into 1½-inch-long pieces.

III. Arrange A in a bowl breast side up, spread C, D, on top.
IV. Pour E over.

COOKING:

1. Steam A–D over boiling water for 35 to 45 minutes or until chicken is tender.
2. Remove C, D, place A in a dish breast side up.

3. Boil ½ cup of soup from A, pour over A and serve.

CHICKEN VELVET SHRIMP
Gee Yung Sha: Peking

雞 蓉 蝦

A. 3 tablespoons vegetable oil
B. 8-oz. shelled shrimp
C. 3 slices ginger
D. 3 scallions
E. ½ teaspoon salt
F. 1 teaspoon sherry
G. 2 teaspoons light soy sauce

H. 3 oz. chicken breast meat
I. 6 egg whites
J. 2 tablespoons cornstarch
K. dash pepper
L. 1 tablespoon vegetable oil
M. 1 oz. cooked ham
N. 6 stalks asparagus

PREPARATION:

I. Devein and wash B. Split each into 2 pieces.
II. Chop C and D fine and mix with E, F, G.
III. Marinate B in C–G mixture 2 hours.
IV. Mince M.

V. Break off tough stems of N; French-cut tips very thin. Precook in boiling water 2 minutes.
VI. Mince H very fine, mix with I, J, K.

COOKING:

1. Heat A in frying pan. Stir-fry B–G mixture 1 minute, then add H–K mixture, stir-fry 2 more minutes. Remove and place in warm bowl.

2. In same frying pan, heat L, add M, N; stir-fry 1 minute, spread over B and serve.

FLUFFY CHICKEN PANCAKE
Fu Yung Gee Pien: Peking

芙 蓉 雞 片

A. ¼ cup peanut oil
B. ½ chicken breast
C. 2 teaspoons sherry

D. salt and pepper to taste
E. few drops sesame oil
F. 4 egg whites

PREPARATION:

I. Bone and mince B.

II. Beat F with chopsticks until foamy; mix in B, C, and D thoroughly.

COOKING:

1. Put A into flat frying pan over medium heat.
2. When slightly hot, add B–F mixture. Tip frying pan so that it is evenly coated by mixture.

3. When firm, turn mixture over; cook until both sides are firm, but do not brown.
4. Add E and serve.

STIR-FRIED CHICKEN WITH WALNUTS
Heh Tao Bao Gee Ding: Peking　核 桃 爆 雞 丁

A. 2 cups peanut oil for deep frying
B. 1 cup walnuts (or cashew nuts)
C. 2 chicken breasts
D. 1 egg white
E. ½ teaspoon salt
F. 2 teaspoons light soy sauce
G. 2 teaspoons sherry
H. ½ teaspoon sugar
I. ½ teaspoon sesame oil
J. 2 teaspoons cornstarch

PREPARATION:

I. Bone C and dice.
II. Beat D and mix with C, E, F, G, H, I, J; mix with C.
III. Pour boiling water over B, let stand for 1 to 2 minutes or until skin comes off easily. Peel off skin. Spread walnuts on paper towel and dry completely before frying.

COOKING:

1. Heat A to 325°. Deep fry B until golden brown, about ½ to 1 minute. (Do not overfry or burn). Remove and drain on paper towel.
2. Heat 3 tablespoons A, add C–J mixture, stir-fry 1 to 2 minutes.
3. Add B, mix well, and serve hot.

STEWED CHICKEN WITH CHESTNUTS
Hung Sao Li-Tze Gee: Shanghai　紅 燒 栗 子 雞

A. 4 tablespoons peanut oil
B. 1 scallion
C. 3 slices ginger
D. 2-lb. fryer
E. 3 tablespoons light soy sauce
F. 1 teaspoon salt
G. 2 teaspoons sugar
H. 2 tablespoons sherry
I. ½ cup water
J. 1 lb. chestnuts

PREPARATION:

I. Wash D thoroughly. Cut into bite-size pieces (do not bone).
II. Make slits on J, cover with water and boil 3 minutes, shell and skin.
III. Cut B into 1½-inch pieces.
IV. Mix together E, F, G, H.

COOKING:

1. Heat A; stir-fry B, C a few times.
2. Add D, stir-fry 3 minutes. Add E–H mixture and mix well.
3. Add I. Bring to boil, simmer 15 minutes.
4. Add J, bring to boil again, simmer 15 minutes more. Serve hot.

CHICKEN BREAST WITH CASHEW NUTS
Yao Goh Gee Ding: Peking　腰 果 雞 丁

A. 3 tablespoons peanut oil
B. 2 chicken breasts
C. 1 egg white
D. ½ teaspoon salt
E. 2 teaspoons light soy sauce
F. 2 teaspoons sherry
G. ½ teaspoon sugar
H. ½ teaspoon sesame oil
I. 2 teaspoons cornstarch
J. 1 cup salted cashew nuts

PREPARATION:

I. Bone B and dice.
II. Beat C and mix with B, D, E, F, G, H, I.

COOKING:

1. Heat A, add B–I, stir-fry 1 to 2 minutes.
2. Add J, mix well, and serve hot.

SHANGHAI FRIED CHICKEN
Yo Ling Gee: Shanghai   油 淋 雞

A. 2-lb. fryer
B. 3 slices ginger, chopped
C. 2 scallions, chopped
D. 3 tablespoons light soy sauce
E. 2 teaspoons anise pepper

F. 2 teaspoons whiskey
G. ⅛ teaspoon five spices powder
H. ½ teaspoon salt
I. 1 pint peanut oil

PREPARATION:

I. Wash A and clean.
II. Mix B, C, D, E, F, G, H.

III. Rub A inside and out with B–H mixture. Let stand 45 minutes.

COOKING:

1. Place A–H on plate, steam over boiling water 30 minutes; remove seasoning, and dry A with paper towel.

2. Fry A in I at 350° until golden brown (about 3 minutes each side).

3. Cut A into bite-size pieces and serve.

SALT-CURED CHICKEN
Yen Tsa Gee: Shanghai   鹽 擦 雞

A. 2- to 3-lb. fryer
B. 1 tablespoon salt

C. 1 teaspoon anise pepper
D. 6 cups chicken broth

E. ¼ cup sherry
F. 1 scallion
G. 3 slices ginger

PREPARATION:

I. Mix B, C.
II. Wash A, dry with paper towel, rub with B–C mixture inside and out. Place in bowl and refrigerate at least ½ day.
III. Mix D, E, bring to boil, cool.
IV. Slice F into thin strips.

V. Cut G crosswise into small pieces.
VI. Marinate A–C in D–E 3 hours, then turn and marinate 3 more hours.
VII. Remove A from sauce, place in bowl and garnish with F, G.

COOKING:

1. Steam A in steamer 30 to 45 minutes. Remove from heat, cool, and cut into bite-size pieces.

Serve. Sauce may be reused; just add chicken broth, if necessary, for marinating.

BRAISED CHICKEN
Hung Sao Gee: Shanghai   紅 燒 雞

A. ½ cup soup stock
B. ⅛ cup sherry
C. ⅛ cup light soy sauce

D. 2-lb. fryer
E. ¼ cup bamboo shoots
F. 8 Chinese mushrooms

G. 1 scallion
H. 3 slices ginger

PREPARATION:

I. Cut D into bite-size pieces.
II. Slice E thin.
III. Wash F, soak in warm water 15 minutes. Drain, cut each in half.

IV. Cut G, H into 1- to 2-inch pieces.
V. Place D in frying pan. Spread E, F, G, H on top.
VI. Mix B, C.

COOKING:

1. In a saucepan, bring A to boil.
2. Add B–C mixture, bring to boil again, pour over D–H mixture.

3. Bring to boil, cover, and simmer until D is tender (about 15 to 20 minutes).

PEKING JELLED CHICKEN
Dung Gee: Peking

凍 雞

A. 2- to 3-lb. chicken
B. 1 lb. pigskin
C. 2 scallions
D. 3 to 4 slices ginger
E. ⅓ cup light soy sauce

F. 2 tablespoons sherry
G. 1½ teaspoons sugar
H. salt to taste
I. Chinese parsley

PREPARATION:

I. Clean and wash A; chop and cut into bite-size pieces.

II. Clean and wash B.

III. Tie C into knot.

COOKING:

1. Place A, B in cooking pot, add 1½ cups water, bring to boil.
2. Add C, D, E, cook 1 minute, lower heat and simmer for 35 minutes.
3. Place A pieces in dish, dice B and discard C, D.
4. Place B back in pot with sauce, simmer for 1½ hours or until sauce is half gone. Drain and save sauce.

5. Mix A with sauce and F, G, bring to boil, lower heat and simmer 5 to 10 minutes or until A is tender. Add a little boiling water if necessary.
6. Add H.
7. Place A in bowl and let stand until jelled.
8. When serving, turn bowl upside down on a plate, garnish jelled chicken with I.

BONG BONG CHICKEN
Bong Bong Gee: Szechuan

棒 棒 雞

A. 2 tablespoons peanut oil
B. hot pepper powder, to taste
C. 1 scallion, chopped
D. 4 to 6 slices ginger, shredded
E. 2 tablespoons light soy sauce
F. 2 tablespoon sesame seed paste
G. 2 tablespoons vinegar

H. 1½ teaspoons sugar
I. ½ teaspoon salt
J. 1 teaspoon sesame oil
K. 1½-lb. fryer (or 2 whole breasts)
L. 1 teaspoon salt
M. Chinese parsley (optional)

PREPARATION:

I. Rub K with L. Cut open. Steam in steamer over boiling water 15 minutes, or until tender. Remove K to dish and cool.

II. Bone K and tear into long thin pieces. (In Szechuan a rolling pin is used to beat the meat to loosen and separate it from the bone.) Arrange K on plate.

III. Mix C, D, E, F, G, H, I, J.

COOKING:

1. Heat A until very hot, remove from heat. Add B, stir well, and add C–J mixture; mix well. Sprinkle over K–L, garnish with M.

BONG BONG CHICKEN WITH CUCUMBER
Hwang Gwa Bong Bong Gee: Szechuan

黃 瓜 棒 棒 雞

Add two small, tender, sweet and sour cucumbers. Wash, cut lengthwise, then slice diagonally into thin pieces. Mix with 1 teaspoon salt and marinate 30 minutes. Squeeze out salt water from cucumber, add 1 tablespoon vinegar and 1 tablespoon sugar, mix well and serve under chicken.

STEAMED CHICKEN
Tze Fung Gee: Shanghai

紙　封　雞

A. 2 chicken breasts (1½ lbs.)
B. 6 Chinese mushrooms
C. ¼ cup thinly sliced Virginia ham
D. 1 scallion

E. 3 slices ginger, shredded
F. 1 teaspoon salt
G. 2 teaspoons sherry

PREPARATION:

I. Bone A, cut into cubes, place in dish.
II. Wash B, soak in warm water 15 minutes; drain and save 1 cup of soak water; discard stems and cut each mushroom in half.
III. Spread B, C over A.

IV. Cut D into 1-inch pieces.
V. Spread D, E, F, G and B water over A mixture.
VI. Cover tightly with aluminum foil.

COOKING:

1. Steam A–G in steamer 1 to 1½ hours or until A is tender.

2. Remove foil and serve hot.

STEAMED WHOLE CHICKEN
Ching Tsen Chwan Gee: Szechuan

清　蒸　全　雞

A. 3-lb. chicken
B. 2 tablespoons chopped scallion
C. 3 slices ginger, chopped

D. 1 tablespoon sherry
E. 1½ teaspoons salt

PREPARATION:

I. Rub A thoroughly inside and out with E.

II. Place prepared A in bowl. Sprinkle with B, C, D.

COOKING:

1. Cook A–D in a steamer over boiling water until tender (about 30 to 45 minutes).

STEAMED CHICKEN BREASTS WITH RICE FLOUR
Fun Tsen Gee: Hupeh

粉　蒸　雞

A. 2 chicken breasts (or 2 lbs. pork chops)
B. 2 teaspoons sherry
C. 2 teaspoons light soy sauce
D. ¾ teaspoon salt

E. ½ cup Cream of Rice
F. 2 scallions
G. 2 slices ginger

PREPARATION:

I. Cut A into 1½-inch squares.
II. Marinate with B, C, D.

III. Mix in E and place in shallow bowl.
IV. Slice F. Scatter F and G over A.

COOKING:

1. Place bowl of A–G in steamer and steam 30 minutes (45 for pork chops). Serve hot.

STEAMED CHICKEN BREASTS WITH RICE FLOUR AND MUSHROOMS
Fun Tsen Dung Gu Gee: Hupeh   粉 蒸 冬 菇 雞

A. 2 chicken breasts
B. 2 teaspoons sherry
C. 2 teaspoons light soy sauce
D. ¾ teaspoon salt

E. ½ cup rice flour
F. 6 dried mushrooms
G. 2 slices ginger

PREPARATION:

I. Bone A and cut into 1½-inch squares. Marinate with B, C, D.
II. Mix E with A–D. Place in shallow bowl.

III. Soak F in hot water until soft. Drain. Cut into small pieces.
IV. Spread F, G over A.

COOKING:

1. Steam A–G 30 minutes.

SMOKED CHICKEN
Shwin Gee: Shanghai   燻 雞

A. 3- to 4-lb. roasting chicken
B. 3 scallions
C. ½ cup brown sugar

D. 2 slices ginger, chopped
E. 2 tablespoons salt
F. few drops sesame oil (optional)

PREPARATION:

I. Wash A thoroughly. Dry with paper towels.
II. Mix D with E.

III. Rub A thoroughly with D–E mixture inside and out. Refrigerate overnight.

COOKING:

1. Place B in A cavity; steam over boiling water 30 minutes.
2. Turn off heat, leave A in steamer another 15 minutes.
3. Line Dutch oven with aluminum foil; sprinkle C over foil. Place a rack over C.

4. Place A on top of rack. Cover and cook over medium heat 10 to 15 minutes.
5. Remove pot from heat, allowing it to cool before uncovering.
6. Cut A into bite-size pieces; serve. If desired, rub A with a little F before cutting.

BARBECUED CHICKEN
Jiang Yo Sao Gee: Shanghai   醬 油 燒 雞

A. 2 chickens (2 to 3 lbs. each)
B. ½ cup light soy sauce
C. 2 tablespoons sherry

D. ¼ teaspoon paprika
E. ¼ cup peanut oil
F. 2 teaspoons sugar

PREPARATION:

I. Wash A; dry with paper towels. Cut into 8 pieces.

II. Mix B, C, D, E, F; marinate A in mixture 1 hour.

COOKING:

1. Get coals red-hot on horizontal grill. Put on A. Cover A with aluminum foil to retain juices. If half hood is on grill, place one end of foil on top of hood (with weights) and allow foil to hang extended over edge of grill. When A browns, turn over. Cooking time: 25 to 40 minutes. Serves 6 to 8.

CHICKEN WITH BROWN BEAN SAUCE I
Jiang Gee: Shanghai

醬 雞

A.	2- to 2½-lb. fryer	E.	¼ cup light soy sauce
B.	2 tablespoons brown bean sauce	F.	½ teaspoon five spices powder
C.	1 teaspoon sugar	G.	1 scallion
D.	2 tablespoons sherry	H.	3 to 4 slices ginger

PREPARATION:

I. Wash A well.

II. Cut G, H in 1-inch to 2-inch pieces.

III. Mix B, C, D, E, F with 1 cup water.

IV. Rub A inside and out with B–F. Save excess mixture.

COOKING:

1. Place A in cooking pot, add any excess B–F mixture. Add G, H.
2. Bring to boil, lower heat, simmer 1 hour. During this time, turn A over 3 or 4 times, basting with sauce.
3. Remove from heat, let cool. When cold, cut A into bite-size pieces and serve.

CHICKEN WITH BROWN BEAN SAUCE II
Jiang Bao Gee: Shanghai

醬 爆 雞

A.	2 tablespoons peanut oil	I.	¼ cup sherry
B.	2- to 3-lb. frying chicken	J.	½ teaspoon salt
C.	2 tablespoons brown bean sauce	K.	½ teaspoon sugar
D.	1 clove garlic, minced	L.	2 teaspoons light soy sauce
E.	1 slice ginger, minced	M.	1 tablespoon cornstarch
F.	7 dried black mushrooms	N.	2 teaspoons heavy soy sauce
G.	½ cup canned bamboo shoots	O.	¼ cup water
H.	¾ cup soup stock		

PREPARATION:

I. Boil B until tender (about 30 minutes). Remove bones and cut B into bite-size cubes.

II. Soak F in warm water 15 minutes. Drain.

III. Mash C with back of spoon.

IV. Mix C, D, E. Set aside.

V. Mix H, I, J, K, L. Set aside.

VI. Mix M, N, O. Set aside.

VII. Slice F and G into ⅛-inch-thick pieces.

COOKING:

1. Heat skillet over high heat. Add A. Heat 30 seconds.
2. Add B and stir-fry 1 minute.
3. Add C–E mixture and stir-fry 1 minute.
4. Add F, G and stir-fry 30 seconds.
5. Add H–L mixture, cover, and cook 1 minute.
6. Add M–O mixture slowly while stirring constantly.
7. Serve as soon as sauce thickens and coats all ingredients well.

SOY SAUCE CHICKEN
Jiang Yo Gee: Shanghai

醬 油 雞

A. 1 slice ginger (½ in. thick) about size of a quarter
B. 1 scallion
C. 1 teaspoon anise pepper
D. 1 to 1½ star anise seeds

E. 2 cups light soy sauce
F. 2 cups chicken broth
G. ½ cup sherry
H. 1 tablespoon sugar
I. 2- to 3-lb. fryer

PREPARATION:

I. Clean and wash I, dry between paper towels.
II. Place A, B, C, D in a piece of cheesecloth, gather at the top, and tie with string.
III. Mix E, F, G, H.

COOKING:

1. Place A–H in 5-qt. saucepan; bring to boil, lower heat and simmer 15 minutes.
2. Turn heat to high, add I; when sauce boils, lower heat, cover pan tightly, and simmer 5 minutes for each pound of I, turning it over every 5 minutes.
3. Turn off heat and leave I in sauce 20 minutes. Do not remove cover during this period.
4. Remove I to dish; cool and cut into bite-size pieces. Pour a little sauce over I to serve. Rest of sauce can be reused many times.

FRIED CHICKEN GIZZARDS
Tza Gee Tzen: Shanghai

炸 雞 珍

A. 1 lb. chicken gizzards
B. 1 cup peanut oil
C. 3 stalks Chinese parsley
D. 1 scallion
E. 1 clove garlic

F. ½ teaspoon anise pepper
G. 1 teaspoon salt
H. 1 tablespoon sherry
I. 1 teaspoon vinegar
J. ½ teaspoon sesame oil

PREPARATION:

I. Clean and wash A, remove all fat, quarter each A; cross slash each piece several times.
II. Cut C, D into 1-inch pieces.
III. Discard skin of E, then slice into thin pieces.
IV. Mix C, D, E, F, G, H, I, J.

COOKING:

1. Cook A in boiling water 1 to 2 minutes. Drain.
2. Heat B to 375°, deep-fry A 1 minute. Pour off B.
3. Add C–J mixture to A, bring to boil, mix well.

STEAMED CHICKEN WITH CAULIFLOWER
Hwa Tsai Tsen Gee: Shanghai

花 荣 蒸 雞

A. 1 to 1½ lbs. chicken meat
B. 1 tablespoon light soy sauce
C. 3 teaspoons sherry
D. 1 tablespoon chopped scallion
E. 1 teaspoon chopped ginger

F. 1 teaspoon salt
G. 1 teaspoon sugar
H. ¼ cup rice flour
I. 1 to 1½ cups cauliflower flowerets
J. ½ teaspoon salt

PREPARATION:

I. Cut A into bite-size pieces, mix with B, C, D, E, F, G and let stand 30 minutes to 1 hour.
II. Mix with H.
III. Mix I, J and arrange in dish.
IV. Arrange A–G mixture on top of I–J.

COOKING:

1. Steam A–J in steamer over boiling water for 25 minutes (or until A is tender).

DICED CHICKEN WITH SWEET SAUCE I
Jiang Bao Gee Ding: Peking   醬 爆 雞 丁

A. ¼ cup peanut oil
B. 1 chicken breast
C. 2 teaspoons light soy sauce
D. 2 teaspoons cornstarch
E. 1 to 2 cloves garlic
F. 2 scallions (white part only), diced
G. 1 tablespoon brown bean sauce
H. 1 teaspoon sugar
I. 2 teaspoons sherry
J. ½ teaspoon sesame oil
K. 4-oz. can water chestnuts, drained and diced

PREPARATION:

I. Bone B and dice, mix well with C, D.
II. Pound E with side of cleaver, discard skin. Mince.
III. Mix G, H, I, J, K.

COOKING:

1. Heat A, add B–D, and stir-fry 1 to 2 minutes. Remove B–D, leaving about 1 tablespoon A in pan.
2. Reheat A, add E, F, stir-fry 1 to 2 minutes. Add G–K mixture, continue stirring for ¾ minute.
3. Return B–D mixture, mix well, add salt to taste.

DICED CHICKEN WITH SWEET SAUCE II
Jiang Bao Gee Ding: Shanghai   醬 爆 雞 丁

A. 4 tablespoons peanut oil
B. 1 scallion, chopped
C. 2 slices ginger, chopped
D. 2 chicken breasts
E. 3 tablespoons brown bean sauce
F. 6 Chinese mushrooms
G. 1 green pepper, cubed
H. 1 sweet red pepper, cubed
I. ½ cup cubed bamboo shoots
J. salt to taste
K. 1 teaspoon light soy sauce
L. 1 teaspoon cornstarch
M. 2 teaspoons sherry
N. 1 teaspoon sugar

PREPARATION:

I. Bone D and cut into cubes. Mix with K, L, M, N.
II. Wash F and soak in warm water 15 minutes. Drain, saving ¼ cup water. Cut each F into quarters.

COOKING:

1. Heat A. Add B, C; stir-fry a few seconds.
2. Add prepared D, stir-fry 2 minutes. Transfer contents of frying pan to plate.
3. Pour excess A back into frying pan. Add E, stir-fry several times.
4. Add F, G, H, I, stir-fry 1 to 2 minutes.
5. Replace D in pan, add water from F. Mix well with F–I mixture and J. Cook 1 more minute. Serve.

SWEET AND SOUR GINGER CHICKEN
Tien Swan Jiang Se Gee: Hunan   甜 酸 薑 絲 雞

A. 1½-lb. frying chicken
B. 2 tablespoons ginger
C. 2 tablespoons distilled vinegar
D. 2 teaspoons sugar
E. 1 teaspoon salt
F. ½ teaspoon sesame oil

PREPARATION:

I. Shred B very fine.
II. Mix B, C, D, E, F well. Let stand ½ hour. Drain, save liquid.

COOKING:

1. Put 2 qts. of water in a pot and bring to a boil.
2. Add A, cover and simmer 15 minutes with occasional turning.
3. Turn off heat, leave A in pot another 20 minutes.
4. Cut A into bite-size pieces.
5. Add B–F mixture to A, mix well, and serve.

DRUNKEN CHICKEN I
Jwei Gee: Shanghai
醉　雞

A. 2-lb. fryer or Cornish hen (or 4 chicken breasts)
B. 1 scallion
C. 2 slices ginger
D. 2 teaspoons salt
E. 1 cup dry sherry or whiskey

PREPARATION:
I. Wash A well.
II. Stuff B, C in cavity.

COOKING:
1. Cover A with boiling water, bring to boil; lower heat, simmer, turning over once, 10 minutes. Remove from heat and leave A in water 5 more minutes.
2. Remove A from water. Cool.
3. Quarter A.
4. Rub prepared A with D; pour E on top. Place in covered container.
5. Refrigerate at least 1 to 2 days. Turn pieces over at least once a day.
6. Cut A into bite-size pieces. Serve.

DRUNKEN CHICKEN II
Jwei Gee: Shanghai
醉　雞

A. 2-lb. fryer
B. 1 tablespoon salt
C. 1 to 1½ cups sherry or whiskey

PREPARATION:
I. Clean and wash A, dry with paper towel, split in halves.
II. Rub A all over with B. Let stand 2 hours; pour off excess liquid.
III. Add ¾ cup C to A, marinate 1 to 2 days in refrigerator. Turn A over a few times.

COOKING:
1. Steam prepared A in steamer over boiling water 25 minutes. Remove from steamer and cool.
2. Pour remainder of C over A. Marinate 3 to 4 hours or leave in refrigerator for few days (can be soaked up to 1 to 2 weeks, the longer, the stronger).
3. Cut into bite-size pieces or bone and cut into strips and serve.

STIR-FRIED CHICKEN LIVERS I
Tsao Gee Gahn: General
炒　雞　肝

A. 3 tablespoons peanut oil
B. ½ lb. chicken livers, sliced
C. 1 tablespoon gin
D. 1 tablespoon light soy sauce
E. 1 tablespoon sherry
F. ¼ cup sliced bamboo shoots
G. ¼ cup sliced water chestnuts
H. 1 teaspoon salt
I. ¼ cup soup stock
J. 1 teaspoon cornstarch
K. ½ teaspoon sugar
L. 2 scallions, sliced

PREPARATION:
I. Mix B with C. Set aside for 10 minutes.   II. Mix F, G, H, I, J. Set aside.   III. Mix D, E. Set aside.

COOKING:
1. Put A in very hot skillet and bring to high heat.
2. When A begins to smoke add B–C. Stir-fry 30 seconds.
3. Add D–E. Stir-fry 30 seconds.
4. Add F–J. Stir-fry until sauce thickens and coats all ingredients well.
5. Add K and half of L. Cook 30 seconds more.
6. Serve with garnish of remaining L.

STIR-FRIED CHICKEN LIVERS II
Tsao Gee Gahn: General

炒 雞 肝

A. 4 tablespoons peanut oil
B. 10 chicken (or duck) livers
C. 1 clove garlic, chopped
D. 1 scallion, chopped
E. 2 slices ginger, chopped
F. 6 dried Chinese mushrooms
G. ¼ cup shredded bamboo shoots
H. ½ teaspoon salt
I. 1 tablespoon light soy sauce
J. ¼ cup chicken broth
K. 2 teaspoons sherry
L. 2 teaspoons cornstarch mixed with ¼ cup water
M. dash pepper and salt

PREPARATION:

I. Cut each B into thin slices. Mix with ½ L and all of M.
II. Wash F, soak in warm water 15 minutes. Drain, saving 2 tablespoons F water. Mix this with remainder of L.
III. Slice F into strips ¼ inch wide.
IV. Mix H, I, J, K.

COOKING:

1. Heat A in frying pan. Add B, stir-fry 1 to 2 minutes. Remove to dish. Pour excess oil back into frying pan.
2. Stir-fry C, D, E 30 seconds.
3. Add F, G, and H–K mixture. Stir well, cook 2 minutes.
4. Return B to frying pan, mix well with F–K. Continue stir-frying 1 minute.
5. Add L, M to thicken. Serve hot.

PINEAPPLE CHICKEN DELIGHT
Bo Lo Gee: Shanghai

菠 蘿 雞

A. 4 tablespoons peanut oil
B. 2 chicken breasts (1 to 1½ lbs.)
C. 1 teaspoon chopped ginger
D. 1 small egg white
E. ½ teaspoon salt
F. 2 teaspoons cornstarch
G. 1 clove garlic, chopped
H. 1 green pepper
I. 2 carrots
J. 1 cup pineapple chunks
K. 2 teaspoons sherry
L. 2 teaspoons light soy sauce
M. 3 teaspoons vinegar
N. 1 teaspoon sugar
O. ½ cup pineapple juice
P. 1 tablespoon cornstarch
Q. 1 to 1½ teaspoons salt

PREPARATION:

I. Bone B and cut into 1-inch cubes. Mix with C, D, E, F and 1 teaspoon A.
II. Wash H, discard stem and seeds, cut into 1-inch cubes.
III. Peel I, cut into ¼-inch thick slices, parboil 3 minutes.
IV. Drain J and save ½ cup juice.
V. Mix K, L, M, N, O, P, Q.

COOKING:

1. Heat 3 tablespoons A, add B–F mixture, stir-fry 2 minutes, remove to a dish.
2. Heat 1 tablespoon A, stir-fry G for ½ minute, add H, I, stir-fry ½ minute.
3. Add B–F mixture and J, stir well for a minute.
4. Add K–Q mixture, continue stirring until it is thickened; serve with rice.

CHICKEN IN PLUM SAUCE
Sue Mei Jiang Gai: Shanghai

蘇 梅 醬 雞

A.   3 tablespoons peanut oil
B.   1 tablespoon chopped scallion
C.   1 teaspoon chopped ginger
D.   2 chicken legs or 1 chicken breast
E.   1½ tablespoons plum sauce

F.   2 teaspoons soy sauce
G.   1 cup sliced carrot
H.   1 cup sliced celery
I.   ½ to 1 teaspoon salt
J.   ½ teaspoon sugar

PREPARATION:

I. Bone and cut into bite-size pieces.

COOKING:

1. Heat A, add B, C, stir-fry ½ minute, add D pieces and brown on all sides.
2. Add E, F, mix well, simmer 15 minutes.

3. Add G, H, I, J, turn heat higher, stir well, then lower heat and simmer for another 5 to 10 minutes (until chicken pieces are tender).

ROCK SUGAR CHICKEN
Bing Tong Gee: Shanghai

冰 糖 雞

A.   4 tablespoons peanut oil
B.   2 chicken legs
C.   2 chicken wings
D.   1½ tablespoons light soy sauce
E.   1 tablespoon sherry
F.   5 Chinese black mushrooms

G.   ½ cup diced bamboo shoots
H.   2 teaspoons salt
I.   2 teaspoons rock sugar
J.   2 scallions
K.   2 teaspoons cornstarch mixed with ¼ cup water

PREPARATION:

I. Cut each B into 4 small pieces, and each C into 2.
II. Mix D, E. Add to B, C. Marinate 5 minutes.

III. Wash F, soak in warm water 15 minutes. Drain. Save mushroom water. Then cut each F into 4 pieces.
IV. Cut each J into inch-long pieces.

COOKING:

1. Heat A, add B–E mixture, brown each side 2 minutes.
2. Add F, G, stir-fry 1 minute.

3. Add ½ cup mushroom water from Step III, H, I; cover, and cook 20 minutes.
4. Add J, mix well, cook another 10 minutes.
5. Thicken with K, serve hot.

CHICKEN BREAST WITH CASHEW NUTS
Yah Goh Gee Ding: Shanghai

腰 果 雞 丁

A.   3 tablespoons peanut oil
B.   2 scallions
C.   2 boned chicken breasts
D.   1 tablespoon hoisin sauce
E.   2 tablespoons light soy sauce
F.   2 teaspoons sherry

G.   2 teaspoons cornstarch
H.   ⅛ teaspoon pepper
I.   1 cup cashew nuts (or blanched peanuts or walnuts)
J.   salt to taste

PREPARATION:

I. Slice C into pieces ½ inch thick.
II. Mix C with D, E, F, G, H thoroughly.

III. Using only white part of B, cut into ¼-inch pieces.

COOKING:

1. Heat A, stir-fry B until slightly brown.
2. Add C–H mixture, stir-fry constantly over medium heat until C changes color (about 2 minutes).

3. Add I, mix well.
4. Add J. Serve hot.

HOT SWEET SAUCE CHICKEN
Jiang Bao Gee Ding: Szechuan　　醬 爆 雞 丁

A. 3 tablespoons peanut oil
B. 1 chicken breast (or ½ lb. veal or lean pork)
C. 1 cup diced bamboo shoots
D. 1 or 2 red-hot peppers or to taste (optional)
E. 2 tablespoons brown bean sauce
F. 1 teaspoon sugar
G. 2 teaspoons sherry
H. 1 teaspoon light soy sauce
I. 2 teaspoons chopped scallion
J. 1 teaspoon chopped ginger
K. 1 teaspoon cornstarch
L. 1 egg white
M. 2 teaspoons cornstarch
N. dash salt

PREPARATION:

I. Bone B and dice, mix with L, M, N.
II. Cut D in half, remove and discard seeds, dice.
III. Mix E, F, G, H, I, J, K thoroughly.

COOKING:

1. Heat A, add B mixture, C and D, stir-fry for 3 to 5 minutes.
2. Add E–K, stir until thoroughly mixed.

BRAISED CHICKEN WINGS
Kwei Fei Gee: Szechuan　　貴 妃 雞

A. 3 tablespoons lard (or vegetable oil)
B. 1 teaspoon rock sugar
C. 6 to 8 chicken wings (1 to 1½ lbs.)
D. 1 tablespoon chopped scallion
E. 1 teaspoon chopped ginger
F. 3 teaspoons light soy sauce
G. 2 teaspoons sherry
H. 1 teaspoon salt
I. ½ cup chicken broth
J. 1 cup sliced bamboo shoots
K. 8 Chinese mushrooms
L. ½ teaspoon sugar
M. 1 teaspoon cornstarch mixed with 2 tablespoons water

PREPARATION:

I. Disjoint C.
II. Wash K and soak in warm water until soft (15 to 30 minutes), drain, and quarter each.
III. Mix D, E, F, G, H, I.

COOKING:

1. Heat A and brown B. Add C pieces, stir-fry 1 minute.
2. Add D–I mixture, bring to boil; lower heat and simmer 25 minutes.
3. Add J, K, L and cook another 3 to 5 minutes (until wings are tender).
4. Thicken with M.

DICED CHICKEN WITH PEANUTS
Kung Bao Gee Ding: Szechuan　　宮 保 雞 丁

A. 4 tablespoons peanut oil
B. 1 chicken breast
C. 1 egg white
D. 2 teaspoons cornstarch
E. 1 tablespoon chopped scallion
F. ½ cup skinless, roasted peanuts (canned are suitable)
G. ½ cup diced bamboo shoots
H. 1 sweet red pepper
I. ½ teaspoon sugar
J. 2 teaspoons sherry
K. 1 tablespoon light soy sauce
L. ½ teaspoon salt

PREPARATION:

I. Bone, dice B. Mix with C, D.
II. Dice H.
III. Mix I, J, K.

COOKING:

1. Heat A. Add B–D mixture, stir-fry 1 to 2 minutes. Remove to dish, pour excess oil back to pan.
2. Add E, F, G, H, stir-fry 1 minute.
3. Return B–D mixture to pan, mix well.
4. Add I–K, stir-fry a few seconds. Add L. If canned F is used, salt to taste.

KUNG BAO CHICKEN DING
Kung Bao Gee Ding: Szechuan

宮 保 雞 丁

A. ¼ cup peanut oil
B. 2 chicken breasts
C. 1 egg white
D. 2 teaspoons cornstarch
E. 1 to 2 scallions, chopped
F. 2 to 4 slices ginger, chopped
G. 2 to 3 red-hot peppers
   (dried hot or pepper flakes)

H. ¼ cup water chestnuts (optional)
I. 1 tablespoon soybean sauce (mien see)
J. 1 teaspoon sugar
K. 2 teaspoons light soy sauce
L. 2 teaspoons sherry
M. 2 teaspoons vinegar
N. ¼ teaspoon sesame oil
O. salt to taste

PREPARATION:

I. Bone B, discard skin, dice and mix with C, D.

II. Split G into halves, discard stem and seeds, cut each into ½-inch pieces.

III. Mix I, J, K, L, M, N.

COOKING:

1. Heat A, stir-fry B–D mixture for 1 to 2 minutes, remove to dish.
2. Leave excess oil in same pan, and heat. Add E, F, G, H (drained and diced); stir-fry 1 to 2 minutes.

3. Add B–D mixture, stir-fry 1 to 2 minutes.
4. Add I–N mixture, continue stirring until well mixed. Add O.

HOT AND SPICY CHICKEN
Ma La Tze Gee: Hunan

麻 辣 子 雞

A. 4 tablespoons peanut oil
B. 1 scallion
C. 2 to 3 red-hot peppers
D. 1 tablespoon shredded ginger
E. 1 tablespoon sherry
F. 2 tablespoons light soy sauce
G. 2-lb. fryer
H. ½ cup chicken broth

I. 1 tablespoon light soy sauce
J. 2 tablespoons wine vinegar
K. 1 tablespoon sugar
L. ½ teaspoon sesame oil
M. ½ teaspoon salt
N. 1 to 2 teaspoons anise pepper
O. 1 tablespoon cornstarch

PREPARATION:

I. Cut G into bite-size pieces, marinate 15 to 20 minutes in D, E, F.
II. Cut B, C diagonally in 1-inch pieces.

III. Grind N to powder.
IV. Mix H, I, J, K, L, M, N.

COOKING:

1. Heat A. Add B, C, stir-fry several times.
2. Add D, E–G mixture to B, C mixture, and stir-fry 1 to 2 more minutes.

3. Add H–N, mix well, cook over low heat until G pieces are tender (about 10 to 12 minutes). Add O to thicken, stir well. Serve with rice.

SWEET AND SOUR CHICKEN
Tien Swan Gee Jiu: General

甜 酸 雞 球

A. 2 eggs, beaten
B. ¾ teaspoon salt
C. ½ teaspoon garlic powder
D. ½ cup all-purpose flour
E. ¼ cup cornstarch
F. ½ cup milk
G. 1 tablespoon honey

H. 1 teaspoon lemon juice
I. 1 teaspoon rice wine or 2 tablespoons sherry
J. 1 teaspoon fresh ginger put through garlic press
K. 2½-lb. chicken
L. Sweet and sour sauce (see Index)

PREPARATION:

I. Bone K and cut into pieces 1 by 2 inches.
II. Mix G, H, I, J.
III. Marinate K in mixture 15 minutes.

IV. Mix A, B, C, D, E, F to make a smooth batter.
V. Dredge K in batter.

COOKING:

1. Fry A–K in peanut oil at 350° F. until light brown. Drain and remove to deep bowl.

2. Heat L and pour over A–K. Serve hot.

FIVE SPICES STEAMED CHICKEN
Fun Tsen Wu Shiang Gee: Hupeh

粉 蒸 五 香 雞

A. 2½-lb. chicken
B. 1 teaspoon salt
C. 1 tablespoon sherry
D. ¼ teaspoon five spices powder
E. 2 tablespoons light soy sauce

F. 4 slices ginger, minced
G. ½ cup rice flour
H. 1 scallion, minced
I. 2 tablespoons vegetable oil
J. ¼ teaspoon sesame oil (optional)

PREPARATION:

I. Cut A into bite-size pieces and add B, C, D, E, F.
II. Place G in paper bag and shake A–F in it.

III. Place A–F in large bowl and garnish with H. Pour I, J over and place in steamer.

COOKING:

1. Cover bowl with aluminum foil and steam 40 minutes. Serve.

DICED WALNUT CHICKEN DING
Heh Tao Gee Ding: General

核 桃 雞 丁

A. 4 tablespoons peanut oil
B. 2 chicken breasts
C. 1 egg white
D. 1 teaspoon cornstarch

E. 1 teaspoon sherry
F. ½ teaspoon salt
G. 1 cup walnuts

PREPARATION:

I. Bone B and dice.
II. Mix B, C, D.

III. Fry G in deep oil. When light brown, take out and drain on paper towel.

COOKING:

1. Heat A until hot.
2. Add B–D. Stir 2 to 3 minutes.
3. Add E, F, G. Mix well and serve hot.

GOLDEN NEEDLES CHICKEN
Jing Tsen Gee: General   金 針 雞

A. 1 tablespoon peanut oil
B. ½ cup golden needles
C. ½ cup cloud ears
D. 7 Chinese mushrooms
E. 2 scallions
F. 4 thin slices ginger, shredded

G. 2 tablespoons light soy sauce
H. 1 tablespoon sherry
I. 2- to 3-lb. frying chicken
J. ½ cup peanut oil
K. ½ teaspoon salt
L. 2 teaspoons cornstarch

PREPARATION:

I. Soak B in hot water 30 minutes. Cut off tips and cut each into 2 pieces.
II. Soak C in warm water; when soft, wash in cold water.

III. Wash D and soak in 1¼ cups hot water 30 minutes (save water); cut each D into 4 pieces.
IV. Slice E into 1-inch strips.

COOKING:

1. Heat A, stir in B, C, D. Add E, F, G, H. Stir well a few seconds. Put in Dutch oven.
2. Brown I in J. Remove and put on top of B–H mixture. Add K and 1 cup mushroom water (save some for Step 4). Cover tightly and simmer 30 minutes.

3. Before serving, cut cooked I into small pieces. Arrange on plate, surrounded by rest of mixture.
4. Use a little mushroom water and L to make gravy in pot. Pour over I. Serve with rice.

CHICKEN CUBES WITH MUSHROOMS
Dung Gu Gee Chiu: General   冬 菇 雞 球

A. 4 tablespoons peanut oil
B. 2 chicken breasts
C. 1 scallion
D. 4 slices ginger
E. 12 Chinese mushrooms
   (or 1 cup bite-size bamboo shoots)

F. 2 teaspoons light soy sauce
G. 1 tablespoon sherry
H. ½ cup chicken broth
I. 1 teaspoon sugar
J. 2 teaspoons cornstarch

PREPARATION:

I. Bone B, cut into 1-inch cubes.
II. Wash E, soak 15 minutes in warm water. Drain, cut each into 3 or 4 pieces.

III. Cut C into 1-inch pieces.
IV. Cut D into long, thin pieces.
V. Mix F, G, H, I.

COOKING:

1. Heat A. Add B, C, D; stir-fry a few seconds.
2. Add E, mix well.

3. Add F–I mixture, stir well, bring to boil. Lower heat, simmer 7 to 10 minutes.
4. Thicken with J mixed with a little water.

DUCK AND OTHER POULTRY

PEKING DUCK

Peking Duck is probably the most unique dish of Northern China and is famous throughout the world. The authentic recipe requires the true Peking Duck which has exceptionally tender meat and a most delicious flavor. In the United States we are very fortunate to have as a substitute the Long Island Duck. This variety received its bloodline from the Chinese duck and is, therefore, considered to be a genuine Peking Duck.

In China, Peking ducks are force fed by hand with the finest of grains and are permitted to have only limited activity so that the meat remains tender and flavorful. On our duck farms similar results are accomplished by mass production techniques with the ducks' activity being restricted and their diet carefully regulated.

Peking Duck is cooked, unlike other duck recipes which are often too fatty, in such a way that the fat melts away from between the skin and the meat. After it has drained off, a crispy brown skin remains. Yet the meat retains its moisture and tenderness.

The skin is served first and is rolled between thin pancakes. A rich brown sauce (Hoisin Sauce) is then spread over the pancakes with the white stem of a scallion which is also served with the pancakes. After the skin has been served, the meat is eaten in similar fashion.

PEKING DUCK
Peking Ya: Peking

北 京 鴨

A. 4-to-6 lb. Long Island duck
B. 1 cup sherry
C. 2 tablespoons honey
D. 1 to 2 bunches of scallion

(use 2½ inches of white stalk only)
E. ½ cup hoisin sauce
F. 1 tablespoon sugar

PREPARATION:

I. Remove fat from A cavity and rinse A with water. Pat A dry with paper towels, and hang in cold, airy spot overnight. In warm climate, pat extra dry and leave in refrigerator overnight.

II. Mix B, C and pour over A. Soak A in sauce for two hours, turning A once or twice.

III. Pat dry A once more and hang it up for another 4 to 6 hours.

IV. Slit the white stalks of D ¾-inch down the stem. Make another slit at right angles to the first cut. Cover with ice water until serving time.

V. Mix E, F well.

COOKING AND SERVING:

1. Preheat oven to 325. Cover tips of wings and legs of A with foil. Line roasting pan with foil. Roast duck over rack, breast side up, 1 hour, then pour off excess oil. Turn A over and roast another hour. Raise oven temperature to 425° and roast A 10 more minutes.

SERVING:

2. Slice skin of A about 1 by 2-inch pieces and cut meat about same size. Arrange both on a platter. Save bones for Duck Bone Soup (see index).

3. Spread a piece of Peking Bo Bing (pancake) with E–F mixture. Then place a piece of skin and scallion on pancake and roll the pancake into a roll and eat it with your hands. Then serve the meat and eat it in the same manner. If preferred, meat and skin can be also served together.

4. Peking Duck can also be served with Chinese Steamed Bread (see Index) or just thin sliced. white bread.

RED-COOKED DUCK
Hung Sao Ya: Peking

紅 燒 鴨

A. 2 tablespoons peanut oil
B. 3 slices ginger
C. 1 or 2 cloves garlic
D. 3- to 4-lb. duck

E. ⅓ cup light soy sauce
F. 2 tablespoons sherry
G. 1 teaspoon sugar
H. 4 to 6 cloves

I. 1 star anise
J. 2 cups water
K. salt to taste

PREPARATION:

I. Clean and wash D, remove fat from cavity, dry between paper towels, chop, and cut into bite-size pieces.

II. Pound C lightly with side of cleaver, discard skin.

COOKING:

1. Heat A, stir-fry B, C ½ minute.
2. Add D, continue stirring for 3 to 5 minutes.

3. Add E, F, G, H, I, J, bring to boil, lower heat and simmer for 1½ hours or until D is tender.
4. Add K and serve.

STEAMED MUSHROOM CORNISH HEN
Tsao Gu Tsen Gee: Peking

草 菇 蒸 雞

A. 2-lb. Cornish hen
B. 3 oz. fresh mushrooms
C. 2 scallions, chopped
D. 3 slices ginger, chopped
E. 1 teaspoon sherry

F. 1 teaspoon sugar
G. 2 tablespoons light soy sauce
H. 1 tablespoon cornstarch
I. ½ teaspoon salt

PREPARATION:

I. Cut A into bite-size pieces and place neatly in shallow bowl for steaming.
II. Cut B into 3 pieces each.

III. Mix B, C, D, E, F, G, H, I and spread over A. Make sure it is spread evenly.

COOKING:

1. Place bowl in steamer and steam 30 to 40 minutes.

SQUAB PEKINESE
Shang Sue Ko Tze: Peking

香 酥 鴿 子

A. 1 qt. vegetable oil for deep frying
B. 2 squab
C. 1 tablespoon light soy sauce
D. 1 clove garlic, chopped
E. 4-oz. can button mushrooms
F. ¾ cup chopped chestnut meat
G. ¼ cup raisins
H. ½ cup chopped ginkgo nuts

I. 1 medium kohlrabi
J. ¼ teaspoon powdered ginger
K. 1 tablespoon heavy soy sauce
L. 1 teaspoon sugar
M. ¼ cup sherry
N. 1 teaspoon salt
O. ½ cup soup stock combined with E water

PREPARATION:

I. Dress and clean B; rub with C and D.
II. Drain E and save water for O.
III. Peel I and shred into small thin pieces.

IV. Mix E, F, G, H, I.
V. Mix J, K, L, M, N, O.

COOKING:

1. Heat A to 325° in deep skillet; deep fry B until golden brown. Rinse under cold water.

2. Place B in casserole; spread E–I mixture over B, then pour J–O mixture over all.
3. Bake in 375° oven 30 minutes or until tender.

SPICED SQUAB
Ru Koh: Peking

乳 鴿

A. 3 squab
B. 1 cup chicken soup
C. dash anise pepper (see Index)
D. 1 star anise
E. ¼ teaspoon cinnamon

F. 1 tablespoon sherry
G. 2 tablespoons light soy sauce
H. 1 teaspoon sugar
I. 1 teaspoon sesame oil (optional)

PREPARATION:

I. Clean and wash A; drain.

II. Place B in 3-qt. saucepan. Mix in C, D, E, F, G, H.

COOKING:

1. Place A in saucepan with B–H mixture; bring to boil; cover and simmer until soup has

nearly evaporated (about 20 to 25 minutes). Add more liquid if necessary.
2. Smear I over A and serve.

SESAME SQUAB
Yo Ling Ru Go: Hunan
油 淋 乳 鴿

A. 3 young squab
B. 1 tablespoon light soy sauce
C. 1 tablespoon sherry
D. ½ teaspoon sugar
E. ½ teaspoon anise pepper

F. 1 teaspoon salt
G. 1 scallion
H. 4 slices ginger, shredded
I. 1 tablespoon sesame oil

PREPARATION:

I. Slit backs of A, remove and discard intestines, and clean giblets. Clean A, dry with paper towels, and place in dish.
II. Mix B, C, D, ½ E, and F.

III. Add A, mix, and let stand 30 minutes.
IV. Cut G into 2-inch pieces. Place on top of A.
V. Place H on top of A.

COOKING:

1. Steam A–H mixture 20 minutes in steamer.
2. Cut each A into quarters, arrange on dish, and top with 2 tablespoons drippings.

3. Heat I. Stir-fry remaining E a few times, strain to remove E. Pour over A.

CHARCOAL ROAST DUCK
Kao Ya: Shanghai
烤 鴨

A. 1 can pickled red-in-snow
B. 4-lb. duck
C. dash black pepper
D. 2 teaspoons sugar

E. 2 tablespoons light soy sauce
F. ½ teaspoon cornstarch
G. hoisin sauce for dipping
H. 1 bunch scallions

PREPARATION:

I. Wash B well, remove fat from cavity, dry with paper towels.
II. Stuff B with A, and sew up openings.
III. Mix C, D, E, F and paint on B.

IV. Slice each H vertically 3 inches down from bulb end; make another 3-inch vertical cut perpendicular to the first cut. Soak H in ice-cold water 10 to 15 minutes. They should spread out like brushes.

COOKING:

1. Attach duck firmly on automatic spit and roast about 2 hours or until B becomes chop-

stick tender; baste occasionally. Serve with G, H.

BARBECUED DUCK
Jiang Yo Sao Yah: Shanghai
醬 油 燒 鴨

A. 2 ducks, 2 to 3 lbs. each
B. ½ cup light soy sauce
C. 2 tablespoons sherry

D. ¼ teaspoon paprika
E. ¼ cup peanut oil
F. 2 teaspoons sugar

PREPARATION:

I. Rinse A, remove fat from cavity, and dry with paper towel.

II. Mix B, C, D, E, F; marinate A in mixture 2 hours, turning a few times.

COOKING:

1. Place A on horizontal grill over red-hot coals. Cover A with 18-inch-wide aluminum foil to retain juices. If half hood is on grill, place one end of foil on top of hood (with weights)

and allow foil to hang extended over edge of grill. When A browns, turn over. Cooking time: 30 to 45 minutes.

CRISPY DUCK I
Tswei Pi Ya: Shanghai 脆 皮 鴨

A. 3-lb. duck
B. 3 slices ginger
C. 1 scallion
D. 1 clove garlic, peeled
E. 2 teaspoons anise pepper

F. 4 tablespoons light soy sauce
G. 1 teaspoon salt
H. 1 tablespoon sherry
I. peanut oil for deep frying

PREPARATION:

I. Wash A well, remove fat from cavity, dry with paper towels.
II. Chop B, C, D very fine.
III. Break up E with back of cleaver or with mortar and pestle.
IV. Mix E, F, G, H with B–D.
V. Rub A inside and out with B–H mixture. Let stand 1 to 2 hours.

COOKING:

1. Place A–H in dish. Steam over boiling water 1½ to 2 hours or until tender. Cool.
2. Remove all ingredients from A; dry A with paper towel.
3. Deep fry A in I until golden brown (about 3 minutes each side).
4. Cut into bite-size pieces. Serve.

CLEAR STEAMED WHOLE ROASTED DUCK
Ching Dun Chwan Sao Ya: Shanghai 清 燉 全 燒 鴨

A. 2- to 3-lb. roasted duck
B. ½ cup thinly sliced bamboo shoots
C. 1 scallion, halved
D. 3 slices ginger

E. 1 tablespoon sherry
F. enough chicken broth to cover duck
G. salt to taste
H. ½ cup thinly sliced baked Virginia ham

PREPARATION:

I. Split open A through the back; place in a bowl. Add B, C, D, E, F, G.

COOKING:

1. Steam A–G in steamer over boiling water 45 minutes or until duck meat is very tender.
2. Remove C, D; place A breast side up on platter; put H on top and serve.

STEAMED WHOLE DUCK
Ching Tsen Chwan Yah: Szechuan 清 蒸 全 鴨

A. 2 teaspoons salt
B. 2 tablespoons sherry
C. ¼ teaspoon pepper
D. 3-lb. duck

E. 1 scallion, chopped
F. 4 slices ginger, chopped
G. 1 cup chicken broth

PREPARATION:

I. Mix A, B, C. Rub D inside and out with mixture.
II. Sprinkle E, F over D.
III. Let D stand 1 to 2 hours.

COOKING:

1. Place prepared D and G in bowl. Steam over boiling water 2½ hours. Serve hot.

TANGERINE PEEL DUCK
Chen Pi Ya: Szechuan   陳 皮 鴨

A.   2 cups peanut oil
B.   3-lb. duck
C.   2 to 3 small pieces tangerine peel
D.   ½ star anise
E.   ½ teaspoon anise peppercorns
F.   1 scallion
G.   2 slices ginger
H.   ⅓ cup light soy sauce

I.   2 tablespoons sherry
J.   1½ teaspoons brown sugar
K.   ½ teaspoon sesame oil
L.   2 teaspoons cornstarch mixed with
     ¼ cup water
M.   1 teaspoon salt
N.   1 to 2 tablespoons honey

PREPARATION:

I. Remove fat from cavity of B. Rub cavity of B with M, and outside with N; let stand 1 to 2 hours; hang up and let drip dry, finish drying with paper towel.

II. Place C, D, E, F, G on a piece of cheesecloth, gather at the top, and tie with a piece of string.

III. Mix H, I, J, K.

COOKING:

1. Heat A to 350°, deep fry B until golden brown (about 2 to 3 minutes); drain on paper towel.

2. Put 1½ cups water in Dutch oven; bring to boil with C–G and H–K and cook 1 minute.

3. Add B, simmer 1 to 2 hours or until B is tender (adding boiling water if necessary). Turn B over a few times during simmering; when done, remove to platter.

4. Thicken gravy with L and pour over A; serve hot.

TANGERINE PEEL DUCK WITH GREENS
Fei Tswei Chen Pi Ya: Szechuan   翡 翠 陳 皮 鴨

Add ½ to 1 lb. any stir-fried green-leafed vegetable. Spread under duck before serving.

DUCK IN BEER SAUCE
Jiu Tzow Ya: Shanghai   酒 糟 鴨

A.   ¼ cup peanut oil
B.   3- to 4-lb. duck
C.   1 tablespoon garlic salt
D.   3 tablespoons light soy sauce
E.   1 cup beer

F.   2 teaspoons cornstarch mixed with
     ¼ cup water
G.   2 teaspoons sugar
H.   2 to 3 tablespoons chopped scallion

PREPARATION:

I. Remove fat from cavity and wash B thoroughly, dry and quarter. Rub each quarter with C.

II. Mix F with G.

COOKING:

1. Heat A in large pot. Brown B, then remove from pot.

2. In same pot, add D, E, and bring to boil.

3. Add B, cover. Turn B over once or twice during cooking, and simmer until done (about 1½ hours). Remove B, allow to cool. When cold, cut into bite-size pieces.

4. Thicken sauce in pot with F–G.

5. Pour this gravy over cold B pieces, and serve, garnished with H.

SOY SAUCE AND CINNAMON DUCK
Jiang Yah: Shanghai
醬 鴨

A. 1 stick cinnamon (½ to 1 inch long)
B. 1 star anise
C. 1 scallion
D. 1 slice ginger (nickel-sized) pounded with side of cleaver
E. 3-lb. duckling (or roasting chicken)

F. 2 tablespoons sherry
G. 5 tablespoons light soy sauce
H. 1 teaspoon rock sugar
I. ½ teaspoon salt
J. 1 to 1½ teaspoons sesame oil
K. 1 teaspoon salt

PREPARATION:

I. Wash E well, remove fat from cavity, and rub inside with K.
II. Place A, B, C, D in a piece of clean cheese-cloth, gather corners and tie with a piece of string.
III. Combine F, G, H, I.

COOKING:

1. Place A–D in large pot, add 2 cups of water, bring to boil, simmer ½ hour (to 45 minutes for chicken) or until there are about 1½ cups liquid left; remove and discard A–D bag.
2. Place E in liquid, add F–I mixture, bring to boil, reduce heat; simmer 1 to 2 hours until E is tender, turning once or twice.
3. Remove E to a dish and rub with J.
4. Cook remaining liquid until about ¼ cup is left; pour over duck and drain, repeating this procedure several times.
5. Cut into bite-size pieces and serve.

CRISPY DUCK
Siang Sue Yah: Szechuan
香 酥 鴨

A. 3- to 4-lb. duck
B. 2 teaspoons anise pepper
C. ¼ teaspoon nutmeg
D. ¼ teaspoon cinnamon
E. ½ teaspoon ground cloves
F. 2 tablespoons salt
G. 2 tablespoons sherry

H. 1 tablespoon chopped scallion
I. 4 slices ginger, chopped
J. 1 egg white
K. 2 teaspoons cornstarch
L. 1 teaspoon flour
M. 2 cups peanut oil

PREPARATION:

I. Wash A thoroughly, remove fat from cavity, dry with paper towels.
II. Mix B, C, D, E, F, G, H, I.
III. Rub A inside and out with B–I mixture; marinate 1 to 2 hours.
IV. Mix J, K, L thoroughly.

COOKING:

1. Place A in dish; steam over boiling water 1½ to 2 hours, or until done.
2. Be sure all of B–I mixture has been removed from A; dry A with paper towel.
3. Rub outside of A all over with J–L mixture.
4. Deep fry A in M at 350° until golden brown (about 3 minutes each side).
5. Cut A into bite-size pieces. Serve with anise pepper salt (see Index) or catsup.

PEKING CRISPY DUCK
Tswei Pi Ya: Peking   脆 皮 鴨

A. 3-lb. duck
B. 1½ tablespoons salt
C. 2 tablespoons sherry
D. 1 tablespoon chopped scallion
E. 1 teaspoon chopped ginger
F. ¼ cup flour

G. 2 small eggs
H. 2 teaspoons light soy sauce
I. 1 tablespoon cornstarch mixed with ¼ cup water
J. 2 cups peanut oil

PREPARATION:

I. Wash A thoroughly.
II. Mix B, C, D, E.

III. Rub A inside and out with B–E.
IV. Beat G, mix with H, I.

COOKING:

1. Place A in dish, steam over boiling water 1 to 2 hours or until tender.
2. Bone A or simply dry between paper towels. Coat lightly with F.
3. Rub A with G–I.

4. Deep fry A in J at 350° until golden brown (about 3 minutes each side).
5. Cut into strips, arrange on plate in a row or cut into bite-size pieces and serve.

SALT-CURED DUCK
Yen Swei Ya: Nanking   鹽 水 鴨

A. 3-lb. duck
B. 1 to 2 tablespoons salt
C. 1 tablespoon anise pepper

D. 3 slices ginger, shredded
E. 2 tablespoons dry sherry

PREPARATION:

I.   Clean A well and remove fat from cavity.
II. Crush C with back of cleaver.
III. Heat frying pan, add B, C, stir-fry over

medium heat 3 to 5 minutes.
IV. Rub A with B, C inside and out.
V. Place A in bowl, refrigerate 1 to 2 days.

COOKING:

1. Wipe A free of excess moisture and B–C mixture. Split A open through breast.
2. Place A in bowl, sprinkle D, E over cavity, steam over boiling water in steamer 45 to 60

minutes. Turn off heat; leave A in steamer until cold. Remove. Remove D.
3. Cut A into bite-size pieces. Serve.

CRISPY CORNISH HEN
Tswei Pi Gee: Shanghai   脆 皮 雞

A. peanut oil for deep frying
B. 2-lb. Cornish hen
C. 2 scallions
D. 4 slices ginger
E. 1½ teaspoons salt
F. 1 teaspoon sherry

G. 1 teaspoon malt sugar
H. 2 tablespoons cornstarch
I. 2 tablespoons water
J. 1 pt. water
K. 6 pineapple rings
L. ¼ cup maraschino cherries

PREPARATION:

I. Stuff B with C, D. Place in 3-qt. saucepan. Add E, J. Cover and boil 20 minutes or until

B is just about done. Drain, save soup.
II. Mix F, G, H, I. Paint mixture on B.

COOKING:

1. Heat A in deep fryer to 350°.
2. Deep fry B until golden brown.

3. Place B on large platter. Remove C, D. Decorate with K, L.

STEWED DUCK WITH CHESTNUTS
Li Tze Dun Ya: Shanghai
栗 子 燉 鴨

A. 4 tablespoons peanut oil
B. 1 scallion
C. 5 slices ginger
D. 3-lb. duck
E. 4 tablespoons light soy sauce

F. 1½ teaspoons salt
G. 3 teaspoons sugar
H. 3 tablespoons sherry
I. ¾ cup water
J. 1 lb. chestnuts

PREPARATION:
I. Wash D thoroughly. Cut into bite-size pieces, with bone in.
II. Make slits in J, cover with water and boil 3 minutes, shell and skin.
III. Cut B into 1½-inch pieces.
IV. Mix E, F, G, H.

COOKING:
1. Heat A; stir-fry B, C a few seconds.
2. Add D, stir-fry 4 minutes.
3. Drain off most of A and duck grease.
4. Add E–H mixture and mix.
5. Add I. Bring to boil, simmer 35 minutes.
6. Add J, bring to boil again, simmer 15 minutes more. Serve hot.

ALMOND DUCK
Shing Jen Ya: Szechuan
杏 仁 鴨

A. 4-lb duck
B. 1 teaspoon salt
C. 5 slices ginger, chopped
D. 3 scallions, chopped
E. 2 tablespoons sherry
F. 2 tablespoons light soy sauce
G. dash anise pepper

H. dash black pepper
I. 4 oz. green peas
J. 2 oz. ham, chopped
K. 4 oz. almonds
L. 4 oz. water chestnuts, sliced
M. 4 eggs
N. 2 tablespoons cornstarch

PREPARATION AND COOKING:
I. Clean and wash A, remove fat from cavity.
II. Mix B, C, D, E, F, G, H in shallow bowl. Rub mixture on A, let stand 2 hours.
III. Place bowl in steamer and steam A for 30 minutes or until just done.
IV. Allow A to cool. Bone A. Separate skin from meat.
V. Cook I in boiling water 3 minutes.
VI. Mix J, K, L, M, N. Make sandwich of J–N mixture between meat (bottom layer) and skin (top layer).
VII. Place duck sandwiches in pan and cook in preheated 350° oven 30 minutes.

PRESSED DUCK
Ban Yah: Nanking
板 鴨

A. 4- to 5-lb. duck
B. 1 teaspoon saltpeter (obtained in drugstore)

C. 6 tablespoons salt
D. 2 teaspoons anise pepper

PREPARATION:
I. Wash A thoroughly, remove fat from cavity, dry with paper towels.
II. Mix B, C, D well. Rub A with B–D mixture inside and out thoroughly.
III. Place a rack in large pan. Place A on rack; refrigerate 3 days. Hang A in sun 1 day.

COOKING:
1. Cut A in halves or quarters. Wash away salt under cold water.
2. Place A pieces in deep plate; steam 1 hour.

Note: Hung or pressed duck can be refrigerated several weeks. Cook when needed. (When processed for commercial sale, it is flattened, or pressed.)

EIGHT PRECIOUS DUCK
Tsen Ba Bao Yah: Shanghai　　　蒸 八 寶 鴨

A. 10 dried shrimp
B. 5 dried mushrooms
C. ¼ cup fresh peanuts
D. ¼ cup barley
E. ½ cup ground pork tenderloin
F. ¼ cup ground fresh scallops
G. 1 teaspoon cornstarch

H. 2 tablespoons vegetable oil
I. ½ cup glutinous rice
J. 2 tablespoons light soy sauce
K. 2 tablespoons sherry
L. 1 teaspoon salt
M. 4-lb. duck

PREPARATION:

I. Soak A, B each in a cup of hot water for 20 minutes. Drain and save water. Cut A, B into small pieces.
II. Soak C in hot water, peel skins.
III. Boil D in water in small pot until soft and done. Drain excess water.

IV. Mix E with F. Add G and mix. Place H in hot skillet. Stir-fry E, F, G.
V. Soak I overnight. Drain and steam 10 minutes.
VI. Place A, B, C, D, E, F, G, H, I, J, K, L in large bowl and mix well. Add ¼ cup extra water. Stuff into M and sew up duck.

COOKING:

1. Place M in steamer and steam for 1 to 2 hours until tender.

STIR-FRIED DUCK WITH SPRING GINGER
Tse Jiang Tsao Ya Pien: Szechuan　　子 薑 炒 鴨 片

A. ½ cup peanut oil
B. ½ duck (or whole duck breast)
C. 1 clove garlic, chopped
D. ¼ lb. spring ginger
E. 3 teaspoons light soy sauce
F. 2 teaspoons sherry
G. ½ teaspoon sugar
H. ¼ to ½ teaspoon sesame oil or to taste

I. 2 teaspoons cornstarch mixed with ¼ cup chicken broth
J. ½ teaspoon salt
K. 1 egg white
L. 2 teaspoons cornstarch
M. 1 teaspoon sugar
N. 1 teaspoon salt

PREPARATION:

I. Bone B, slice meat into very thin pieces, mix with J, K, L.
II. Peel skin of D and slice D into thin pieces;

mix thoroughly with M, N; squeeze out water before using.
III. Mix E, F, G, H, I.

COOKING:

1. Heat A, add B mixture, stir-fry 1 minute; remove to dish.
2. Heat 1 tablespoon A in same pan, add C, stir-fry ½ minute, add D, continue stirring

1 minute.
3. Add B, stir well.
4. Add E–I, continue stirring until gravy is thickened.

PICKLED GINGER DUCK
Tse Jiang Ya Pien: Szechuan　　子 薑 鴨 片

A. 3 tablespoons peanut oil
B. 1 breast of roasted duck or
   2 roasted duck legs
C. 1 walnut-sized piece pickled ginger
D. 1 clove garlic, chopped
E. 2 teaspoons sherry
F. 2 teaspoons light soy sauce

G. 1 teaspoon brown bean sauce
H. 1 or 2 pickled peppers, diced
I. ¼ cup chicken broth
J. 1 scallion
K. 1 green pepper
L. 1 teaspoon sugar
M. Chinese hot sauce to taste

PREPARATION:

I. Bone B and cut into long strips.
II. Cut C into thin slices.
III. Mix D, E, F, G, H.

IV. Cut J into 1-inch-long strips.
V. Discard stem and seeds of K; wash and cut
   into long strips.

COOKING:

1. Heat A, stir-fry B 1 minute, add C, mix well.
2. Add D–H mixture, stir thoroughly; add I,
   lower heat and simmer 3 minutes or until

   gravy has almost evaporated.
3. Turn heat high, add J, K, stir ½ minute, add
   L, M and serve.

FIVE SPICES PIGEON
Wu Shiang Koh Tze: Hunan　　五 香 鴿 子

A. 2 cups vegetable oil
B. 2 pigeons, about 1 to 1½ lbs. each
C. 1 teaspoon five spices powder

D. 2½ tablespoons light soy sauce
E. ¾ teaspoon salt

PREPARATION:

I. Clean B well, dry with paper towels.

II. Mix C, D, E and paint B with mixture, inside
   and out. Let stand 2 to 4 hours.

COOKING:

1. Heat A to 350° in 3-qt. saucepan, and deep fry B 15 to 20 minutes. Use toasted salt and anise pepper mixture as dip (see Index).

PORK

Countless ways have been found to prepare pork, and often it is preserved quickly after slaughter, either by salting or smoking.

For stir-fried dishes, the following cuts are used: pork tenderloin, pork shoulder, fresh butt, boned shoulder, and chops. Ground pork is used in Lion's Head, Pork Balls with Glutinous Rice, Peking Smoke Rolls, and other dishes. Belly pork or uncured bacon, which is rarely used by the American housewife, has alternating layers of lean meat and fat, with the skin on one side. This cut closely resembles our salt pork.

Pork may be considered cooked when it has turned white. When used in soup, thin slices are usually done after 8 minutes of boiling. When recooking pork, since additional cooking will only cause it to lose flavor, it should be added to a dish at the last possible moment.

PORK ROLLS ON SPINACH
Ro Guen Bo Tsai: Peking

肉 捲 菠 荣

A. ½ cup vegetable oil
B. 6 eggs
C. 2 scallions
D. 3 slices ginger
E. 1 lb. ground pork
F. 2 teaspoons sherry
G. ½ teaspoon salt

H. dash black pepper
I. 2 teaspoons cornstarch
J. ½ teaspoon salt
K. 1 qt. soup stock
L. 10-oz. package spinach
M. ½ teaspoon salt

PREPARATION:

I. Mince C, D; mix with E, F, G, H, I.

II. Break B into bowl, add J, beat mixture slightly.

COOKING:

1. Put 2 tablespoons A in 8-inch nonstick skillet, heat and spread; using low heat, add a cooking ladle of B, J mixture to form a skin about 8 inches in diameter. Make 6 such skins.
2. Take C–I mixture and divide into 6 equal portions; put 1 portion onto each egg skin and roll 6 pork rolls.
3. Using medium heat, fry rolls in remaining A, turning to ensure even cooking. Add ½ cup K, cover and simmer 10 minutes; remove from skillet and allow to cool.
4. Place rest of K in skillet; bring to boil, add L, M. Be sure that L is completely covered. Scoop out L, drain; place in shallow bowl.
5. Slice rolls diagonally ¼ inch thick, place neatly over L.

PEKING SMOKE ROLL
Chuen Jien: Peking

捲 尖

A. 1 teaspoon peanut oil
B. 3 eggs
C. 2 teaspoons cornstarch mixed with 2 tablespoons water
D. ½ teaspoon salt
E. ½ lb. ground pork
F. 1 egg white

G. 1 tablespoon chopped scallion (white only)
H. ½ teaspoon chopped ginger
I. 1 teaspoon light soy sauce
J. ⅛ teaspoon five spices powder
K. ½ teaspoon salt
L. sesame oil, as needed

PREPARATION:

I. Mix E, F, G, H, I, J, K well.

II. Beat B, add C, D, mix thoroughly (makes about 1 cup mixture).

COOKING:

1. Grease bottom of 10-inch frying pan with A.
2. Heat over medium heat, add ¼ cup B–D; tip pan so that egg mixture covers it evenly; when skin is done (about 1 to 2 minutes), skin will slide off the pan. Make 4 egg skins; add more oil to frying pan if necessary.
3. When skins cool completely, place ¼ of E–K mixture on each, fold skin, and make into a 5-inch roll.
4. Place rolls on round cake rack and steam over boiling water 8 to 10 minutes.
*5. Smoke rolls over sawdust for 5 to 10 minutes, brush L on rolls, slice each into 4 or 5 pieces and serve.

* Fire should burn in grill until only red coals (charcoal) remain. Cover coals with ashes. Sprinkle sawdust on coals so that it smokes but does not catch fire. If a flame appears extinguish it with a few drops of water. If not enough smoke is produced, add more sawdust. Place rolls on a wire rack and hold rack over smoke. If a charcoal grill is used, place aluminum foil so that it hangs down from hood, thereby cutting out air and allowing more concentrated smoking.

SLICED PORK WITH VEGETABLES
Er Dung Ro Pien: Peking
二 冬 肉 片

A. 3 tablespoons peanut oil
B. ½ lb. pork tenderloin
C. 1 small egg white
D. 1 teaspoon cornstarch
E. few drops sesame oil
F. ½ teaspoon chopped ginger
G. 1 tablespoon chopped scallion
(white part only)

H. 1 cup sliced bamboo shoots
I. ½ cup button mushrooms
J. 1 tablespoon light soy sauce
K. 2 teaspoons sherry
L. ½ cup chicken broth
M. ½ teaspoon salt
N. 2 teaspoons cornstarch mixed with I liquid

PREPARATION:

I. Slice B into 1- by 2-inch pieces, mix well with C, D, E.

II. Drain I and save liquid for N.
III. Mix J, K, L, M.

COOKING:

1. Heat A, add B–E mixture, stir-fry 1 to 2 minutes, remove to dish; leave oil in pan.
2. Heat oil in pan, stir-fry F, G ½ minute; add H, I, continue frying 1 minute.
3. Add B–E mixture to J–M mixture, bring to boil, cook 1 minute. Thicken with N and serve.

PORK SLICE WITH ANISE PEPPER SALT
Jiao Yen Ro Pien: Peking
椒 鹽 肉 片

A. 2 cups peanut oil
B. ½ lb. pork tenderloin
C. 1 egg white

D. 2 tablespoons flour
E. anise pepper salt for dipping (see Index)

PREPARATION:

I. Slice B in pieces about ⅛ inch thick. II. Beat C, mix with D. III. Dip each B slice into B–D mixture.

COOKING:

1. Heat A in saucepan.
2. Deep fry B–D until golden brown, about 30 to 60 seconds.
3. Serve with E.

STIR-FRIED PORK WITH SNOW PEAS
Shieh Do Ro Pien: Peking
雪 豆 肉 片

A. 3 tablespoons peanut oil
B. ¼ lb. pork, thinly sliced
C. ½ egg white
D. 1 teaspoon cornstarch
E. ¼ teaspoon sesame oil
F. 1 clove garlic, minced

G. 1 tablespoon chopped scallion
H. ½ cup thinly sliced bamboo shoots
I. 6 Chinese mushrooms
J. ¼ lb. snow peas
K. ½ teaspoon sugar
L. Salt to taste and dash of MSG

PREPARATION:

I. Mix B, C, D, E.
II. Wash I and soak in warm water 15 minutes, drain (save water), discard stems, slice each into 4 to 6 pieces. Discard tips of J.

COOKING:

1. Heat A, add B–E mixture, stir-fry 2 minutes.
2. Add F, G, H, I, stir-fry 1 minute.
3. Add J, stir ½ minute, add K, L, and 2 tablespoons I liquid, mix well, cover and cook 1 minute.

STIR-FRIED PORK WITH TOMATO
Fan Cheh Ro Pien: Shanghai
蕃 茄 肉 片

A. 3 tablespoons peanut oil
B. 1 clove garlic
C. 1 scallion
D. ½ lb. pork
E. 1 tablespoon light soy sauce
F. ½ teaspoon sugar
G. ½ teaspoon salt

H. ½ teaspoon sesame oil
I. 2 teaspoons cornstarch
J. 2 to 3 tomatoes
K. ½ teaspoon sugar
L. ½ teaspoon salt
M. 1 teaspoon cornstarch

PREPARATION:

I. Slice D into thin pieces 2- by ½-inch.
II. Mix D with E, F, G, H, I.
III. Pound B with side of cleaver, discard skin.
IV. Cut C into 1- to 2-inch pieces.

V. Place J in boiling water for few seconds, remove skin. Slice each J into 8 to 10 pieces, mix with K, L, M.

COOKING:

1. Heat A, brown B, C, lightly, add D–I mixture, stir-fry 1 to 2 minutes or until D is done.
2. Add J–M mixture, mix well. Serve.

STIR-FRIED PORK WITH LOTUS ROOTS
Gno Tsao Tsu Ro: Hupeh
藕 炒 豬 肉

A. 2 tablespoons peanut oil
B. 1 clove garlic, minced
C. ½ slice ginger, minced
D. ½ lb. pork loin, sliced
E. 1 tablespoon gin or sherry
F. 1 tablespoon light soy sauce

G. ½ lb. lotus roots
H. 1 cup soup stock or water
I. 1 tablespoon cornstarch or water chestnut flour
J. 1 tablespoon heavy soy sauce
K. 2 scallions, cut in 1-in. pieces

PREPARATION:

I. Scrape G with potato peeler. Halve roots lengthwise and slice into thin slivers along the grain.
II. Mix B, C. Set aside.

III. Mix E, F. Set aside.
IV. Mix H, I, J and add 3 tablespoons water. Set aside. Stir well before using.

COOKING:

1. Put A in very hot skillet and bring to high heat.
2. Add B, C. Stir-fry rapidly 15 seconds to brown B slightly.
3. Add D and stir-fry 2 minutes.
4. Add E, F and stir-fry 15 seconds.
5. Add G and stir-fry 30 seconds.
6. Cover and cook 8 minutes.
7. Add H–J mixture slowly. Stir-fry until sauce thickens and coats all ingredients well. (If water chestnut flour (I) is used, sauce will thicken almost immediately.)
8. Serve with garnish of K.

STIR-FRIED PORK WITH CLOUD EARS AND EGGS
Ywing Er Ro Sih Tsao Don: General　雲 耳 肉 絲 · 炒 蛋

A. 2 tablespoons peanut oil
B. ½ lb. pork loin, sliced
C. 1 teaspoon cornstarch
D. ½ teaspoon salt
E. 1 tablespoon sherry
F. 3 tablespoons light soy sauce
G. 2 teaspoons heavy soy sauce

H. 1 slice ginger, minced
I. 12 cloud ears
J. 2 tablespoons peanut oil
K. 4 eggs
L. 3 tablespoons water
M. 4 scallions, sliced

PREPARATION:

I. Soak I in warm water 15 minutes. Drain. Discard water. Wash well. Cut into small pieces.

II. Marinate B in mixture of C, D, E, F, G, H.
III. Beat K lightly. Set aside.

COOKING:

1. Put A in very hot skillet and bring to high heat.
2. Add B and C–H marinade; add I. Stir-fry until pork is done. Remove from skillet and set aside.
3. Add J to skillet and heat over high heat.

4. Add K. Scramble until set.
5. Return B–I (from Step 2) to skillet. Mix well.
6. Add L (add more L if desired) and half of M and stir-fry 1 minute.
7. Serve with garnish of remaining M.

SWEET AND SOUR PINEAPPLE SPARERIBS
Tien Swan Bo Lo Pai Gu: Peking　甜 酸 菠 蘿 排 骨

A. 2 cups peanut oil
B. 1 to 1½ lbs. spareribs
C. 2 cloves garlic
D. 1 red-hot pepper
E. 2 small green peppers
F. ½ teaspoon salt
G. 1 cup pineapple chunks

H. 2 tablespoons brown sugar
I. 3 tablespoons vinegar
J. 2 tablespoons light soy sauce
K. ½ cup G pineapple juice
L. 1 tablespoon cornstarch
M. ½ teaspoon salt
N. ⅓ cup cornstarch

PREPARATION:

I. Cut each B into 1½-inch pieces, cover with boiling water and cook 5 minutes; drain, dry with paper towel, mix with M and coat with N.

II. Pound C with side of cleaver, discard skin.
III. Wash D, E, discard stems and seeds, cut into cubes.

COOKING:

1. Heat A to 325°, deep fry B until golden brown (about 2 minutes), arrange on platter.
2. Leave 1 tablespoon A in pan, add C and brown.

3. Add D, E, stir-fry 1 minute, add F.
4. Add G, mix well and place around B.
5. Mix H, I, J, K, L, stir over heat until thickened. Pour over B and serve.

SWEET AND SOUR SPARERIBS
Tang Tsu Pai Gu: Shanghai   糖 醋 排 骨

A. 2 to 3 cups peanut oil
B. 1 to 2 lbs. spareribs
C. 1 tablespoon sherry
D. 3 tablespoons sugar
E. 3 tablespoons vinegar
F. 3 tablespoons catsup
G. 1 tablespoon light soy sauce
H. 1 teaspoon cornstarch mixed with ¼ cup water
I. 2 teaspoons light soy sauce

PREPARATION:
I. Cut B into 1- to 1½-inch pieces, mix with C, I.
II. Mix D, E, F, G, H thoroughly.

COOKING:
1. Heat A to 325°, deep fry B pieces until golden brown (about 2 to 3 minutes or until ribs are done).
2. Pour off excess A, leave B in pot.
3. Add D–H mixture, bring to boil, cook over low heat 3 to 5 minutes.

BRAISED SPARERIBS
Hung Sao Pai Gu: Shanghai   紅 燒 排 骨

A. 2 tablespoons peanut oil
B. 1 scallion
C. 2 slices ginger
D. 1 lb. spareribs
E. 2 tablespoons light soy sauce
F. 1 tablespoon sherry
G. 1 teaspoon sugar
H. salt to taste

PREPARATION:
I. Cut D into 1½-inch pieces.
II. Cut B, C into 1-inch pieces.
III. Mix E, F, G.

COOKING:
1. Heat A. Add B, C, stir-fry a few seconds.
2. Add D, stir-fry 1 minute.
3. Add E–G; mix well.
4. Add about 1 cup boiling water, bring to boil, then simmer 30 to 45 minutes or until D is tender and very little gravy is left. Add H.

ONION SPARERIBS
Yang Tsung Tsu Pai: Wushih   無 錫 洋 葱 豬 排

A. ⅓ cup peanut oil
B. 1 lb. spareribs
C. 1 lb. onions
D. 1 tablespoon sherry
E. ¼ cup catsup
F. 1½ tablespoons vinegar
G. 1½ tablespoons sugar
H. 1 tablespoon light soy sauce
I. ¼ cup water

PREPARATION:
I. Pound B with back of cleaver several times; cut each rib into 2-inch pieces.
II. Peel C and slice into ½-inch pieces.
III. Mix E, F, G, H, I.

COOKING:
1. Heat A, add B and brown 1 to 2 minutes; remove B to dish.
2. Heat 2 tablespoons A, add C, and brown 1 minute.
3. Return B, add D, stir well.
4. Add E–I, bring to boil, lower heat and simmer for 10 to 15 minutes, depending on the tenderness of the ribs.

STEAMED SPARERIBS
Swan Tsai Tsen Pai Gu: Szechuan   酸 荣 蒸 排 骨

A. 1 lb. spareribs
B. 3 teaspoons brown bean sauce
C. 1 tablespoon water
D. ½ teaspoon salt
E. 1 cup shredded pickled mustard greens
F. ½ teaspoon sugar
G. ½ cup rice flour
H. 1 or 2 red-hot peppers (optional)

PREPARATION:

I. Cut A into 1-inch pieces.
II. Mix A, B, C, D, marinate 30 to 60 minutes.
III. Chop E, mix with F and 1 tablespoon G. Add H.
IV. Place rest of G in paper bag. Add marinated A, and shake, coating each piece with G.
V. Line soup dish with E, top with A mixture.

COOKING:

1. Steam A over boiling water in steamer 1 hour, or until meat is tender.

STEAMED SPARERIBS WITH RICE FLOUR
Fun Tsen Woo Siang Pai Gu: Anhwei   粉 蒸 五 香 排 骨

A. 1½ lbs. spareribs
B. 2 teaspoons light soy sauce
C. ½ teaspoon sugar
D. 1 teaspoon salt
E. ⅛ teaspoon five spices powder
F. 1 teaspoon sherry
G. 2 tablespoons chopped scallion
H. 1 teaspoon chopped ginger
I. ¼ cup rice flour

PREPARATION:

I. Cut A into 1½-inch pieces.
II. Mix A, B, C, D, E, F, G, H, let stand 1 hour.
III. Add I to A–H mixture, arrange on dish.

COOKING:

1. Steam over boiling water 45 to 60 minutes.

SPARERIBS WITH SZECHUAN SAUCE
Yu Shiang Pai Gu: Szechuan   魚 香 排 骨

A. 1 tablespoon peanut oil
B. 1 lb. spareribs
C. 1 tablespoon brown bean sauce
D. 2 teaspoons light soy sauce
E. 1 tablespoon sherry
F. 2 teaspoons vinegar
G. 1 teaspoon sugar
H. 1 tablespoon chopped scallion
I. 1 teaspoon chopped ginger
J. 1 tablespoon light soy sauce
K. 1 clove garlic, minced
L. 1 teaspoon cornstarch

PREPARATION:

I. Cut B into 1½-inch pieces, mix with J, K, L.
II. Mix C, D, E, F, G, H, I for sauce.

COOKING:

1. Heat A, stir-fry B 1 to 2 minutes.
2. Add 1 cup water, bring to boil 1 minute, lower heat, and simmer 45 minutes or until B is tender.
3. Add C–I, turn up heat and stir well 1 minute or until gravy is almost gone.

STIR-FRIED KIDNEY WITH WALNUTS
Heh Tao Yao Hwa: Peking
核 桃 腰 花

A. 2 cups peanut oil
B. 4 pork kidneys
C. ½ to 1 cup shelled walnuts
D. 1 teaspoon salt

E. 1 egg
F. ½ teaspoon salt
G. Dash pepper and MSG
H. 2 tablespoons cornstarch

PREPARATION:

I. Split B lengthwise, wash, remove all white veins and any outer membranes. Make tiny crisscross patterns on top of B, then cut each into 8 to 10 slices.
II. Rub with D, squeeze out any blood; rinse thoroughly with water, drain.

III. Add B to 1 qt. boiling water, cook 1 minute, drain and dry between paper towels.
IV. Beat E, mix thoroughly with F, G, H.
V. Add B to E–H and coat each piece well.
VI. Pour boiling water over C, let soak 1 to 2 minutes, peel off skins to avoid bitter taste, and dry completely before frying.

COOKING:

1. Heat A to 375°, deep fry prepared B until golden brown, drain on paper towel.
2. Deep fry C until golden brown (about ½ to 1 minute) in 325° oil; do not burn by over-frying.
3. Mix fried B and C. May be served with Szechuan ground pepper.

STIR-FRIED KIDNEY
Tsao Yao Hwa: Shanghai
炒 腰 花

A. 4 tablespoons peanut oil
B. 1 cup sliced bamboo shoots
C. 2 tablespoons dried cloud ears
D. 1 to 2 cloves garlic
E. 2 pairs pork kidneys
F. 1 teaspoon salt
G. 2 teaspoons light soy sauce

H. 2 teaspoons sherry
I. ½ teaspoon salt
J. 1 teaspoon sugar
K. 1 teaspoon cornstarch
L. ½ teaspoon sesame oil
M. Dash pepper and MSG
N. 2 scallions

PREPARATION:

I. Split E lengthwise, wash, remove all white veins and any outer membranes; make tiny crisscross patterns on top of E, then cut each into 6 to 8 slices. Rub with F, squeeze out any blood; rinse thoroughly with water, drain.
II. Dip E in boiling water 1 minute, drain dry between paper towels.

III. Mix E with G, H, I, J, K, L, M.
IV. Cover C with hot water 30 minutes, discard water, and wash and clean C thoroughly. Then slice each into several pieces.
V. Using white part of N only, cut into 1- to 1½-inch pieces.
VI. Pound D with side of cleaver, discard skin.

COOKING:

1. Heat 1 tablespoon A, add B, C, N; stir-fry ½ to 1 minute, remove to dish.
2. Heat rest of A to smoking. Add D, stir once or twice, add E–M, stir-fry 1 minute.
3. Add B, C, N, mix well; serve hot.

KIDNEY IN PEANUT BUTTER SAUCE
Hwa Sun Jiang Yaw Pien: Szechuan

花 生 醬 腰 花

A. 3 slices ginger
B. 1 scallion
C. 2 tablespoons sherry
D. 2 pairs pork kidneys
E. 2 cups shredded iceberg lettuce hearts
F. 1 tablespoon sesame sauce from Chinese grocery
G. 2 tablespoons peanut butter

H. 1 teaspoon Chinese hot sauce or to taste
I. 1½ tablespoons light soy sauce
J. 1½ teaspoons sugar
K. 3 teaspoons salt
L. 1½ tablespoons vinegar
M. 1 teaspoon sesame oil
N. 3 tablespoons water
O. ¼ teaspoon MSG (optional)

PREPARATION:

I. Split D lengthwise, wash, remove any white veins and outer membranes; rub with 1 teaspoon K, rinse with water; cover with cold water and soak 1 to 2 hours; drain, slice into thin pieces, rub with 1 to 1½ teaspoons K, rinse well and drain.

II. Mix F, G, H, I, J, ½ teaspoon K, L, M, N, and steam over boiling water 5 minutes to soften the paste.

COOKING:

1. Add A, B, C to 1 qt. boiling water; boil 2 minutes.
2. Add D slices, continue stirring. When water boils, turn off heat and drain.
3. Arrange E on a plate, spread D on top.
4. Pour F–N over D and serve.

YU SIANG KIDNEY
Yu Siang Yao Hwa: Szechuan

魚 香 腰 花

A. ¼ cup peanut oil
B. 4 pork kidneys
C. 1 teaspoon salt
D. ½ cup shredded bamboo shoots
E. 4 Chinese mushrooms
F. 1 tablespoon chopped scallions
G. 1 teaspoon chopped ginger
H. 1 clove garlic, minced
I. 2 teaspoons light soy sauce

J. 3 teaspoons brown bean sauce
K. 2 teaspoons sherry
L. 1 teaspoon sugar
M. ½ teaspoon salt
N. 2 teaspoons cornstarch mixed with ⅓ cup water
O. 2 teaspoons vinegar
P. Chinese hot sauce to taste (optional)
Q. 2 to 3 tablespoons cornstarch

PREPARATION:

I. Wash and remove any outer membranes of B. Split lengthwise and with sharp scissors remove all the white veins; make tiny crisscross patterns on top, then cut each B into 8 to 10 slices.

II. Rub with C, squeeze out any blood and rinse thoroughly with water. Drain. Add B to 1 qt. boiling water. Cook 1 minute. Drain. Dry between paper towels.

III. Mix B with 1 teaspoon K, dash salt and pepper.

IV. Place Q in paper bag, add B mixture and shake until B pieces are coated with Q.

V. Wash D and soak in water 15 minutes; drain and shred.

VI. Mix I, J, K, L, M, N, O.

COOKING:

1. Heat A until smoking, then lower heat, add B, stir-fry 1 minute, remove to dish.
2. Heat excess oil in same pan, add D, E, F, G, H, stir-fry 1 minute.
3. Add I–O, stir in B until all is mixed and gravy has thickened. Add P if desired.

RED-COOKED PORK WITH CHESTNUTS
Tsu Ro Mun Li Tze: Shanghai

豬 肉 燜 栗 子

A. 2 tablespoons peanut oil
B. 1 boned pork shoulder (about 2 lbs.)
C. 2 scallions
D. ⅓ cup light soy sauce
E. 2 teaspoons sugar
F. 1 cup water
G. 1 lb. fresh chestnuts

PREPARATION:,

I. Cut B into 1½-inch cubes.
II. Slit G, cover with boiling water and simmer 5 minutes; drain, shell and skin.
III. Cut C into 1-inch pieces.

COOKING:

1. Heat A in pot.
2. Add B, C, and brown slightly.
3. Add D, E, F, simmer 1 hour.
4. Add G, cook until done (about 15 to 20 more minutes).

RED-COOKED PORK WITH BAMBOO SHOOTS (FAMILY STYLE)
Jia Shiang Hung Sao Ro: General

紅 燒 肉

A. 1 lb. pork butt
B. 1½ cups water
C. 4 slices ginger
D. 1 scallion
E. 1 tablespoon sherry
F. 1½ cups bite-size pieces bamboo shoots
G. ⅓ cup light soy sauce
H. 1 teaspoon sugar
I. salt to taste

PREPARATION:

I. Cut A into 1-inch cubes.
II. Cut D into 1-inch pieces.

COOKING:

1. Cover A with B in saucepan, bring to boil. Remove foamy froth.
2. Add C, D, E, cook 20 minutes.
3. Add F, G, H, bring to boil; lower heat, simmer until A is soft (about 30 minutes). Add I.

STEAMED MINCED PORK WITH WATER CHESTNUTS (OR WATER CHESTNUT MEATCAKE)
Ma Ti Tsen Tsu Ro: General

馬 蹄 蒸 豬 肉

A. ½ lb. ground pork
B. 9 canned water chestnuts, chopped fine
C. 1 teaspoon cornstarch
D. 2 tablespoons water
E. 1 tablespoon light soy sauce
F. ½ teaspoon sugar
G. ½ teaspoon salt

PREPARATION:

I. Mix A, B, C, D, E, F, G, well.

COOKING:

1. Flatten A–G in a flat serving dish suitable for steaming.
2. Place dish in steaming utensil and steam 25 minutes.
3. Remove from steaming utensil and serve.

VIRGINIA HAM WITH CHICKEN BREASTS
Ring Twei Gee Pien: Peking

雲 腿 雞 片

A. 3 tablespoons peanut oil
B. 1 lb. chicken breasts
C. 3 Chinese mushrooms
D. 1 oz. Virginia ham
E. ½ cup diced bamboo shoots
F. 2 scallions
G. 3 slices ginger, chopped

H. dash pepper
I. 1 teaspoon sugar
J. salt to taste
K. 2 egg whites
L. 2 tablespoons cornstarch
M. 2 teaspoons sherry

PREPARATION:

I. Soak C in hot water 15 minutes. Drain, reserving water. Remove and discard stems; cut C into 3 pieces each.

II. Bone and slice B into pieces 2 by 2 by ⅛ inches.

III. Mix K, L, M with some C soak water; coat B with mixture.

IV. Cut D about size of B. Cut E similarly.

COOKING:

1. Heat A in frying pan; add prepared B, stir-fry 1 minute, add C, D, E, F, G, stir-fry 1 more minute. Then add H, I and C water so that meat does not scorch. Adjust with J.

GOLDEN HAM ROLLS
Ho Twei Don Chuen: Hupeh

火 腿 蛋 捲

A. ¼ cup vegetable oil
B. 8 eggs
C. ½ lb. lean pork, minced
D. ½ lb. ham, minced
E. 3 slices ginger, minced
F. 2 scallions, minced

G. dash pepper
H. 1½ teaspoons cornstarch
I. 2 teaspoons sherry
J. 1 lb. celery cabbage
K. 1 qt. soup stock
L. 1 teaspoon salt

PREPARATION:

I. Cut J, separating stems from leaves, chop stems, and cut leaves into 1½-inch squares; keep separate.

II. Mix C, D, E, F with G, H, I and stems of J.

III. Break B into bowl, add ½ of L; beat mixture slightly.

COOKING:

1. Put 2 tablespoons A in 8-inch nonstick skillet, heat and spread, using low heat; add a cooking ladle of B mixture to form a skin about 8 inches in diameter. Make 8 such skins.

2. Divide C–J into 8 equal portions; put 1 portion onto each egg skin and roll 8 ham rolls.

3. Using medium heat, fry rolls in remaining A, turning to ensure even cooking.

4. Add ½ cup K, cover and simmer 10 minutes. Remove from skillet and allow to cool.

5. Place rest of K in skillet; bring to boil, add saved J leaves and rest of L; bring to boil again 1 minute, or until J is just done. Spoon out pieces of J and drain; place in shallow bowl.

6. Slice B–I diagonally in pieces ¼ inch thick; place neatly over J. (B–I pieces should be golden-edged, with pink centers set over light green J base.)

RED-COOKED FRESH HAM
Hung Sao Bing Tang Ti Pong: Shanghai

冰 糖 蹄 膀

A. ½ cup heavy soy sauce
B. 2 tablespoons sherry
C. 1 star anise

D. 1 tablespoon rock sugar
E. 2½ lbs. fresh ham
F. salt to taste

PREPARATION:

I. Clean and wash E thoroughly.

COOKING:

1. Bring 3 cups water in cooking pan to boil.
2. Add A, B, C, D. Keep boiling.
3. Add E, bring back to boil and cook in bubbling A–D sauce 5 to 10 minutes; lower heat and simmer 2 hours (or until E is tender).

4. Turn E over 2 or 3 times during cooking so that it will absorb A–D sauce evenly. Add boiling water if necessary.
5. Add F, if necessary, after first hour of cooking.

RED-IN-SNOW WITH PORK
Shieh Li Hung Ro Si: Shanghai

雪 裏 紅 肉 絲

A. 3 tablespoons peanut oil
B. ½ lb. pork, shredded
C. 1 teaspoon cornstarch
D. 2 teaspoons light soy sauce
E. ½ teaspoon sugar
F. 1 tablespoon chopped scallion

G. 1½ cups shredded bamboo shoots
H. ½ (5-oz.) can (or preserved) red-in-snow
I. ½ teaspoon salt
J. ½ teaspoon sugar
K. ¼ cup water

PREPARATION:

I. Mix B, C, D, E, F.

II. Mix I, J, K.

COOKING:

1. Heat A, stir-fry B–F 2 minutes.
2. Add G, H, and I–K. Mix well.

3. Cover, lower heat, and cook 3 minutes.

FRIED FRESH HAM
Go Sao Ti Pong: Peking

鍋 燒 蹄 膀

A. 2 lbs. fresh ham
B. 1 tablespoon chopped scallion
C. 1 teaspoon chopped ginger
D. 1 clove garlic, chopped
E. 1 tablespoon light soy sauce

F. 1 egg
G. 1 tablespoon cornstarch
H. 1 qt. vegetable oil
I. anise pepper salt for dipping (see Index)

PREPARATION AND COOKING:

I. Cover A with boiling water, simmer 1 hour; remove to dish, save water for soup.
II. Mix B, C, D, E and rub over A.
III. Steam over boiling water until meat is tender (about 1 hour); remove A from juice and remove bone, if any.

IV. Mix F, G well and dip A in mixture.
V. Deep fry in H at 350° until A is golden brown (about 5 to 10 minutes).
VI. Cut into 2½-inch by 1-inch strips; serve with I.

HOT SPICED FRESH HAM
Swan La Ti Pong: Szechuan

酸　辣　蹄　膀

A. 3 tablespoons peanut oil
B. 3 slices ginger
C. 1 or 2 cloves garlic
D. 1 or 2 red-hot peppers
E. 2 green peppers
F. 2½-lb. fresh ham, with skin
G. ¼ cup light soy sauce

H. 1 teaspoon salt
I. 1 cup chicken soup
J. 1 scallion (white part only), chopped
K. 3 tablespoons sugar
L. ¼ cup vinegar
M. 2 teaspoons cornstarch mixed with
   ¼ cup water

PREPARATION:

I. Place F in 2 qts. boiling water, bring back to boil, lower heat and simmer 1½ hours or until skin is tender. Remove from pot and cool.
II. Bone cooked F and cut into ½-inch pieces with skin on.

III. Cut each B into 4 pieces.
IV. Pound C with side of cleaver, discard skin and chop.
V. Wash D, E, split open, discard seeds and cut into cubes.
VI. Mix J, K, L, M.

COOKING:

1. Heat A to smoking, add B, C, stir-fry ½ to 1 minute.
2. Add D, E, stir-fry ½ minute, then remove to dish.
3. Heat excess oil, stir-fry F pieces, add G, H, stir 2 to 3 minutes longer.
4. Add I, bring to boil, cover and cook 3 to 5 minutes.
5. Return B–E mixture, mix well.
6. Thicken with J–M; serve hot.

LION'S HEAD
Sih Tze Do: Shanghai

獅　子　頭

A. 3 tablespoons peanut oil
B. ½ lb. hearts of celery cabbage
C. 1 cup soup stock
D. 3 dried black mushrooms
E. ⅔ small onion, chopped
F. 2 teaspoons heavy soy sauce

G. 2 tablespoons sherry
H. 2 tablespoons light soy sauce
I. 1 teaspoon salt
J. 1½ teaspoons sugar
K. 1 lb. ground pork
L. 2 slices ginger, minced

PREPARATION:

I. Cut B into quarters (lengthwise).
II. Soak D in warm water 15 minutes. Discard water. Cut into small pieces.
III. Mix F, G, H, I, J. Marinate K in F–J.

IV. Mix D, E, L well. Add F–K mixture. Stir well. Let stand for 5 minutes.
V. Form into 5 meatballs.

COOKING:

1. Put A in very hot skillet and bring to high heat.
2. Add B and stir-fry 2 minutes. Distribute leaves evenly on bottom of skillet.
3. Place meatballs on B. Add C.
4. Bring to boil. Cover. Simmer over low heat 15 minutes.

SPICED PORK WITH SOY SAUCE
Jiang Ro: Shanghai

醬 肉

A. 1- to 1½-lb. pork butt
B. 1 teaspoon salt
C. 1 scallion
D. 3 slices ginger
E. 1 piece stick cinnamon, ½ inch long
F. 1 star anise
G. 1 cup chicken broth
H. 2 tablespoons sherry
I. 3 tablespoons light soy sauce
J. 1 teaspoon rock sugar

PREPARATION:

I. Clean and wash A, dry with paper towel, rub with B, let stand 2 hours.

II. Place C, D, E, F in piece of clean cloth, gather corners and tie with string. Mix H, I, J.

COOKING:

1. Place A–B in pot.
2. Place C–F in G, bring to boil, add to A, bring to boil, cook 2 to 3 minutes.
3. Add H–J, simmer 1 to 1½ hours (until pork is tender). Turn A once or twice during cooking.
4. Cool, slice, and serve.

PORK WITH BRAISED BEAN AND VEGETABLES
Shueh Tsai Mao Do Ro Si: Shanghai

雪 荣 毛 豆 肉 絲

A. 3 tablespoons peanut oil
B. ½ lb. pork (or beef), shredded
C. 1 tablespoon light soy sauce
D. 2 teaspoons cornstarch
E. ½ teaspoon sugar
F. 1 tablespoon chopped scallion
G. 1 cup shredded bamboo shoots
H. 10-oz. can braised bean and vegetables from Chinese grocery

PREPARATION:
I. Mix B with C, D, E, F.

COOKING:
1. Heat A. Stir-fry B–F mixture 1½ minutes.
2. Add G, stir-fry 1 more minute.
3. Add H, mix well, continue stirring 1 minute.

RED BEAN CURD CHEESE PORK
Nam Yu Tsu Ro: Shanghai

南 乳 豬 肉

A. 1 lb. pork butt
B. 1 scallion tied into a knot
C. 2 slices ginger
D. 1 tablespoon sherry
E. 1 teaspoon sugar
F. 2 tablespoons mashed red bean curd cheese
G. salt to taste
H. 1½ cups water

COOKING:

1. Mix all ingredients in pot, bring to boil and simmer 45 minutes.
2. Place mixture in dish and steam in steamer over boiling water 30 minutes or until meat is very soft and tender.
3. Before serving, pour all gravy into pot, discard B, C, boil down gravy until very thick, pour over A and serve.

MEATBALL PUFFS WITH SWEET AND PUNGENT SAUCE
Tien Swan Ro Jiu: Shanghai
甜 酸 肉 球

A. ½ lb. pork tenderloin
B. ¼ cup glutinous rice flour
C. 2 cups peanut oil for deep frying
D. 1 large green pepper
E. 1 cup pineapple chunks
F. 3 tablespoons vinegar
G. 1½ tablespoons sugar
H. 3 tablespoons catsup
I. 2 teaspoons cornstarch

J. ½ cup E pineapple juice
K. 2 teaspoons light soy sauce
L. 2 teaspoons sherry
M. ¼ teaspoon ground anise pepper
N. ¼ cup flour
O. 1 teaspoon baking powder
P. dash salt
Q. 5 tablespoons water

PREPARATION:

I. Cut A into cubes, steam over boiling water 5 minutes, drain. Mix with K, L, M and marinate 15 minutes.
II. Mix B and N, O, P, Q, stir into a batter.

III. Wash D, discard seeds and stem, cut into cubes.
IV. Mix F, G, H, I, J.

COOKING:

1. Dip A mixture into B batter and deep fry at 350° until golden brown (about 2 to 3 minutes); drain on paper towel.

2. Heat 1 tablespoon C, add D, stir-fry 15 seconds, add dash of salt.
3. Add E, F–J, stir until thickened.
4. Add A mixture, stir well and serve with rice.

STIR-FRIED PORK LIVER
Tsao Tsu Gahn: Shanghai
炒 豬 肝

A. 1 tablespoon peanut oil
B. 2 scallions
C. 1 cup sliced bamboo shoots
D. 4 to 6 Chinese mushrooms
E. ¼ cup peanut oil
F. ½ lb. pork liver

G. 1 tablespoon light soy sauce
H. 2 teaspoons sherry
I. 1½ teaspoons cornstarch
J. ½ teaspoon sugar
K. ¼ teaspoon salt (or to taste)
L. dash pepper

PREPARATION:

I. Wash and clean F, remove any white veins and spots, cut into slices about ⅛ inch thick, dip in boiling water 30 seconds, drain.
II. Mix F with G, H, I, J, K, L.

III. Cut B into 1½-inch pieces (white part only).
IV. Wash D and soak in warm water 15 minutes or until soft, drain; discard stems, cut each into 3 or 4 pieces.

COOKING:

1. Heat A; add B, C, D, stir-fry ½ minute, remove to dish.
2. Heat E until smoking, add F–L, stir-fry 1 minute, return B–D, mix well, and serve.
   Note: When stir-frying liver, the oil has to be very hot. As a safety measure, either turn off heat when adding liver (turning heat on again right away), or cover frying pan as soon as liver is added, and shake pan over heat.

EGGPLANT SANDWICH
Chieh Pien Ja Ro: Shanghai

茄 片 夾 肉

A. peanut oil for deep frying
B. 1-lb. eggplant
C. 10 dried shrimp
D. 1 scallion, chopped (white part only)
E. ½ lb. ground pork
F. 2 teaspoons light soy sauce

G. 1 teaspoon sugar
H. 3 teaspoons cornstarch
I. ¼ teaspoon pepper
J. 1 teaspoon salt
K. 1 large egg
L. bread crumbs

PREPARATION:

I. Peel B and cut diagonally in thin slices.
II. Soak C in water 15 minutes or until soft, drain and mince.
III. Mix C, D, E, F, G, H, I, J thoroughly.

IV. Make sandwich with B pieces by spreading them with C–J mixture.
V. Beat K well, mix with additional ½ teaspoon salt.
VI. Dip each B sandwich in K, then coat with L.

COOKING:

1. Heat A to 350°, deep fry B sandwiches until golden brown, and serve.

STUFFED MUSHROOM SANDWICH
Dung Gu Heh Tze: Suchow

冬 菇 盒 子

A. 20 large Chinese mushrooms
B. 2 tablespoons light soy sauce
C. 2 teaspoons sherry
D. 1 teaspoon sugar
E. ⅓ cup chicken broth
F. 1 lb. any fresh green vegetable (Chinese cabbage, spinach, etc.)

G. 1 tablespoon peanut oil
H. 2 dashes salt to taste
I. 2 teaspoons cornstarch mixed with ¼ cup water
J. ¼ lb. ground pork
K. 1 teaspoon sherry
L. 2 teaspoons cornstarch

PREPARATION:

I. Wash A in cold water and soak in warm water 15 minutes; drain (if chicken broth or soup stock are not available, use mushroom water); discard stems, dry between paper towels; sprinkle A with ½ L.
II. Slice F diagonally in 1-inch lengths.

III. Mix H, J, K and rest of L well, divide into 10 portions.
IV. Stuff ½ A with H, J, K, L mixture, cover stuffing with remaining A to make 10 sandwiches.

COOKING:

1. Place stuffed A in saucepan; add B, C, D, E, bring to boil and cook 3 to 5 minutes until meat is done.
2. Parboil F, stir-fry in G 1 minute; add rest of H. (If spinach is used, heat should be turned off as soon as spinach is dropped into boiling water, and the spinach stirred well and then drained.)
3. Arrange F on dish, place stuffed A on top.
4. Thicken sauce with I and pour over A.

STEAMED PORK
Tsen Tsu Ro: Szechuan

蒸 豬 肉

A. 1 lb. pork
B. 1½ tablespoons light soy sauce
C. 1 tablespoon brown bean sauce
D. 1 teaspoon sugar
E. 2 teaspoons sherry

F. 1 teaspoon chopped ginger
G. 1 tablespoon chopped scallion
H. 2 tablespoons water
I. ½ teaspoon anise pepper
J. ⅓ cup rice flour

PREPARATION:

I. Cut A into slices 1½ by ⅛ inches.
II. Mix with B, C, D, E, F, G, H, I and marinate ½ hour.
III. Mix with J.

COOKING:

1. Steam all ingredients in steamer over boiling water 30 to 45 minutes.

DOUBLE-COOKED PORK WITH HOISIN SAUCE
Hwei Gwo Ro: Szechuan

回 鍋 肉

A. 3 tablespoons peanut oil
B. 1 tablespoon chopped scallion
C. 2 tablespoons hoisin sauce
D. ½ lb. pork

E. 2 small green peppers
F. 1 to 2 small sweet red peppers
G. salt to taste
H. 1 tablespoon water

PREPARATION:

I. Cover D with water, bring to boil, lower heat, cook 30 minutes. Broth may be saved for soup.
II. Discard E seeds, cut each E into eighths, each eighth into quarters.
III. Discard F seeds, cut each same as E.
IV. Cut cooked D in slices 1½ by ¾ inches.

COOKING:

1. Heat A, add B, stir-fry a few seconds.
2. Add C, mix well.
3. Add D slices, stir a few times.
4. Add E, F, G, H. Continue stir-frying 1 minute.

STIR-FRIED PORK WITH KOHLRABI
Da To Tsai Tsao Ro Si: Szechuan

大 頭 菜 炒 肉 絲

A. 3 tablespoons peanut oil
B. 8 dried shrimp
C. ¼ lb. pork, shredded
D. 2 teaspoons light soy sauce
E. ¼ teaspoon sugar
F. 1 teaspoon cornstarch

G. 2 slices ginger, shredded
H. 1 teaspoon chopped scallion
I. 1 bunch kohlrabi
J. ½ to 1 teaspoon sesame oil
K. salt to taste

PREPARATION:

I. Peel I, slice thin, shred. II. Mix C, D, E, F, G, H. III. Wash B and soak in water 15 minutes, chop.

COOKING:

1. Heat A, add B and C–H, stir-fry 1½ minutes.
2. Add I and stir-fry another 2 to 3 minutes.
3. Add J, K to taste.

SZECHUAN PORK WITH ASPARAGUS
Lu Sun Tsu Ro: Szechuan

蘆 筍 豬 肉

A. 3 tablespoons peanut oil
B. ½ lb. pork
C. 2 teaspoons light soy sauce
D. 1 teaspoon cornstarch
E. 1 bunch asparagus (½ lb.)
F. 1 tablespoon chopped scallion
G. 1 teaspoon chopped ginger
H. 1 clove garlic, minced
I. 2 teaspoons light soy sauce

J. 2 teaspoons brown bean sauce
K. ½ teaspoon salt
L. 2 teaspoons sherry
M. 2 teaspoons vinegar
N. 1 teaspoon sugar
O. 2 teaspoons cornstarch mixed with ¼ cup water
P. Chinese hot sauce or anise pepper to taste (optional)

PREPARATION:

I. Slice B thin, shred, mix with C, D and 1 teaspoon A.
II. Cut E into 1- to 1½-inch-long pieces.

III. Bring 1 qt. water to boil, add asparagus and parboil 2 to 4 minutes depending on thickness of pieces. Drain. Mix I, J, K, L, M, N, O.

COOKING:

1. Heat remaining A, add B–D mixture, stir-fry 1 to 2 minutes. Remove to a dish, pour excess oil back to pan.
2. Add E, F, G, H, stir-fry 1 minute.

3. Return B–D to pan, stir-fry 1 to 2 minutes.
4. Add I–O mixture, stir until thickened.
5. Add P to taste.

YU SIANG* SHREDDED PORK
Yu Siang Ro Si: Szechuan

魚 香 肉 絲

A. 3 tablespoons peanut oil
B. ½ lb. pork (or beef)
C. 2 teaspoons light soy sauce
D. 1 teaspoon cornstarch
E. 8 water chestnuts
F. 1 cup shredded bamboo shoots
G. 4 Chinese mushrooms
H. 1 tablespoon chopped scallion
I. 1 teaspoon chopped ginger
J. 1 clove garlic, minced

K. 2 teaspoons light soy sauce
L. 2 teaspoons brown bean sauce
M. ½ teaspoon salt
N. 2 teaspoons sherry
O. 2 teaspoons vinegar
P. 1 teaspoon sugar
Q. 2 teaspoons cornstarch mixed with ¼ cup water
R. Chinese hot sauce to taste (optional)

PREPARATION:

I. Slice B thin, then shred, mix with C, D and 1 teaspoon A.
II. Slice E thin, then shred.

III. Wash G and soak 15 minutes in warm water; shred.
IV. Mix K, L, M, N, O, P, Q (fish sauce).

COOKING:

1. Heat A. Add B–D, stir-fry 1 to 2 minutes. Remove to dish, pour excess oil back into pan.
2. Stir-fry E, F, G 1 minute, add H, I, J and mix well.

3. Return B–D mixture to pan, stir 1 to 2 minutes.
4. Add K–Q, stir until thickened.
5. Add R to taste.

* "Fish sauce" highly desired in cooking fish. It also combines well with meats.

PORK WITH PRESERVED KOHLRABI
Tza Tsai Ro Si: Szechuan

榨 菜 肉 絲

A. 3 tablespoons peanut oil
B. ½ lb. shredded pork
C. 2 teaspoons cornstarch
D. 2 slices ginger
E. 1 tablespoon chopped scallion
F. 1 teaspoon light soy sauce
G. ½ cup shredded preserved kohlrabi
H. 1 cup shredded bamboo shoots
I. 1 teaspoon sugar
J. ¼ teaspoon salt

PREPARATION:

I. Chop D fine.   II. Mix B, C, D, E, F well.   III. Combine I, J.   IV. Rinse and clean G.

COOKING:

1. Heat A and B–F mixture. Stir-fry about 3 minutes.
2. Put G, H into same pan. Stir-fry 1 minute.
3. Add I, J to cooked mixture. Mix well and serve.

CELLOPHANE NOODLES WITH MINCED MEAT
Ma Yee Song Sue: Szechuan

螞 蟻 上 樹

A. 1 qt. peanut oil
B. ½ lb. ground pork (or beef)
C. 2 teaspoons brown or yellow bean sauce
D. 2 teaspoons sherry
E. 2 teaspoons light soy sauce
F. ½ teaspoon sugar
G. 1 red-hot pepper
H. ½ cup chicken broth
I. 2 teaspoons cornstarch
J. 2-oz. pkg. cellophane noodles
K. 1 tablespoon chopped scallion
L. 1 teaspoon chopped ginger

PREPARATION:

I. Divide J into 4 portions; deep fry in A at 375°. As soon as J expands (in a few seconds), remove to plate.
II. Mix B, C, D, E, F.
III. Discard seeds and stem of G, chop.
IV. Mix H, I well.

COOKING:

1. Reheat 2 tablespoons A, stir-fry B–F and G 2 or 3 minutes.
2. Add H, I, mix well, and cook until thickened; place in dish.
3. Just before serving, spread B–F over J and garnish with K, L.

PORK BALLS WITH GLUTINOUS RICE (Pearl Balls)
Tsen Tsu Ro Chiu: Hupeh

珍 球 肉 球

A. 1 cup glutinous rice
B. ½ lb. ground pork
C. 6 dry shrimp
D. 1 tablespoon light soy sauce
E. ½ teaspoon sugar
F. ½ teaspoon cornstarch
G. 1 egg
H. ¼ teaspoon salt

PREPARATION:

I. Wash A and soak in cold water 25 minutes. Drain.
II. Wash and soak C in hot water 15 minutes; chop fine.
III. Mix B, C, D, E, F, G, H.
IV. Take 1 teaspoonful B–H mixture and roll into ball; roll over A until well covered. Repeat until all of B–H is used.

COOKING:

1. Arrange meatballs on a plate and steam about one hour.
2. After steaming, the rice should have a pearl-like appearance.
3. Serve hot or cold.

FIRE POT (OR CHAFING DISH)
Ho Go: General
火 鍋

A. 2 qts. meat stock, canned
chicken broth, or stock
B. 1 scallion, sliced
C. 1 slice ginger, slivered
D. ½ lb. pork loin
E. ¾ lb. boned chicken

F. 1 lb. fresh shrimp
G. 2 cups spinach
H. 2 cups lettuce
I. 2 cups Chinese cabbage
J. 1 cup watercress, tough stems cut off
K. 12 raw eggs in shell

PREPARATION:

I. Slice D, E as thinly as possible and place each on separate plate.
II. Shell F and cut in half lengthwise.
III. Wash and drain G, H, I, J. Cut into bite-sized pieces and place each ingredient in separate bowl.
IV. Place K unbroken on table.
V. Mix B, C and set aside.

COOKING:

1. Heat A just to boiling in regular pot.
2. Transfer A to lit chafing dish or fire pot.
3. Add B–C.
4. Cook D, E, F, G, H, I, J, K in soup as follows: Each person cooks his own portions of meats and vegetables on a skewer in the soup in fire pot or chafing dish. K boils in soup.
5. Arrange soy, oyster, duck (plain), etc., sauces in small bowls around the table for use as "dips" as desired. Serves 8 to 10.

GOLDEN STRIPS WITH PRESSED BEAN CURD
La Jiao Tsao San Sih: Hupeh
辣 椒 炒 三 絲

A. ¼ cup peanut oil
B. 3 medium pork chops
C. 2 to 3 hot green Italian peppers or
1 to 2 large sweet green peppers
D. 4 eggs
E. 4 cakes pressed bean curd

F. ¼ cup chicken soup
G. salt, to taste
H. ½ teaspoon salt
I. 2 teaspoons light soy sauce
J. 2 teaspoons sherry

PREPARATION:

I. Beat D, add H, heat just enough A in skillet to oil pan. Add 2 tablespoons D mixture and tip pan to ensure making thin egg skins without holes. Turn skins over, being careful not to scorch them. Cut skins into strips ¼-inch wide by 2 inches long. Continue procedure until all D has been used.
II. Cut E into ¼-inch strips.
III. Bone B, discard bones; cut meat into ½-inch by 2¼-inch strips.
IV. Split C, discard seeds and stems; cut into ¼-inch by 2-inch strips.
V. Mix B with I, J.

COOKING:

1. Heat rest of A in skillet; add B mixture; stir-fry 1 minute.
2. Add C, continue to stir-fry 1 minute.
3. Add D, E strips and F. Cover and simmer 1 to 2 minutes; adjust with G.

SHREDDED PORK WITH BEAN SPROUTS AND SCALLIONS
Nying Ya Ro Si: Hunan   銀 芽 肉 絲

A. 4 tablespoons peanut oil
B. ½ lb. bean sprouts
C. 2 scallions
D. 4 slices ginger, shredded
E. 1 teaspoon salt

F. ½ lb. pork (or veal or beef), shredded
G. 1 tablespoon light soy sauce
H. 1 teaspoon sherry
I. 1 teaspoon cornstarch
J. ½ teaspoon sugar

PREPARATION:

I. Mix F thoroughly with G, H, I, J.
II. Wash B, drain. Trim and discard tail roots.

III. Slice C into 1½-inch pieces

COOKING:

1. Heat 1 tablespoon A. Add B, C, D, stir-fry a few seconds.
2. Add E, stir-fry 1 minute. Drain off liquid, place B–E mixture on plate for later use.

3. Heat remaining A until very hot. Add F–J, stir-fry 2 minutes.
4. Add B–E mixture, mix well, and serve hot.

PORK BUTT STEWED WITH MUSHROOMS AND BAMBOO SHOOTS
Tsu Ro Sao Er Dung: General   豬 肉 燒 二 冬

A. 3 tablespoon peanut oil
B. 1 scallion
C. 2 slices ginger
D. 1 lb. pork butt
E. 8 dried Chinese mushrooms

F. ¼ cup light soy sauce
G. ½ teaspoon salt
H. 1 teaspoon sugar
I. 2 cups mushroom soak water
J. 1 cup bite-size pieces bamboo shoots

PREPARATION:

I. Cut D into bite-size pieces.
II. Wash E, soak 15 minutes in 2 cups water. Drain, saving water. Cut E in quarters.

III. Cut B into 1-inch pieces.
IV. Mix F, G, H.

COOKING:

1. Heat A in frying pan, add B, C, stir-fry 1 minute.
2. Add D, E, stir-fry 2 to 3 more minutes.

3. Add F–H, I. Bring to boil.
4. Simmer 45 minutes. Add J, cook another 30 to 45 minutes. Serve.

SIMPLE SPICY PORK CHOPS
Sao Tsu Pai: General   燒 豬 排

A. 3 tablespoons vegetable oil
B. 3 lbs. pork chops
C. 2 onions
D. 5 to 10 drops tabasco

E. ¼ cup light soy sauce
F. 1 teaspoon sugar
G. dash paprika (optional)

PREPARATION:

I.   Cut B into 12 to 15 pieces.
II. Slice C.
III. Mix D, E.

IV. Marinate B in D–E 20 minutes. Drain, saving liquid.

COOKING:

1. Heat A in large frying pan.
2. Using high heat, stir-fry B 10 minutes.
3. Add C, cook 3 minutes, cover pan, lower heat to medium.

4. Add D–E, F, G. Continue cooking 15 to 25 minutes (depending on thickness of chops) until done. Salt to taste.

PORK CHOPS WITH BEAN CURD
Tsu Pai Do Fu: General   豬 排 豆 腐

A. 3 tablespoons peanut oil
B. 2 scallions, sliced
C. 2 slices ginger, slivered
D. 2 medium pork chops
E. 6 dried black mushrooms

F. 4 cakes bean curd
G. 12 cloud ears (optional)
H. 2 tablespoons light soy sauce
I. ½ teaspoon sugar
J. ½ cup water from E

PREPARATION:

I. Soak E in warm water 15 minutes; drain, saving water, and slice.
II. Soak G in cold water 15 minutes; wash and drain.

III. Cut each F into 16 pieces.
IV. Slice D into strips.
V. Mix B, C.

COOKING:

1. Put A into very hot skillet and bring to high heat.
2. Fry B, C ½ minute.

3. Add D, E. Cook until D is thoroughly done (pork will turn white).
4. Add F, G, H, I, J. Cook 5 minutes.
5. Serve hot on rice.

RED-COOKED PORK STOMACH
Hung Sao Tsu Du: General   紅 燒 豬 肚

A. 1 pork stomach
B. 4 tablespoons light soy sauce
C. 2 tablespoons heavy soy sauce
D. ⅛ teaspoon five spices powder

E. 2 teaspoons sugar
F. 1 scallion
G. 2 slices ginger
H. ½ cup chicken broth

PREPARATION:

I. If A is not ready to cook, wash well with 3 tablespoons salt and ½ cup vinegar; rinse with hot water; repeat 2 or 3 times until clean.

COOKING:

1. Put A in pot, add B, C, D, E, F, G, H. Bring to boil.
2. Lower heat, simmer 2½ hours. Add more water if necessary.

3. Slice into bite-size pieces. Serve hot or cold with Chinese hot sauce (optional).

RED-COOKED PORK TONGUE
Hung Sao Tsu Suh: General   紅 燒 豬 舌

A. 2 pork tongues (about 1 lb.)
B. 1 tablespoon whiskey
C. 1 star anise
D. ½ teaspoon anise pepper
E. 3 teaspoons sauterne

F. 2 tablespoons light soy sauce
G. 1 tablespoon heavy soy sauce
H. 2 teaspoons sugar
I. ¼ cup water

PREPARATION:

I. Place A in cold water and clean. Drain; place in pot; add boiling water to cover. Bring to boil, add B, boil 5 to 7 minutes. Drain and let it stay in cold water 1 minute. Slice off white skin. Wash and drain.

COOKING:

1. Place prepared A in pot, add C, D, E, F, G, H, I, bring to boil, lower heat and simmer 45 minutes.
2. Turn A over and simmer another 45 minutes, adding water if necessary.
3. Chill, slice, and serve.

JELLIED PIGS' KNUCKLES
Dung Tee: General

凍蹄

A. 2 pigs' knuckles (1½ lbs.)
B. 2½ cups water
C. 1 chunk ginger, ¾ inch long

D. 2 tablespoons sherry
E. ½ cup light soy sauce
F. 1 tablespoon rock sugar

PREPARATION:

I. Cover A with cold water, bring to boil; continue boiling several minutes. Discard water, rinse A and pot under cold water.

II. Peel C skin; pound with back of cleaver.

COOKING:

1. Cover A with B, bring to boil.
2. Add C, D, cook 30 minutes. Scoop froth off top, discard.
3. Add E, F, lower heat, simmer 2 hours. During this time, turn A over every 30 minutes.

Remove A from pot, saving gravy (there should be about 1 cup gravy left).
4. Bone A, chop very fine. Remove fat from gravy and add gravy to meat, mix well.
5. Pour into loaf pan, refrigerate until jelled. Slice and serve.

SPICED FRESH PICNIC HAM
Hung Sao Wu Siang Ro: General

紅燒五香肉

A. 2 tablespoons peanut oil
B. 2½-lb. fresh picnic ham (shank half)
C. 4 tablespoons heavy soy sauce
D. ½ star anise
E. ½ teaspoon anise pepper

F. 1 teaspoon sugar
G. 1 scallion
H. 4 slices ginger
I. 1 cup water (or meat broth)
J. salt to taste

COOKING:

1. Heat A in 3-qt. saucepan. Brown all sides of B.
2. Add C, D, E, F, G, H, turn B in this mixture a few times.

3. Add I, bring to boil; lower heat, simmer until B is tender (about 2 hours). During this time, turn B over 2 or 3 times so that it will absorb juice evenly. Add water or broth if needed. Adjust with J.

SPICED FRESH PICNIC HAM WITH HARD-COOKED EGGS
Lu Dan: General

鹵蛋

During last hour of simmering in Step 3, add to B 6 to 10 peeled, hard-cooked eggs in which several 1½-inch slashes have been made around the middle portions. The eggs may be served as hors d'oeuvres.

STUFFED EGGPLANT
Rahng Chieh Tze: General

饟 茄 子

A. 1- to 1½-lb. eggplant
B. 8 water chestnuts, chopped
C. 1 scallion, chopped
D. 2 slices ginger, chopped
E. 2 teaspoons sherry

F. ½ lb. ground pork
G. 2 teaspoons light soy sauce
H. 1 teaspoon sugar
I. ½ teaspoon salt
J. ¼ cup chicken broth

PREPARATION:

I. Peel A, cut in half, remove seeds.
II. Mix B, C, D, E, F, G, H, I.

III. Stuff A with B–I.
IV. Place stuffed A in bowl; pour J over it.

COOKING:

1. Place in steamer and steam over boiling water 45 minutes.

STUFFED CUCUMBER
Rong Hwong Gwa: General

饟 黃 瓜

A. 2 large cucumbers
B. ½ lb. ground pork
C. ½ teaspoon sesame oil
D. 1 slice ginger, minced
E. 10 water chestnuts, chopped

F. 2 tablespoons light soy sauce
G. 1 scallion, sliced
H. 1 tablespoon lard
I. ¼ teaspoon salt
J. 1 teaspoon chopped Chinese parsley

PREPARATION:

I. Peel A; cross-cut into 2-inch slices; scoop out seeds.
II. Mix B, C, D, E, F, G, H, I.

III. Fill centers of A with B–I mixture. Arrange on a plate.

COOKING:

1. Steam A–I 20 minutes in a steamer.
2. Garnish with J.

3. Serve hot.

BEEF

Beef cooked in Chinese style can be a real delight. When cooked to peak flavor it literally melts in your mouth. In China, beef is not primarily raised for food. Therefore, the meat is much tougher and often requires drastic tenderizing effort. Thus with the high quality beef offered in the States, the taste, flavor and quality of a beef dish can be far superior to any similar dish offered in China.

BROILED STEAK, MANDARIN STYLE
Sao Niu Pa: Peking

燒 牛 扒

A. 2 cloves garlic
B. 6 slices ginger
C. 2 scallions
D. 3 tablespoons light soy sauce

E. 1 tablespoon sugar
F. 1 teaspoon peanut oil
G. salt, pepper to taste
H. 1 flank or sirloin steak

PREPARATION:

I. Chop A, B, C very fine.
II. Combine A, B, C, D, E, F, G, mix well.

III. Marinate H in sauce mixture half a day.
IV. Preheat broiler.

COOKING:

1. Broil H 5 to 8 minutes on each side.

SAVORY BEEF LIVER WITH ONIONS
Yang Tsung Mun Niu Gan: Shantung   洋 葱 燜 牛 肝

A. ¼ cup vegetable oil
B. 1 lb. beef liver
C. 3 slices ginger, minced
D. 2 tablespoons light soy sauce
E. 1 tablespoon sherry
F. ½ teaspoon salt

G. dash black pepper
H. ⅓ cup flour
I. 2 stalks celery, diced
J. 1 onion
K. ½ teaspoon sugar

PREPARATION:

I. Dice B, removing membrane and tough fibers.
II. Cut J in half and slice into rings.

III. Marinate B in C, D, E, F, G 30 minutes. Mix in H.

COOKING:

1. Heat A in frying pan. Add B–H, fry 5 to 7 minutes over medium heat until browned.

2. Add I, J, K, lower heat, cover, and simmer 12 to 15 minutes. Gradually add ⅓ cup water while simmering. Serve hot.

FRAGRANT GROUND CHUCK BALLS
Shang Ching Niu Ro Ruan: Shanghai   香 芹 牛 肉 丸

A. 3 tablespoons peanut oil
B. 1 clove garlic
C. ½ lb. ground chuck beef
D. salt to taste
E. 2 teaspoons light soy sauce
F. 2 teaspoons cornstarch
G. 1 egg

H. 1 tablespoon sherry
I. ½ teaspoon sugar
J. dash pepper
K. ¼ teaspoon vinegar
L. 1 lb. celery hearts with leaves
M. ½ cup chicken soup

PREPARATION:

I. Mash B with flat side of cleaver; discard skin.
II. Mix C thoroughly with D, E, F, G, H, I, J, K,

roll into 10 meatballs.
III. Shred L; parboil in M 1 to 2 minutes; drain and set aside; save M.

COOKING:

1. Place A in frying pan, brown B, remove.
2. Add C–K to pan with A, brown 1 to 2 minutes.

3. Add L, M; cover and simmer 3 minutes or until meatballs are done.

PRESSED BEAN CURD AND CELERY WITH STIR-FRIED BEEF
Do Fu Gahn Ching Tsai Ro Si: Shanghai   豆 腐 乾 芹 菜 肉 絲

A. 3 tablespoons peanut oil
B. ½ lb. beef (or lamb)
C. 1 clove garlic, chopped
D. 2 slices ginger, chopped

E. 1 tablespoon light soy sauce
F. 2 teaspoons sherry
G. 2 teaspoons cornstarch
H. 1 teaspoon peanut oil

I. 3 stalks celery
J. 2 cakes pressed bean curd
K. 1 teaspoon sugar
L. ½ teaspoon salt

PREPARATION:

I. Slice B, then shred very thin.
II. Mix B, C, D, E, F, G, H and marinate 20 to 30 minutes.

III. Slice I diagonally 2½ by ¼ inches.
IV. Slice J into thin pieces.

COOKING:

1. Heat A, add B–H, stir-fry 1 to 1½ minutes.
2. Remove to dish, pour excess A back into pan.

3. Reheat A, add I, J, stir-fry 1 to 2 minutes; add K, L; mix well with B–H and serve.

BEEF TONGUE WITH TOMATO SAUCE
Cheh Tze Niu Suh: Shanghai

茄 汁 牛 舌

A. 3 tablespoons peanut oil
B. 2 large onions
C. 1 cup catsup
D. 3 teaspoons salt
E. ½ to 1 teaspoon black pepper

F. 6 cloves
G. 2 tablespoons white vinegar
H. 4- to 5-lb. beef tongue (fresh, not pickled)
I. 2 qts. soup stock

PREPARATION:

I. In Dutch oven, boil water. Add H, boil 10 to 15 minutes. Remove, cool in cold water. Trim gristle and bone off thick end. H may now be skinned easily. Discard water.

II. Peel B and shred.
III. Mix C, D, E, F, G.

COOKING:

1. Put A into Dutch oven and heat; stir-fry B until brown.
2. Add C–G, simmer 1 minute.
3. Add H and half of I; cover tightly and simmer 3 to 3½ hours or until H is chopstick tender. Add more soup when needed.
4. Slice and serve.

RED-COOKED BEEF TONGUE
Hung Sao Niu Seh To: General

紅 燒 牛 舌

A. 4- to 5-lb. beef tongue (fresh, not pickled)
B. 1 cup light soy sauce
C. 2 cloves star anise

D. 1 tablespoon sugar
E. 3 tablespoons sherry
F. salt to taste

PREPARATION AND COOKING:

I. In Dutch oven, boil water. Add A, boil 10 to 15 minutes. Remove, cool in cold water. Trim gristle and bone off thick end. A may now be skinned easily. Discard water.
II. Place A, B, C, D, E in Dutch oven. Bring to boil. Cover and simmer about 3 to 3½ hours —until chopstick can puncture A. Add water when needed.
III. Adjust with F, slice and serve.

STEAMED BEEF
Fun Tsen Niu Ro: Szechuan

粉 蒸 牛 肉

A. 1 lb. beef tenderloin
B. 1½ tablespoons light soy sauce
C. 1 tablespoon brown bean sauce
D. 1 teaspoon sugar
E. 1 tablespoon sherry

F. 1 teaspoon sesame oil
G. 1 teaspoon chopped ginger
H. ½ teaspoon salt
I. 2 tablespoons water
J. ⅓ cup rice flour

PREPARATION:

I. Slice A against the grain into thin pieces, mix with B, C, D, E, F, G, H, I and marinate 30 minutes.
II. Mix A–I well with J in dish.

COOKING:

1. Steam in steamer over boiling water 30 to 45 minutes or until beef is tender and soft. Serve hot.

STEAMED BEEF WITH PUMPKIN
Nan Gwa Niu Ro: Szechuan

南 瓜 牛 肉

Add 1½ cups peeled, sliced pumpkin in 1½- by ¾-inch pieces, mixed with ½ teaspoon salt and 2 teaspoons butter or margarine. Arrange pumpkin pieces in dish and place A–J mixture on top of pumpkin. In Step 1, steam in steamer 30 to 45 minutes or until pumpkin is soft.

STEAMED BEEF WITH SWEET POTATO
Fun Tsen Tien Sao Niu Ro: Szechuan

甜 藷 牛 肉

Add 2 sweet potatoes (about ½ to 1 lb.), peeled and cut into bite-size pieces. Mix with ½ teaspoon salt and 2 teaspoons margarine, arrange on dish and place A–J mixture on top of sweet potato.

STEAMED BEEF WITH BEAN CURD
Niu Ro Tsen Do Fu: General

牛 肉 蒸 豆 腐

A. ½ lb. beefsteak, shredded
B. 2 teaspoons light soy sauce
C. ¼ teaspoon ginger juice (see Index)
D. 1 teaspoon cornstarch
E. 4 cakes bean curd, cubed

F. 1 teaspoon light soy sauce
G. 1 teaspoon sherry
H. 1 tablespoon chopped scallion
I. 1 tablespoon cornstarch

PREPARATION:

I. Mix B, C, D, marinate A in it 15 minutes.
II. Mix E, F, G, H, place in dish.

III. Mix I with 2 tablespoons water.
IV. Spread A–D over E–H.

COOKING:

1. Steam A–H 15 minutes over boiling water.
2. Pour gravy into small saucepan, thicken with I mixture.

3. Return thickened gravy to main dish, add pepper to taste, serve with rice.

YU SIANG STEAK
Yu Siang Niu Ro Si: Szechuan

魚 香 牛 肉 絲

A. 6 tablespoons peanut oil
B. 1-lb. flank steak
C. 6 stalks asparagus, chopped
D. 1 scallion, chopped
E. 2 slices ginger, chopped
F. 1 clove garlic, minced
G. 4 teaspoons light soy sauce
H. 2 teaspoons brown bean sauce
I. ½ teaspoon salt

J. 1½ tablespoons sherry
K. 4 teaspoons vinegar
L. 2 teaspoons sugar
M. 1½ tablespoons cornstarch mixed with ¼ cup water
N. ¼ teaspoon meat tenderizer
O. 1 tablespoon light soy sauce
P. 2 teaspoons cornstarch
Q. Chinese hot sauce (optional)

PREPARATION:

I. Slice B across grain, 3/16-inch thick, sprinkle on N and mix well; let stand at room temperature ½ hour, then mix with O, P and 2 teaspoons A.

II. Bring 1 quart water to boil, add C and parboil 2 or 3 minutes, drain.
III. Mix G, H, I, J, K, L, M.

COOKING:

1. Heat remaining A, add prepared B, stir-fry 1 to 2 minutes; remove to dish and pour excess oil back.
2. Add C, D, E, F, stir-fry 1 minute.

3. Return prepared B to pan, stir-fry 1 minute.
4. Add G–M mixture, stir until thickened.
5. Add Q to taste; serve hot.

PINEAPPLE STEAK
Bo Lo Niu Ro: General
菠 蘿 牛 肉

A. 3 tablespoons peanut oil
B. ½ lb. beefsteak
C. 1 teaspoon peanut oil
D. 2 teaspoons cornstarch
E. 1 tablespoon light soy sauce
F. ½ teaspoon sugar

G. 6 slices ginger, shredded
H. 1 scallion
I. 2 8¼-oz. cans sliced pineapple
J. 1 tablespoon sherry
K. salt to taste
L. toasted almonds

PREPARATION:

I. Cut B into thin slices; mix well with C, D, E, F.

II. Cut H into 1½-inch pieces.
III. Drain I and cut each ring into 6 pieces.

COOKING:

1. Heat A; add B–F and G, H; stir-fry 1 to 1½ minutes.

2. Add I, J; stir well.
3. Add K; garnish with L and serve.

STIR-FRIED STEAK WITH GREEN PEPPERS AND TOMATOES
Jiao Cheh Niu Ro: General
椒 茄 牛 肉

A. 3 tablespoons peanut oil
B. 1 clove garlic
C. 1 scallion, white part only, chopped
D. 4 slices ginger
E. ¼ teaspoon salt
F. ½ lb. flank steak
G. 2 medium tomatoes
H. 2 medium green peppers

I. 1 medium onion
J. ½ teaspoon sugar
K. 2 teaspoons sherry
L. 2 teaspoons light soy sauce
M. ⅛ teaspoon black pepper
N. ¼ cup bouillon
O. 1 tablespoon cornstarch

PREPARATION:

I. Slice F into strips ⅛ inch by 1½ inches.
II. Cut each G into 10 wedges. Slice each H diagonally after discarding seeds.
III. Peel I, cut in half, slice thin.

IV. Pound B with back of cleaver, discard skin; then chop.
V. Slice D into long, thin pieces.
VI. Mix J, K, L, M, N.
VII. Mix O with 2 tablespoons cold water.

COOKING:

1. Heat A. Add B, C, D, E, stir-fry a few seconds.
2. Add F slices, stir-fry 1 minute.
3. Add G–I, stir-fry 1 more minute.

4 Add J–N. Keep stirring until all ingredients are well mixed.
5. Add O, stir until gravy thickens. Serve hot with rice.

PAPER-WRAPPED BEEF
Tze Bao Niu Ro: Szechuan
紙 包 牛 肉

A. ½ lb. beef tenderloin or steak
B. 4 slices ginger, chopped
C. 2 tablespoons oyster sauce

D. ¼ cup Cream of Rice
E. Chinese hot sauce to taste

PREPARATION:

I. Slice A into small pieces.
II. Mix B, C, D, E, add A, and marinate 30 minutes.

III. Divide mixture into several portions. Wrap each in waxed paper (shaped like small envelope).

COOKING:

1. Steam 30 to 45 minutes over hot water. Serve.

STIR-FRIED BEEF WITH CELERY
Szechuan Ching Tsai Niu Ro Si: Szechuan   芹 荣 牛 肉 絲

A. ¼ cup peanut oil
B. ½ lb. beef tenderloin
C. 2 teaspoons brown bean sauce
D. 2 teaspoons light soy sauce
E. ½ teaspoon salt
F. 2 teaspoons sherry

G. 1 teaspoon sugar
H. 4 stalks celery
I. 1 tablespoon chopped scallion
J. 1 teaspoon chopped ginger
K. ½ teaspoon Szechuan ground pepper

PREPARATION:

I. Cut B into thin slices, then shred.   II. Mix C, D, E, F, G.   III. Cut H diagonally into thin pieces.

COOKING:

1. Heat A, add B and stir until almost dry. (If too much water comes out of B, remove to another pan and stir-fry until dry.)

2. Add C–G, mix well.
3. Add H and stir-fry 1 or 2 minutes.
4. Add I, J, K, mix well and serve.

STIR-FRIED CELERY HEARTS WITH BEEF
Ching Tsai Niu Ro: General   芹 荣 牛 肉

A. 4 tablespoons peanut oil
B. ½ lb. beefsteak
C. 1 tablespoon light soy sauce
D. 2 teaspoons sherry
E. ½ teaspoon sugar
F. 2 teaspoons cornstarch

G. 3 slices ginger
H. 1 tablespoon chopped scallion
I. 4 celery hearts
    (about 2 cups after slicing, below)
J. ¼ teaspoon salt

PREPARATION:

I. Cut B into thin slices. Mix with C, D, E, F, G, H. Cut I diagonally into ½-inch-thick slices.

COOKING:

1. Heat A, add B–H, stir-fry 1 minute, remove to dish. Return excess oil to pan.
2. Turn up heat, add I to same pan, stir-fry a

few seconds, add 2 tablespoons water, mix well; cover and cook ½ minute.
3. Return B to pan, stir well, add J. Mix well and serve.

PEPPER STEAK
Ching Jao Tsao Niu Ro: General   靑 椒 牛 肉

A. 3 tablespoons peanut oil
B. 1 lb. flank steak
C. 2 green peppers
D. 2 tablespoons water
E. 1 tablespoon light soy sauce
F. 1 teaspoon oyster sauce

G. 1 tablespoon sherry
H. 2 teaspoons cornstarch
I. ½ teaspoon sugar
J. 1 scallion, chopped
K. 4 slices ginger, shredded

PREPARATION:

I. Cut B into narrow strips about 2 inches by ¼ inch, against the grain.
II. Cut C into strips. Discard seeds.

III. Mix B with E, F, G, H, I, J, K. Let stand 15 minutes.

COOKING:

1. Heat A in skillet until hot.
2. Add B and stir-fry 1 minute. Remove and set aside.

3. Using the same pan, add C and stir.
4. Add D, cover and simmer ½ minute.
5. Add E–K mixture, stir 1 minute and serve.

BEEF WITH PRESERVED KOHLRABI
Niu Ro Tza Tsai: Szechuan
牛 肉 榨 荣

A. 3 tablespoons peanut oil
B. ½ lb. boneless beef
C. 2 teaspoons cornstarch
D. 2 slices ginger
E. 1 tablespoon chopped scallion
F. 1 teaspoon light soy sauce

G. 1 teaspoon peanut oil
H. 1 cup shredded bamboo shoots
I. ½ cup preserved kohlrabi
J. 1 teaspoon sugar
K. ½ teaspoon salt

PREPARATION:

I. Shred B very fine.
II. Chop D fine.
III. Mix B, C, D, E, F, G. Mix well.

IV. Combine J, K.
V. Wash and clean I; slice thin and shred.

COOKING:

1. Heat A and add B–G. Stir-fry about 1½ minutes. Remove from pan.
2. Put H, I into same pan. Stir-fry 1 minute.

3. Return cooked B–G and J–K. Mix well and serve.

STEAK WITH ONIONS
Yang Tsung Niu Ro: General
洋 葱 牛 肉

A. 3 tablespoons peanut oil
B. 1 medium onion, sliced
C. 1 clove garlic, minced
D. 3 slices ginger, minced

E. 2 teaspoons cornstarch
F. 1 tablespoon light soy sauce
G. ½ lb. flank steak
H. 1 teaspoon salt

PREPARATION:

I. Slice G into thin, bite-size pieces.

II. Mix C, D, E, F, G.

COOKING:

1. Put A in very hot skillet and bring to high heat.
2. Add B and stir-fry until tender.

3. Add C–G. Stir-fry until brown on outside but slightly rare inside. Add H and serve.

RED-COOKED SHANK OF BEEF
Hung Sao Niu Ro: General
紅 燒 牛 肉

A. 2 tablespoons peanut oil
B. 2-lb. shank of beef
C. 1 scallion
D. 3 slices ginger
E. 2 cloves garlic

F. ⅓ cup light soy sauce
G. 1 teaspoon sugar
H. 1 tablespoon sherry
I. salt, pepper to taste
J. water to cover B

PREPARATION:

I. Cut B into bite-size pieces.
II. Cut C into 1-inch pieces.

III. Pound E with side of cleaver, remove skin.

COOKING:

1. Heat A in saucepan. Stir-fry B, C, D, E 1 minute.
2. Add F, G, H, I, stir well.

3. Add J. Bring to boil, lower heat, and simmer until tender (about 2 to 3 hours.) Add more boiling water if necessary.

COLD CUT SHANK OF BEEF
Hung Sao Niu Ro Pien: General   紅 燒 牛 肉 片

Place whole, uncut B in saucepan, cook with other ingredients until done. Then cool, slice thin, and serve cold.

PEAS WITH GROUND BEEF
Niu Ro Ching Do: General   牛 肉 青 豆

A. 2 tablespoons peanut oil
B. 1 tablespoon chopped scallion
C. 2 slices ginger, chopped
D. ½ lb. ground beef
E. 2 teaspoons cornstarch

F. 1 teaspoon sherry
G. 1 teaspoon light soy sauce
H. 1 pkg. frozen peas
I. 1 teaspoon salt

PREPARATION:

I. Defrost H and drain.

II. Mix D, E, F, G well.

COOKING:

1. Heat A in frying pan.
2. Add B, C, stir-fry several seconds.
3. Add D–G, stir-fry until it changes color

(about 2 to 3 minutes).
4. Add H, I. Stir thoroughly 1 minute. Serve hot.

STIR-FRIED BEEF WITH SPINACH
Niu Ro Bo Tsai: General   牛 肉 菠 菜

A. 3 tablespoons peanut oil
B. ½ lb. beef
C. 2 slices ginger, chopped
D. 1 tablespoon chopped scallion
E. 2 teaspoons cornstarch
F. 1 tablespoon light soy sauce

G. ½ teaspoon sugar
H. 1 tablespoon peanut oil
I. 10-oz. pkg. spinach
J. ½ teaspoon salt
K. 2 teaspoons cornstarch
L. 1 tablespoon water

PREPARATION:

I. Shred B very fine.   II. Mix B, C, D, E, F, G.   III. Mix J, K, L.

COOKING:

1. Heat A. Add B–G, stir-fry 1½ minutes. Remove from pan and place on plate.
2. Add H to same pan.
3. Add I, stir well, add ½ tablespoon hot water,

cover and cook 1 minute.
4. Return B–G to H–I, stir a few seconds, add J–L. Stir well until gravy is thickened. Serve with fried cellophane noodles (see Index).

BEEF WITH TOMATOES AND ONION
Niu Ro Tsao Fan Chieh: General   牛 肉 炒 蕃 茄

A. 3 tablespoons peanut oil
B. 1 lb. flank steak or beef tenderloin
C. 1 teaspoon cornstarch
D. 2 tablespoons light soy sauce

E. 1 tablespoon sherry
F. 2 tablespoons chopped scallions
G. 3 slices ginger
H. ½ teaspoon sugar

I. dash pepper
J. 1 medium onion, sliced
K. 2 medium tomatoes
L. ½ teaspoon salt

PREPARATION:

I. Cut B into strips about 2 inches by ¼ inch, against the grain.

II. Mix with C, D, E, F, G, H, I.

III. Soak K in boiling water until skin is easy to peel off; cut K into 10 wedges each.

COOKING:

1. Heat A in skillet until hot.
2. Stir-fry B–I in A for about 1½ minutes. Remove B.

3. Add J; stir until tender.
4. Add K; stir until heated through.
5. Add L, stir 1 minute, and serve hot.

LAMB AND VEAL

Lamb is very popular in the northern and western provinces. Since it has a strong flavor of its own, it is generally cooked in strong flavored sauces such as combinations of garlic, red peppers, and onions. Veal is relatively scarce throughout China because China is not a cattle-producing country.

THE DOWAGER'S FAVORITE OR SWEET LIKE HONEY *
Ta Sih Mi: Peking

他 司 蜜

A. ⅓ cup sesame oil
B. ½ lb. meat from leg of lamb
C. 1 tablespoon sugar
D. 1 tablespoon brown bean sauce
E. ½ tablespoon sugar
F. 2 teaspoons cornstarch
G. 2 teaspoons vinegar

H. 2 teaspoons light soy sauce
I. 2 teaspoons sherry
J. ½ teaspoon ginger juice (see Index)
K. 2 teaspoons cornstarch mixed with ½ cup water
L. 1 clove garlic, chopped
M. 1 tablespoon chopped scallion

PREPARATION:

I. Cut B into pieces 2 inches long, mix well with D, E, F. Mix G, H, I, J, K, L, M.

COOKING:

1. Heat A and stir-fry B mixture 2 minutes; remove to a dish and drain off A.

2. In a saucepan, heat 1 tablespoon A, and C, stirring until it boils; add G–M, stir until thickened.

3. Return B mixture, cook 1½ minutes; serve with Man To bread (see Index) or rice.

* There is a legend that the famous Dowager Tse Hsi, of the Ching Dynasty loved to eat and that the palace kitchen was kept very busy concocting new recipes for her. One day the Dowager tasted a dish that was both fragrant and sweet, as well as tasty. She had the chief cook called in and asked him what he called this new creation. The chef, who had been preoccupied with working out the recipe, did not have a name for it. He said to the Dowager: "Your venerable Lady, what would you name it?" The Dowager still tasting the sweetness of the new creation answered: "It's sweet like honey." And the chef smilingly said: "Ah, that is the name of this new creation."

LAMB STEW
Hung Sao Yang Ro: Peking

紅 燒 羊 肉

A. 2 tablespoons vegetable oil
B. 1 scallion
C. 1 teaspoon chopped ginger
D. 1 clove garlic, chopped
E. 1½ lbs. leg of lamb

F. 1 teaspoon sugar
G. ½ teaspoon sesame oil
H. 2 tablespoons heavy soy sauce
I. 2 tablespoons light soy sauce
J. 5 carrots (optional)

PREPARATION:

I. Cut E into small pieces.
II. Cut B into 1-inch pieces.

III. Crush D with back of knife. Remove skin.
IV. Cut J into 1-inch pieces.

COOKING:

1. Heat A; stir-fry B, C, D a few seconds.
2. Add E, stir.
3. Add F, G, H, I. Mix well.

4. Bring to boil; simmer 1½ hours or until E is tender. Add J half an hour before E is done. Add chicken broth if necessary.
5. Serve hot.

LAMB CHAFING DISH (FONDUE)
Sa Yang Ro: Peking

涮 羊 肉

A. 10 cups chicken stock
B. 2 lbs. leg of lamb
C. 1 lb. celery cabbage
D. 10-oz. package spinach
E. 10 to 20 cakes bean curd (optional)
F. 1 oz. cellophane noodles
G. 2 or 3 scallions, minced
H. 3 tablespoons light soy sauce

I. ½ teaspoon sesame oil (optional)
J. vinegar*
K. peanut butter*
L. 2 slices ginger
M. 3 tablespoons Chinese parsley, minced (optional)
N. 4 cups soup stock from lamb bones or additional chicken stock

PREPARATION:

This recipe requires a fondue dish or an electric hot plate or an electric deep frying pan. (Each guest is supplied with a porcelain spoon and chopsticks, and will cook his own food at the table.)

I. Cut off bone and slice paper thin.
II. Cut C into 1½-inch strips.

III. Cut E into 1-inch squares.
IV. Soak F in hot water 20 minutes.
V. Place each of the above ingredients in separate bowls on the table.
VI. Prepare sauces by mixing G, H, I or by using J or K, individually or blended together, in any desirable mixture.

COOKING:

1. Place A in deep frying pan or fondue dish as described above. Add L, cover with lid and use high heat to bring to boil.
2. Each guest cooks his own ingredients in a corner of the cooking utensil. When the soup boils again, the cooked food and some of the soup should be ladled out into a bowl and garnished with M.
3. Whenever required, N should be added to cooking utensil.

* Amounts to be determined by individual preference at the table. However, one cup of each should suffice.

MUTTON GELATIN
Yang Gow: Peking

羊 糕

A. 2½-lb. leg of lamb, shank half
B. 2 qts. water
C. 3 cloves garlic
D. ¼ cup light soy sauce

E. dash black pepper
F. 1 teaspoon salt
G. salt to taste

PREPARATION AND COOKING:

I. Bone A, cut into 2-inch squares. Place bone and meat in Dutch oven and add B.
II. Add C, D, E, F. Bring to boil. Lower heat and simmer 3 hours.
III. Remove bones and C.

IV. Shred A chunks. Meat juice at this time should be around 1 qt.; add G.
V. Mix shredded A and juice. Place in mold. Allow to cool, then place in refrigerator to jell.
VI. Skim off fat. Cut gelatin into squares.

STIR-FRIED VEAL CUTLET WITH WALNUTS
Heh Tao Shiao Niu Ro Ding: Peking

核 桃 牛 肉 丁

A. 1 cup shelled walnut halves
B. 2 cups peanut oil
C. 1 egg white

D. ½ teaspoon salt
E. 2 teaspoons light soy sauce
F. 2 teaspoons sherry
G. ½ teaspoon sugar

H. ¼ to ½ teaspoon sesame oil
I. 2 teaspoons cornstarch
J. 1 lb. veal cutlet, diced

PREPARATION:

I. Pour boiling water over A, let stand 1 to 2 minutes or until skin is easy to peel off. After skin is off, spread out on paper towel; dry completely before frying.
II. Beat C and mix well with D, E, F, G, H, I.
III. Add J and mix well.

COOKING:

1. Deep fry A in B at 325° until golden brown, about ½ to 1 minute (do not overfry and burn walnuts); drain on paper towel.

2. Heat 3 tablespoons B, add C–J, stir-fry 3 to 5 minutes or until J is tender.
3. Add A. Mix well, and serve hot.

STIR-FRIED LAMB WITH SCALLIONS
Chung Bao Yang Ro: Peking

葱 爆 羊 肉

A. 2 tablespoons peanut oil
B. 2 teaspoons sesame oil
C. 1 clove garlic
D. 1 lb. lean lamb
E. 4 to 6 scallions, white part only
F. 2 teaspoons sherry

G. 1 tablespoon light soy sauce
H. ¼ teaspoon ground anise pepper
I. 1 teaspoon peanut oil
J. 2 teaspoons vinegar
K. few drops sesame oil
L. salt to taste

PREPARATION:

I. Pound C with side of cleaver, discard skin.
II. Cut D into very thin slices 2 inches by 1 inch.

III. Split E lengthwise, then cut into 1- to 2-inch pieces.
IV. Mix D, E, F, G, H, I, and marinate 15 minutes.

COOKING:

1. Heat A, B, C in pan until very hot.
2. Add D–I, stir-fry 2 to 3 minutes.

3. Add J, K, L and serve.

STIR-FRIED LAMB (SZECHUAN)
Jiang Bao Yang Ro Pien: Szechuan　　醬 爆 羊 肉 片

A. ½ cup peanut oil
B. 1 lb. lean lamb meat
C. 1 teaspoon cornstarch
D. ½ teaspoon salt
E. 1 clove garlic
F. 1 scallion
G. 3 slices ginger, shredded
H. 2 teaspoons light soy sauce

I. 1 teaspoon sugar
J. 2 teaspoons brown bean sauce
K. 2 teaspoons sherry
L. ½ teaspoon sesame oil
M. 2 teaspoons cornstarch mixed with ¼ cup water
N. ½ teaspoon meat tenderizer

PREPARATION:
I. Slice B into thin pieces 2 inches long, mix with N, let stand 15 minutes.
II. Mix B with C, D.

III. Pound E with side of cleaver, discard skin.
IV. Cut F in 1½-inch pieces.
V. Mix H, I, J, K, L, M.

COOKING:
1. Heat A until smoking, add B–D, stir-fry 1 minute, remove to dish.
2. Heat 2 tablespoons A in frying pan, add E, F, G, stir-fry a few seconds.

3. Return B–D, stir-fry ½ minute.
4. Add H–M, stir until sauce is thickened.

SPICED LEG OF LAMB
Wei Yang Ro: Shanghai　　燴 羊 肉

A. ½ leg of lamb (about 2 lbs.)
B. 1 star anise
C. ½-inch piece cinnamon
D. 1 scallion
E. 3 slices ginger
F. 1 tablespoon sherry

G. 2 cups water
H. ¼ tablespoon heavy soy sauce
I. 4 tablespoons light soy sauce
J. 2 teaspoons sugar
K. ½ teaspoon sesame oil
L. 1 tablespoon chopped scallion

PREPARATION AND COOKING:
I. Bone A, clean and wash. Place in Dutch oven.
II. Wrap B, C in cloth, tie tightly with string, add to A.
III. Add D, E, F, G to A, bring to boil; skim froth off top and discard.
IV. Lower heat and simmer ½ hour.

V. Add H, I, J, bring to boil, simmer another hour or until meat is tender and gravy becomes thick. Turn meat over once or twice during cooking and add more water if necessary.
VI. Discard B, C, D, E; add K, stir in well.
VII. Slice A on platter, pour gravy over slices, garnish with L and serve.

BARBECUED LAMB
Jiang Yo Sao Yang Pai: Shanghai　　醬 油 燒 羊 排

A. 3- to 4-lb. leg of lamb
B. ½ cup light soy sauce

C. 1 tablespoon sherry
D. ¼ teaspoon paprika

E. 2 teaspoons sugar

PREPARATION:
I. Mix B, C, D, E.

II. Marinate A 1 to 2 hours.

COOKING:
1. Place A on horizontal grill over red-hot coals. Cover A with 18-inch-wide aluminum foil to retain juices. If half hood is on grill, place one end of foil on top of hood (with weights) and

allow foil to hang extended over edge of grill. When A browns, turn over. Cooking time: 1 to 1½ hours.

VEAL CUTLET WITH LETTUCE AND SCALLIONS
Sun Tsai Shiao Niu Ro Pien: Shanghai
生 菜 牛 肉 片

A. 4 tablespoons peanut oil
B. 2 to 3 scallions
C. 1 small head iceberg lettuce
D. 4 slices ginger, shredded
E. 1 teaspoon salt
F. ½ lb. veal cutlet

G. 2 teaspoons light soy sauce
H. 1 teaspoon sherry
I. 2 teaspoons cornstarch
J. ½ teaspoon sugar
K. dash pepper
L. 1 teaspoon peanut oil

PREPARATION:

I. Slice F thin, then shred; mix with G, H, I, J, K, L.

II. Cut B into 2-inch pieces.

III. Quarter C, then shred.

COOKING:

1. Heat 2 tablespoons A, add B, C, D, stir-fry ½ to 1 minute, add E, stir-fry 1 minute. Drain, remove to dish.

2. Heat remaining A, add F–L, stir-fry 2 to 3 minutes.

3. Return A–E, mix well and serve hot.

STIR-FRIED VEAL CUTLET WITH TOMATO AND PEPPERS
Jiao Chieh Shiao Niu Ro Pien: Shanghai
椒 茄 牛 肉 片

A. 3 tablespoons peanut oil
B. 1 clove garlic, chopped
C. 1 tablespoon chopped scallion
D. ½ lb. veal cutlet
E. 2 teaspoons light soy sauce
F. ½ teaspoon sugar

G. 2 teaspoons cornstarch
H. few drops sesame oil
I. 1 large green pepper
J. 2 tomatoes
K. ½ teaspoon sugar
L. ½ teaspoon salt

PREPARATION:

I. Slice D thin into 2- by ¼-inch strips. Mix well with E, F, G, H.

II. Slice I diagonally into ½-inch strips, discarding seeds.

III. Place J in boiling water a few seconds, remove skin and cut each into 8 to 10 wedges.

IV. Mix K, L.

COOKING:

1. Heat 2 tablespoons A, add B, C, stir-fry a few seconds.

2. Add D–H, stir-fry 2 minutes, remove to dish.

3. Heat 1 tablespoon A, add I, stir-fry 1 minute.

4. Add D–H, J, K, L, continue stirring until everything is well mixed, serve hot.

STIR-FRIED VEAL CUTLET WITH BROCCOLI
Gai Lan Shiao Niu Ro: General
芥 蘭 牛 肉

A. 3 tablespoons peanut oil
B. 1 tablespoon chopped scallion
C. 1 clove garlic, chopped

D. ½ lb. veal cutlet
E. 2 teaspoons light soy sauce
F. 2 teaspoons cornstarch

G. ½ teaspoon sugar
H. few drops sesame oil
I. 1 bunch broccoli

PREPARATION:

I. Slice D thin into about 1- by 2-inch pieces, mix with E, F, G, H.

II. Cut flowerets of I about 1½ inches long. (Save stems for other dishes.) Drop into boiling water; when water returns to boil, turn off heat, drain, and let cold water run over it several seconds.

COOKING:

1. Heat A, add B, C, stir-fry ½ to 1 minute; add D, E–H; stir-fry 2 minutes.

2. Add I, mix well and serve.

VEAL CUTLET WITH SZECHUAN SAUCE
Yu Shiang Shiao Niu Ro Pien: Szechuan   魚 香 牛 肉 片

A. 3 tablespoons peanut oil
B. ½ lb. veal cutlet
C. 2 teaspoons light soy sauce
D. 1 teaspoon cornstarch
E. 1 teaspoon peanut oil
F. ½ lb. asparagus
G. 1 or 2 cloves garlic, chopped
H. 1 teaspoon chopped ginger
I. 1 tablespoon chopped scallion

J. 2 teaspoons brown bean sauce
K. 1 teaspoon sugar
L. 2 teaspoons light soy sauce
M. 2 teaspoons sherry
N. 2 teaspoons vinegar
O. ½ teaspoon salt
P. 2 teaspoons cornstarch mixed with
    ¼ cup water

PREPARATION:

I. Slice B thin, then shred, mix with C, D, E.
II. Break F into 1- to 1½-inch pieces; wash well.

III. Bring 1 to 2 qts. water to boil, add F, parboil
2–3 minutes, drain. Mix J, K, L, M, N, O, P.

COOKING:

1. Heat A, add B–E, stir-fry 2 minutes, remove
to a dish, pour excess oil back into pan.
2. Turn on heat, stir-fry F, G, H, I 1 minute.
3. Return B to pan, stirring 1 to 2 minutes.

4. Add J–P, stir until mixture is thickened.
5. Add Szechuan pepper or Chinese hot sauce to
taste.

DICED VEAL CUTLET WITH HOT PEPPERS
La Tze Shiao Niu Ro Ding: Szechuan   辣 子 牛 肉 丁

A. 4 tablespoons peanut oil
B. 1 lb. veal cutlet, diced
C. 1 egg white
D. 2 teaspoons cornstarch
E. ½ teaspoon salt

F. 2 cloves garlic, chopped
G. 1 green pepper
H. 2 red-hot peppers
I. 1 teaspoon chopped ginger
J. 1 tablespoon chopped scallion

K. 1 teaspoon salt
L. 2 tablespoons light soy sauce
M. 1 tablespoon vinegar
N. 2 teaspoons sugar
O. Sesame oil to taste

PREPARATION:

I. Mix B, C, D, E.
II. Wash and discard stems and seeds of G, H;
dice.

III. Mix I, J, K.
IV. Mix L, M, N, O.

COOKING:

1. Heat 3 tablespoons of A; add B–E; stir-fry 3
to 5 minutes or until meat is done; remove
from pan.
2. Add 1 tablespoon A, add F, G, H, stir-fry ½

minute.
3. Add I–K, stir a few seconds.
4. Return B to pan, add L–O, mix well and serve.

VEGETABLES

A wide variety of vegetables is available in China as well as in the United States. They are an integral part of many dishes or can be served separately as an accompaniment to main courses of fish and meat.

SWEET AND SOUR CUCUMBERS I
Tien Swan Hwang Gwa: Peking

甜 酸 黃 瓜

A. 2 tablespoons vegetable oil
B. 3 medium cucumbers
C. 4 slices ginger
D. 4 tablespoons cider vinegar

E. 1 teaspoon light soy sauce
F. 1 teaspoon sesame oil
G. 3 tablespoons sugar
H. 1 teaspoon salt

PREPARATION:

I. Wash and cut B in half lengthwise. Remove seeds. Cut into 1- to 1½-inch slices.

II. Mix C, D, E, F, G, H.

COOKING:

1. Heat A in skillet. Stir-fry B one minute (do not cook thoroughly).
2. Add C–H, allow mixture to boil.

3. Remove to bowl and cool.
4. Marinate 30 minutes or more and serve.

SWEET AND SOUR CUCUMBERS II
Tien Swan Huang Gwa: Szechuan

甜 酸 黃 瓜

A. 1 tablespoon sesame oil
B. 2 to 3 medium cucumbers
C. 1 teaspoon light soy sauce
D. 4 tablespoons cider vinegar

E. 3 tablespoons sugar
F. 1 teaspoon salt
G. 1 to 2 red-hot peppers

PREPARATION:

I. Wash and cut B in half lengthwise. Remove seeds. Cut each half into 3 cross-sections, dry with paper towels.

II. Halve G, discard seeds and stems, and shred diagonally.

COOKING:

1. Heat A, stir-fry B 1 minute.
2. Add C, D, E, F, stir well, and bring to boil.
3. Add G, stir a few seconds.

4. Remove mixture to a bowl, cover, and let stand 3 to 4 hours.
5. Before serving, remove B and G from mixture. Shred B, garnish with G.

STEAMED MUSHROOMS
Ching Tsen Dung Gu: Peking

清 蒸 冬 菇

A. 2 oz. Chinese mushrooms
B. 2 scallions, chopped

C. 3 slices ginger, chopped
D. 1 teaspoon sherry

E. 1 teaspoon sugar
F. Salt and MSG to taste

PREPARATION:

I. Soak A in warm water 20 minutes. Drain and cut off stems. Place in deep dish for steaming.

II. Mix A, B, C, D, E.

COOKING:

1. Place dish in steamer and steam 35 minutes. Add F and serve.

PEKING PICKLES
La Bai Tsai: Peking

辣 白 菜

A. 1 tablespoon peanut oil
B. ½ teaspoon anise pepper
C. ¼ cup sugar
D. ¼ cup vinegar
E. 1 to 2 lbs. celery cabbage

F. 1½ tablespoons salt
G. 4 slices ginger, shredded
H. ½ to 1 teaspoon red pepper flakes (to taste)

PREPARATION:

I. Remove E leaves from main stem. Rub each with F, and spread out uniformly in an 8- by 12-inch cake pan. Cover with waxed paper topped by another 8- by 12-inch pan.

Place a heavy weight over second pan. Let stand at least 6 hours or overnight.

II. Remove E leaves from pan, squeeze out water. Cut each into ½- to 1-inch pieces, place in a bowl, and add G, H.

COOKING:

1. Heat A, stir-fry B a few seconds. Add C, D, bring to boil.
2. Pour A–D over E–H mixture, mix well, and marinate 2 hours.

3. Pour juice back in pot, bring to boil. Pour over E–H again; marinate 4 more hours.
4. To serve, discard B (it is easily visible), drain, and arrange pickles on a dish.

SZECHUAN PICKLES
Pow Tsai: Szechuan
泡 菜

A. 6 cups bite-size American cabbage pieces, from center portion
B. 2 carrots
C. 1 red-hot pepper
D. 1 slice ginger (about ½-inch)

E. 2 cloves garlic
F. 3 tablespoons salt
G. 6 cups boiling water
H. 2 tablespoons dry sherry

PREPARATION:

I. Peel B; cut into sticks 1 to 2 inches long.
II. Discard C seeds and stem, cut C into long, thin diagonal pieces.
III. Slice D into 4 to 5 pieces.
IV. Peel E, discard skin.
V. Wash A, B, drain. Dry thoroughly with paper towels. Place in a 2-qt. jar with C, D, E.

VI. Dissolve F in G, cool thoroughly, and add to mixture.
VII. Add H, cover jar tightly. Let stand 3 days, when pickle will be ready to serve. Pickle juice may be reused indefinitely. With each use, add ½ tablespoon salt, and pickle will be ready to serve in one day.

CHINESE COLE SLAW
Lun Ban Bai Tsai Si: Tientsin
凉 拌 白 荣 絲

A. ½ cup shredded carrots
B. 2 cups shredded celery cabbage
C. 15 to 20 whole peppercorns

D. 1 to 2 teaspoons salt and dash MSG
E. 1 handful Chinese parsley
F. 1 teaspoon sesame oil

PREPARATION:

I. Combine A, B, C, D and mix well. Place in jar and allow to stand 6 hours.
II. Cut E into 1-inch pieces.

III. Drain water from A–D; add E, F, mix and serve.

EGGPLANT BUTTER
Tsen Chieh Nee: Shantung
蒸 茄 泥

A. 1-lb. eggplant
B. 1 tablespoon sesame sauce or peanut butter
C. 1 clove garlic, minced

D. 1 teaspoon sesame oil
E. ½ teaspoon salt and ¼ teaspoon MSG

PREPARATION:

I. Peel A and remove stem. Cut into small pieces. Place in deep platter.

COOKING:

1. Steam A 20 minutes or until it is soft and breaks up easily. Mix with B, C, D, and E to taste. Serve.

BRAISED SOYBEAN SPROUTS
Hung Sao Hwang Do Ya: Shanghai
紅 燒 黃 豆 芽

A. 2 tablespoons peanut oil
B. 1 tablespoon chopped scallion
C. ¼ cup diced Virginia ham

D. 1 lb. soybean sprouts
E. 1 tablespoon light soy sauce
F. 1 teaspoon sugar

G. ½ teaspoon salt and ¼ teaspoon MSG (optional)
H. ½ cup water

PREPARATION:

I. Remove tail part of D. Wash well, drain.
II. Mix E, F, G, H.

COOKING:

1. Heat A, add B, stir-fry a few seconds.
2. Add C, stir-fry ½ minute, add D, mix well.

3. Add E–H, bring to boil, lower heat and simmer 35 minutes.

Bean sprouts have been popular in China for centuries. Although their discoverer is not known, bean sprouts, as a food, is listed in *The Herb and Foodstuff Encyclopedia* of the Ming Dynasty.

Bean sprouts are rich in Vitamins A, B, and C. In sprout form as compared to the bean itself, its vitamin content is greatly increased.

HOW TO RAISE BEAN SPROUTS
Fa Do Ya: General 發 豆 芽

A. 1 cup mung beans
B. ½-gallon milk carton
C. 2 pieces paper towel

D. 1 8-oz. coffee jar filled with pebbles, wt. about 1½-2 lbs.

PREPARATION:

1. Rinse A and cover A with water overnight.
2. Use ice pick and poke 30–40 holes in bottom of B. Then poke 3 to 4 holes in sides of B about ½ inch from bottom.
3. Pour soaked A into B.
4. Fold C into 4½-inch square. Wet and cover A.

5. Place D on top of C.
6. Water A 4 times a day (once each meal and just prior to bedtime). Depending on the temperature of the room, sprouts will be ready in 5–7 days. Wash and remove hulls. One cup of beans will make 2 to 2½ lbs. sprouts.

ONE-MINUTE BEAN SPROUTS
Ching Tsao Do Ya: General 清 炒 豆 芽

A. 3 tablespoons peanut oil
B. 4 slices ginger, shredded
C. 1 scallion

D. ½ lb. bean sprouts
E. 1 teaspoon salt and dash MSG
F. ½ teaspoon sugar

PREPARATION:

I. Remove tail part of D. Wash well, drain.

II. Cut C into 1-inch pieces.

COOKING:

1. Heat A, add B, C, and stir-fry several seconds.
2. Add D, stir-fry 30 seconds.

3. Add E, F, stir well several times. D will be crisp and ready to serve in exactly 1 minute.

BRAISED CHESTNUTS WITH CELERY CABBAGE
Hung Sow Li Tze Bai Tsai: Shanghai 紅 燒 栗 子 白 菜

A. ¼ cup peanut oil
B. 4 cups, 1-inch-wide pieces, center portion celery cabbage
C. 12 Chinese mushrooms
D. 2 teaspoons sugar

E. 3 tablespoons soup stock (or mushroom water)
F. 2 tablespoons light soy sauce
G. 1 cup chestnuts
H. salt to taste

PREPARATION:

I. Make slits in G, cover with water. Boil 10 minutes, then shell and cut into halves.

II. Wash C, and soak 15 minutes in warm water. Drain, saving water. Cut each C in half.

COOKING:

1. Heat A, add B, C, stir-fry about 5 minutes.
2. Add D, E, F, cover, cook over low heat 5 minutes.

3. Add G, cook another 5 minutes. Add H.

HOT AND SOUR CELERY CABBAGE
Swan La Tsai: Szechuan

酸 辣 荣

A. 4 tablespoons peanut oil
B. 1 teaspoon anise pepper
C. 3 red-hot peppers
D. 1 lb. center portion celery cabbage
E. ⅓ cup white vinegar

F. ½ teaspoon salt
G. 1 tablespoon light soy sauce
H. ½ to 1 teaspoon sesame oil
I. 1 teaspoon cornstarch
J. Dash MSG

PREPARATION:

I. Cut D into pieces 1 to 1½ inches wide.
II. Cut C endwise, discard seeds and stem, then slice diagonally in thin pieces.
III. Mix E, F, G, H, I, J.

COOKING:

1. Heat A. Add B, stir-fry 1 minute, remove B from pan. Discard.
2. Add C, stir-fry a few seconds, add D. Continue stir-frying 2 to 3 minutes.
3. Add E–J, mix well. Cover, cook 2 minutes. Serve hot.

HOT AND SOUR CELERY CABBAGE
Swan La Tsai: Shanghai

酸 辣 荣

A. 2 teaspoons sesame oil
B. 1 hot chili pepper, chopped
C. ¼ cup vinegar
D. 1 tablespoon sugar

E. 1 to 2 lbs. celery cabbage
F. 1 to 2 teaspoons salt
G. ¼ teaspoon MSG

PREPARATION:

I. Using center stalk portion of E (removing top leafy part), cut into 2-inch cross-section pieces. Pour boiling water over E, drain. Repeat pouring and draining process 4 times, then cool. When cold, mix with F and G.
II. Mix C, D.

COOKING:

1. Heat A. Add B, fry until golden brown.
2. Add C–D, mix well.
3. Pour A–D over cold E and G. Serve as hors d'oeuvres.

CAULIFLOWER WITH HAM SAUCE
Yung Twei Hwa Tsai: Shanghai

雲 腿 花 荣

A. 4 cups bite-size pieces cauliflower
B. ⅔ cup soup stock
C. ½ teaspoon salt and dash MSG
D. ½ cup chopped Virginia ham

E. 4 slices ginger, chopped
F. 1 tablespoon chopped scallion
G. 2 teaspoons cornstarch mixed with ¼ cup water

COOKING:

1. Mix A, B in saucepan, bring to boil; cook covered 5 minutes.
2. Add C, stir well.
3. Remove A to dish, leaving liquid in saucepan.
4. Add D, E, F, bring to boil.
5. Thicken with G.
6. Pour sauce over cooked A.

PRESERVED RED-IN-SNOW
Yen Shieh Li Hung: Shanghai
淹 雪 裏 紅

Wash 1 to 2 lbs. fresh red-in-snow well, dry with paper towels, and let stand 2 days in an airy place. Rub thoroughly with ½ cup salt, place in a clean jar, and cover tightly. Let stand 2 weeks before cooking. Stir-fry with pork, beef, or veal, or cook in meat soup.

BROCCOLI WITH MUSHROOMS
Gai Lan Dung Gu: General
芥 蘭 冬 菇

A. 1 bunch broccoli
B. 4 tablespoons peanut oil
C. 8 to 10 Chinese mushrooms
D. 2 tablespoons chopped scallion
E. 1½ teaspoons salt and dash MSG
F. 1 teaspoon sugar

PREPARATION:

I. Use only flower parts of A cut into pieces 1 to 2 inches long. Marinate stems and save for other recipes.

II. Wash C, soak in warm water 15 minutes. Drain, saving water.

III. Cut each C into 2 or 3 pieces.

COOKING:

1. Drop tips of A into boiling water. When water boils again, remove from heat. Drain, and let cold water run over.

2. Heat B, stir-fry C, D 1 minute.

3. Add A, E, F, and ¼ cup C water. Continue stir-frying 1 to 2 minutes. Serve hot.

MUSHROOMS WITH BAMBOO SHOOTS
Yang Chow Tsao Er Dung: Yangchow
楊 州 炒 二 冬

A. 3 tablespoons peanut oil
B. 2 cups sliced bamboo shoots
C. 12 large Chinese mushrooms
D. 1½ tablespoons light soy sauce
E. 1 teaspoon sugar
F. 2 teaspoons sherry
G. ½ teaspoon ginger juice (see Index)
H. ⅓ cup chicken broth or mushroom water
I. 2 teaspoons cornstarch mixed with ¼ cup water
J. few drops sesame oil
K. ¼ teaspoon MSG (optional)

PREPARATION:

I. Wash C in cold water, then soak in warm water 15 minutes; drain, save water; cut each C into halves.

II. Mix D, E, F, G.

COOKING:

1. Heat A, add B, C, stir-fry 1 minute.
2. Add D–G, H and K, cook 1 to 2 minutes.

3. Thicken with I.
4. Add J and serve.

CABBAGE HEARTS WITH BAMBOO SHOOTS
Sun Sih Tsai Shing: Yangchow
筍 絲 荣 心

A. 4 tablespoons vegetable oil
B. 2 lbs. Chinese cabbage hearts
C. 1 cup sliced bamboo shoots
D. 1 teaspoon salt
E. 1 tablespoon sherry
F. 1 teaspoon sugar
G. ¼ cup chicken soup mixed with 2 teaspoons cornstarch

PREPARATION:

I. Wash and clean B, cut into 1½-inch segments.

II. Slice C into pieces ¼ inch thick, ½ inch wide and 1½ inches long.

COOKING:

1. Place A in frying pan; when hot, add B, C; stir-fry 1 minute.

2. Add D, E, F and stir-fry 1 minute.
3. Add G and simmer 1 to 2 minutes.

CABBAGE HEARTS WITH CHICKEN FAT
Gee Yo Tsai Shing: Szechuan   雞 油 荣 心

A. 2 tablespoons peanut oil
B. 1½ lbs. Chinese cabbage hearts
C. ½ cup chicken broth
D. ½ teaspoon sugar
E. ½ to 1 teaspoon salt and

dash MSG to taste
F. 1 tablespoon cornstarch mixed with
¼ cup water
G. 1 teaspoon chicken fat

PREPARATION:

I. Remove tough leaves of B, cut tender part in 1½-inch lengths, and parboil in boiling water 1 minute. Drain and squeeze out water.

COOKING:

1. Heat A, stir-fry B a few seconds.
2. Add C, cook 2 to 3 minutes.
3. Add D, E and stir well.

4. Thicken with F.
5. Add G and serve.

BRAISED BAMBOO SHOOTS
Hung Mun Sun: Szechuan   紅 燜 筍

A. 2 tablespoons peanut oil
B. 1 cup sliced bamboo shoots
C. 1½ tablespoons brown bean sauce
D. 1 teaspoon sugar
E. ½ cup chicken broth

F. 2 teaspoons sherry
G. 1 teaspoon cornstarch mixed with
2 tablespoons water
H. sesame oil
I. salt to taste

COOKING:

1. Heat A, add B, stir-fry 1 to 2 minutes.
2. Add C, D, E, continue stirring 1 minute.

3. Add F, mix well, cover and cook 2 to 3 minutes.
4. Thicken with G, add H, I.

STEAMED EGGPLANT WITH MINCED MEAT
Chieh Nee: Szechuan   蒸 茄 泥

A. 2 tablespoons peanut oil
B. ½ cup ground pork
C. 1 small hot pepper
D. 1 clove garlic, chopped

E. 1 tablespoon preserved celery cabbage
F. 1-lb. eggplant
G. 1 teaspoon salt

PREPARATION:

I. Peel F, split in half, steam over boiling water 20 minutes or until soft; mash.
II. Discard stem and seeds of C, chop.

III. Cover E with cold water, stir so that any sediment will sink to bottom; remove E from water.

COOKING:

1. Heat A, add B, C, D, E, stir-fry 1 to 2 minutes.

2. Add F, G, stir well and serve.

BARBECUED EGGPLANT
Kow Cheh Tze: Szechuan

烤 茄 子

A. 1-lb. eggplant
B. ¼ cup peanut butter
C. 1 teaspoon salt and dash MSG

D. dash garlic salt or 1 clove garlic, chopped
E. ⅓ cup water

PREPARATION AND COOKING:

I. Skin A, cut into 8 lengthwise pieces and place on aluminum foil.

II. Mix B, C, D, E to form paste. Paint mixture on A. Wrap with the foil. Grill 15 minutes on medium heat, 7½ minutes on each side.

KOHLRABI OR CABBAGE PICKLES
Pow Tsai: Szechuan

泡 菜

A. 1 lb. kohlrabi or cabbage
B. 1 red-hot pepper (optional)
C. 4 slices ginger

D. 2 cloves garlic
E. 1 tablespoon salt

F. 2 cups boiling water
G. 1 tablespoon wine

PREPARATION:

I. Peel A and discard skin. Slice A into bite-size pieces or use center portion of cabbage and cut into bite-size pieces.

II. Discard B seeds and stem. Cut B diagonally into thin, long pieces.
III. Peel D, discard skin.

COOKING:

1. Mix A, B, C, D, place in jar.
2. Dissolve E in F. Cool thoroughly, add to jar.
3. Add G, cover jar tightly, and let stand 2 to 3 days, when pickle will be ready to serve.

Pickle juice can be used over and over, each time, adding ½ tablespoon salt, and pickle will be ready to serve in only one day. Refrigerate between use.

MARINATED BROCCOLI STEMS
Pao Gai Lan: General

泡 芥 蘭

A. 3 to 4 broccoli stems
B. 1 teaspoon salt

C. 1 clove garlic, minced
D. 1 teaspoon olive oil or

sesame oil

E. 2 teaspoons distilled white vinegar

PREPARATION:

I. Peel skin from A; slice thin, diagonally.
II. Place A, B in a jar and shake well. Let stand overnight.
III. Mix C, D, E.

IV. Drain salt water from A.
V. Add C–E mixture. Shake well.
VI. Let stand several hours before serving.

COOKING:

1. Heat A, add B, stir-fry a few seconds, turn off heat.
2. Add C–E (be careful that oil does not spatter), bring to a boil.

3. Pour hot mixture over F, let stand overnight before serving. Shake the jar a few times so that the juice is absorbed evenly.

FRIED SALTY PUMPKIN STICKS
Tza Nahn Gwa: General

炸 南 瓜

A. 1 qt. peanut oil
B. ½- to 1-lb. pumpkin
C. ½ cup flour
D. 5 tablespoons water

E. 1 teaspoon salt
F. 2 teaspoons light soy sauce
G. pepper to taste

PREPARATION:

I. Peel B and discard seeds and soft pulp and strings; cut into finger-size sticks.

II. Mix C, D, E, F into a paste.
III. Add B sticks to C–F until each is coated well.

COOKING:

1. Heat A to 350°.
2. Deep fry B–F, ⅓ at a time, until golden brown (about 2 minutes). The pumpkin sticks will float when they are done. Serve hot or cold, with or without G.

VEGETARIAN DISHES

In China there are three types of people who are connoisseurs of vegetarian menus. The Buddhist monk, or nun, whose religious beliefs require that he eat only food derived from vegetables, or the fervent Buddhist layman who adheres to the strict dietary rules for given religious dates. These two types not only consider fish, eggs, milk, or butter to be nonvegetarian but even their cooking utensils must be thoroughly scrubbed to remove all possible contamination by animal fat. This dietary practice is entirely in keeping with the purity and asceticism of Buddhism as practiced throughout China.

The third type is not a true vegetarian in any sense of the word. But after a feast of meats and heavy foods, many people crave the simplicity and lightness of vegetable dishes, an easily digestible change of pace.

These three groups have lent their talents and ingenuity in creating dishes like Vegetarian Chicken, Duck, Ham, and Steak.

VEGETARIAN ROAST DUCK
Sue Sao Ya: Shanghai   素 燒 鴨

A. 1 tablespoon peanut oil
B. 4 large mushrooms
C. 1 cup finely shredded bamboo shoots
D. 2 teaspoons light soy sauce
E. ½ teaspoon sugar
F. ½ teaspoon salt
G. 1 tablespoon mushroom water
H. 1½ teaspoons cornstarch

I. 1 teaspoon sugar
J. 2 teaspoons light soy sauce
K. ½ teaspoon sesame oil
L. ½ teaspoon salt
M. 2 tablespoons mushroom water
N. 8 pieces fresh bean curd skin
O. 2 cups peanut oil

PREPARATION:

I. Wash B and soak in warm water 15 minutes; drain and save water; shred B very fine.

II. Mix D, E, F, G.

III. Mix H, I, J, K, L, M.

COOKING:

1. Heat A, add B, stir-fry a few seconds, add C, mix well.
2. Add D–G, stir well and cook 1 minute.
3. Dip pastry brush into H–M and brush 1 piece of N generously.
4. Spread ¼ of A–G on top; place second piece of N over this; brush again with H–M and spread ¼ A–G over this.
5. Repeat procedure until fourth layer is finished.
6. Fold into 2- to 3-inch roll, tie with thread; place on a plate and steam over boiling water 10 minutes; cool completely.
7. Heat O to 375°, deep fry A–N until golden brown (1 to 2 minutes), cool. Slice and serve as hors d'oeuvres or serve with rice.

VEGETARIAN STEAK WITH MUSHROOMS AND BAMBOO SHOOTS
Mien Jing Tsao Er Dung: Shanghai   麵 筋 炒 二 冬

A. 3 tablespoons peanut oil
B. 1 scallion, chopped
C. 2 slices ginger, chopped
D. 10-oz. can vegetarian steak
E. 1 cup diced bamboo shoots
F. 6 Chinese mushrooms
G. ¼ cup dry lily flowers

H. ¼ cup cloud ears
I. 2 tablespoons light soy sauce
J. ½ teaspoon sugar
K. ½ teaspoon salt
L. 1 teaspoon cornstarch mixed with ¼ cup water
M. ½ teaspoon sesame oil

PREPARATION:

I. Cut D into bite-size pieces.
II. Wash F, soak 15 minutes in warm water. Drain, saving water; cut each F in quarters.
III. Soak G 15 to 20 minutes in cold water; discard water. Remove hard tips, cut each G in half.

IV. Place H in pan large enough to allow it to double when expanded. Cover with 1 cup hot water, soak 15 to 30 minutes. Discard water; wash H well.

COOKING:

1. Heat A, stir-fry B, C a few seconds. Add D, E, F, G, H, stir-fry 2 minutes.
2. Add I, J, K and 3 tablespoons F water; cover, cook 5 minutes over low heat.
3. Stir in L until gravy is thick.
4. Remove from heat, add M, and mix thoroughly.

VEGETARIAN SWEET AND SOUR MEATBALLS
Tien Swan Sue Ro Jiu: Shanghai　　甜 酸 素 肉 球

A. 1 cup peanut oil
B. 1 cup walnut halves
C. ¼ cup glutinous rice flour
D. ¼ cup flour
E. 1 teaspoon baking powder
F. dash salt
G. 1 green pepper
H. 1 red pepper

I. 1 scallion, chopped
J. 2 tablespoons vinegar
K. 2 tablespoons sugar
L. 2 tablespoons catsup
M. 1 tablespoon light soy sauce
N. ½ teaspoon salt
O. 2 teaspoons cornstarch mixed with
　¼ cup water

PREPARATION:

I. Pour boiling water over B, let stand 2 minutes; peel, dry completely on paper towel.
II. Mix C, D, E, F with 5 tablespoons water to make batter.

III. Wash G, H; discard stems and seeds; cut G, H into cubes.

COOKING:

1. Heat A to 325°; deep fry B 15 to 30 seconds until golden brown; do not burn; drain on paper towel.
2. Dip fried B in C–F batter; then deep fry again in A until golden brown; drain on paper towel.
3. Heat 1 tablespoon A, add G, H, I, stir-fry ½ minute, add salt to taste.
4. Mix J, K, L, M, N, O in a saucepan over medium heat, stirring until thickened.
5. Add B and G–I, stir well and serve.

VEGETARIAN STIR-FRIED SLICED FISH
Tsao Sue Yu Pien: Shanghai　　炒 素 魚 片

A. 1 cup peanut oil for deep frying
B. 12 wood ears
C. ¼ lb. snow peas
D. 1 medium tomato
E. 1 teaspoon salt

F. ½ teaspoon sugar
G. 1 teaspoon cornstarch mixed with
　⅓ cup water
H. 1 large cooked potato (about ½ lb.)
I. 1½ tablespoons flour

PREPARATION:

I. Peel H, cut in half, then into ¼-inch slices; coat with I, deep fry in A at 375° until golden brown (1 to 2 minutes); drain on paper towel.

II. Wash B thoroughly and cook in boiling water ½ hour; drain and shred.
III. Remove tips of C.
IV. Cut D into 8 to 10 pieces.

COOKING:

1. Heat 2 tablespoons A, add B, C, stir-fry 1 minute; add 1 tablespoon water, cover and cook 1 minute.
2. Add D, stir-fry ½ minute.
3. Add E, F, G and stir until thickened.
4. Add H, mix well and serve.

VEGETARIAN HAM DRIED BEAN CURD
Sue Ho Twei Do Fu: Shanghai   素 火 腿 豆 腐

A. 1 tablespoon sugar
B. ¼ cup light soy sauce
C. 1 cup water

D. 20 sheets dried bean curd
E. 1 to 2 teaspoons sesame oil
F. 4 cakes bean curd skin

PREPARATION:

I. Soak D in water 2 minutes; drain, cut into 1-inch squares.

COOKING:

1. Place A, B, C in pot, bring to boil.
2. Add D and cook 15 minutes over medium heat.
3. Add E, mix well and cool.
4. Place ½ of A–E mixture in middle of 2 pieces of F.
5. Fold F over tightly and make into 5-inch roll.
6. Wrap 1 square foot waxed paper around the roll; tie with a string. Make 2 rolls like this.
7. Stand endwise on a plate.
8. Steam over boiling water 45 minutes.
9. Cool completely before unwrapping waxed paper; slice and serve.

VEGETARIAN RINGING BELL
Tza Shang Ling: Shanghai   炸 響 鈴

A. 1 tablespoon peanut oil
B. 3 Chinese mushrooms
C. 1 carrot
D. ½ cup shredded bamboo shoots
E. 1 tablespoon light soy sauce
F. 1 teaspoon sugar
G. 1 to 2 teaspoons sherry
H. 1 medium potato

I. ½ teaspoon salt and ¼ teaspoon MSG
J. 8 pieces fresh bean curd skin
K. 3 tablespoons flour mixed well with 2 tablespoons water
L. 2 cups peanut oil
M. tomato sauce (to taste)

PREPARATION:

I. Peel H and cut into small pieces; using little water, cook until soft; mash, mix with I, making a thick paste.
II. Wash B and soak in warm water 15 minutes, drain, and shred very thin.
III. Peel C, slice and shred.
IV. Mix E, F, G.
V. Mix K with dash of salt.

COOKING:

1. Heat A, add B, C, D, stir-fry 1 to 2 minutes; add E–G, mix well.
2. Spread H–I paste on each J; put 2 pieces on top of each other.
3. Place ¼ B–G mixture across J, about 2 inches below top, spread out 1½ inches wide.
4. Fold top over and roll, cut each roll diagonally into 5 pieces.
5. Dip ends in K mixture.
6. Deep fry in L at 350° until golden brown (about 2 minutes).
7. Serve with M.

VEGETARIAN STIR-FRIED CRAB MEAT
Tsao Sue Pong Sha Ro: Shanghai   炒 素 螃 蟹 肉

A. ½ cup peanut oil
B. ½ cup mashed cooked carrot
C. ⅔ cup mashed potato
D. 1 cup finely shredded bamboo shoots
E. 8 Chinese mushrooms

F. ¼ lb. snow peas
G. ½ teaspoon sugar
H. 1½ teaspoons salt
I. 2 teaspoons wine vinegar

PREPARATION:

I. Wash E and soak in warm water 15 minutes; shred very fine.

II. Discard tips of F, shred.
III. Mix G, H.

COOKING:

1. Heat A, add B, C, stir-fry until crispy (about 4 minutes).
2. Add D, E, F, stir-fry 2 minutes.

3. Add G, H, mix well.
4. Add I and serve.

NOODLES, PANCAKES, BREAD

In Northern China, noodles are a common food staple. They are cheaper than rice and need few meat or vegetable dishes to accompany them; also a small quantity of meat can be added to produce a complete dish. The Chinese have always regarded noodles as a symbol of longevity because of their great length, and therefore seldom cut them. Noodles frequently are served at birthday celebrations and festivals because of their symbolic nature.

Like all noodles, the Chinese types come in a variety of shapes and sizes; some are small, often as fine as thread. Various kinds of American egg noodles are reasonably good substitutes.

Dry noodles should never be washed before cooking and should be stored in a cool, dry place. Both dry and fresh noodles should be added slowly to rapidly boiling water, separated with a fork, and cooked until they are barely tender (4 to 6 minutes), never overcooked. If other ingredients are to be added just before serving, the noodles should be set aside before they are fully cooked and then reheated when the final ingredients are incorporated into the dish. The boiled noodles should then be drained and rinsed with cold water in a colander, and separated with a fork or chopsticks.

PEKING SCALLION PANCAKE
Chung Yo Bing: Peking

葱 油 餅

A. 1 cup and 2 tablespoons
  flour
B. ½ cup warm water (100°)
C. 1½ teaspoons sesame oil

D. 3 to 4 scallions, chopped
E. Salt to taste
F. 6 teaspoons peanut oil

PREPARATION:

I. Mix 1 cup A with B. Blend well and knead with rest of A until dough is smooth and elastic.

II. Divide A into 6 parts. Take one part and knead into a ball. Then, using remainder of A, roll dough out on a floured board into a 6-inch diameter pancake. Brush with ¼ tea-spoon C, sprinkle with D and E. Then starting from one side, roll into a long roll.

III. Pick up one end of the long roll and roll over again into a roll. Then with both hands roll this lightly into a ball. Roll ball again on the floured board as in Step II. (Repeat with 5 remaining parts of the dough.)

COOKING:

1. Grease hot frying pan with 1 teaspoon F. Lower heat.
2. Over low heat pan-fry each cake individually

until golden brown (about 2 to 3 minutes on each side).

PEKING TA LU MEIN
Ta Lu Mein: Peking

大 鹵 麵

A. 3 tablespoons peanut oil
B. ½ teaspoon chopped ginger
C. 1 tablespoon chopped
  scallion
D. 13-oz. can chicken broth,
  diluted with water to make
  2½ cups
E. ½ lb. pork, shredded
F. 3 black mushrooms
G. 10 dried shrimps
H. 20 golden needles
I. 1 tablespoon dried cloud
  ears

J. 1½ tablespoons light soy
  sauce
K. 1 tablespoon sherry
L. salt to taste
M. 3 tablespoons cornstarch
  mixed with ½ cup water
N. 1 egg beaten
O. 2 teaspoons sesame oil
P. ½ teaspoon star anise
  peppercorn
Q. ½ lb. cooked noodles

PREPARATION:

I. Rinse and soak F in hot water 20 to 30 minutes or until soft (save water and add to D). Shred F.

II. Clean and wash G; soak in water 20 minutes.

III. Rinse H and soak in hot water 30 minutes. Cut each into 2 to 3 pieces, discard hard tips.

IV. Soak I in warm water; when soft, clean and wash in cold water.

COOKING:

1. Heat pan, add A; when hot, add B, C. Stir-fry 30 seconds.
2. Add D, E, F, G, H, I, J, K; bring to boil. Cook 1 to 2 minutes, add L.
3. Thicken with M.
4. Turn flame very low; stir in N. Turn up flame, cook until egg becomes firm. Then turn flame very low.
5. Heat O, add P. Stir over medium heat until P turns dark brown; discard P. Add O to B–N mixture, stir well. Serve over Q in individual bowl.

PORK LO MEIN
Tsu Ro Lo Mein: General   豬 肉 撈 麵

A. 3 tablespoons peanut oil
B. 4 Chinese mushrooms
C. 1 tablespoon chopped scallions
D. ¼ lb. pork (or beef or chicken)
E. 2 tablespoons light soy sauce
F. 1 teaspoon salt
G. 1 cup shredded celery cabbage

H. 1 cup thinly shredded bamboo shoots
I. 1 cup thinly shredded celery
J. ¼ cup mushroom water
K. 10 snow peas
L. 1 teaspoon cornstarch mixed with
   1 tablespoon water
M. ½ lb. fresh or dried thin noodles

PREPARATION:

I. Cook M in 2 qts. boiling water 5 to 8 minutes. Drain and run under cold water a few seconds; drain again.

II. Mix cooked M with ½ E, ⅓ A, and ½ teaspoon F. Put mixture in baking dish and bake in 375° oven 25 minutes.

III. Wash B and soak in warm water 15 minutes. Cut in thin shreds 2 inches long.

IV. Cut D in thin shreds 2 inches long.

COOKING:

1. Heat A in frying pan until hot, stir in B, C, add D and stir-fry 2 minutes. Add E, F, stir-fry 1 minute.

2. Add G, H, I and mix well. Add J, cover and cook 2 minutes. Add K and continue to stir-fry 1 minute.

3. Add L, stir well.

4. Pour over baked crispy M and serve.

PANCAKES
Bo Ping: Peking   薄 餅

A. 2 cups flour
B. 1 teaspoon salt

C. 1 cup boiling water
D. ¾ cup sesame oil

PREPARATION:

I. Sift A, B into bowl.

II. Add C, stir well with chopsticks.

III. Knead A–C on floured board until dough is smooth. Divide into 2 parts.

IV. Roll A–C with hands into a long roll, divide into 8 parts.

V. Take one part only, shape into a ball. Roll it into a very thin round piece about 8 inches in diameter.

VI. Brush A–C piece with D; then make into a long roll; again shape it into a ball.

VII. Again roll A–C ball into 8-inch thin piece. Brush with D. Put 2 pieces together.

VIII. Repeat with each 12 parts. Makes 24 pancakes.

COOKING:

1. Heat frying pan over low heat, grease, and fry each pancake until done (3 to 5 minutes); turn each over 2 or 3 times. Separate the two pieces when done. Serve with Peking Duck, Szechuan Yu – Siang Shredded Pork, or Szechuan Doubled Cooked Pork with Hoisin Sauce. Pancakes can be made beforehand. Steam in steamer 5 minutes, just prior to serving.

PEKING FLOWER ROLL
Hwa Jwen: Peking

花 捲

A. 4 cups flour
B. ¼ cup sugar
C. 1 teaspoon salt
D. 1½ cups lukewarm water

E. 1 tablespoon sugar
F. 1 pkg. dry yeast
G. 1 teaspoon sesame oil

PREPARATION:

I. Sift A, B, C together in large bowl.

II. Mix D with E, stir in F slowly, mixing well.

III. Make hollow in center of flour mixture, add D–F and mix thoroughly.

IV. Knead on floured board until dough is smooth and elastic.

V. Place dough in well-greased bowl, cover and let rise at room temperature until it doubles in bulk (about 45 minutes).

VI. Remove from bowl and knead again for a few minutes; divide into two parts.

VII. Roll one part into a rectangle, about 14 by 7 inches; brush ½ of G over dough. Follow same procedure with remaining half of dough.

VIII. Form each half into a round roll, like a jellyroll; then cut each roll into 16 one-inch segments.

IX. With the loose ends against each other, press two segments together lightly to make a flat bun. Press chopstick through the buns to make them stick together; then remove.

X. Place each bun on a 2½- by 2½-inch square of waxed paper, let them rise at room temperature again until dough looks light and almost doubles in bulk (about 45 minutes).

COOKING:

1. Leave on paper and place buns in steamer; steam over boiling water 15 minutes. When buns are completely cooked, they will resemble butterflies. Makes 16 rolls.

SNOW-WHITE STEAMED BREAD
Shwieh Bai Man To: Peking

雪 白 饅 頭

A. 2 pkges. dry yeast
B. ½ cup warm water
C. ¾ tablespoon sugar
D. 1 cup warm milk
E. ½ cup warm water

F. ½ cup peanut oil
G. ½ cup sugar
H. 1 teaspoon salt
I. 1 box cake flour
J. 1 teaspoon vegetable oil

PREPARATION:

I. Combine A, B, C in large bowl; let stand until spongy (about 10 minutes).

II. Add D, E, F, G, H, blend well.

III. Stir in I and knead until dough is smooth and firm. Brush top of dough with J; cover with wet clean dish towel. Let stand until doubled in size (about 45 to 60 minutes).

IV. Punch dough down with fist and let it stand a few more minutes; then turn dough onto lightly floured board and knead.

V. Divide into 4 parts; then divide each part into 8 to 10 pieces. Dough can be used to make Bao Tze (see Index).

VI. Place each piece on top of a 2-inch-square piece of waxed paper; cover with a clean towel and let rise about 1½ hours before steaming.

COOKING:

1. Steam over boiling water 15 minutes. Bread can replace rice and is particularly good with red-cooked dishes. Also, it can be sliced and served with Peking Duck (see Index) or with peanut butter and jam. Bread can be frozen and resteamed.

CHINESE BREAD
Man To: Peking   饅　頭

A. 4 cups flour
B. 1 teaspoon salt
C. ¼ cup sugar
D. 1¼ cups warm water

E. 2 tablespoons sugar
F. 1 pkg. dry yeast
G. 2 tablespoons melted butter or margerine

PREPARATION:

I. Sift A, B, C in large bowl.
II. Mix D, E in measuring cup.
III. Stir in F slowly. Mix well.
IV. Add G to D–F.
V. Hollow out center of A–C. Add D–G. Mix thoroughly.
VI. Knead lightly on floured board until dough

is smooth and elastic.

VII. Place in greased bowl, cover, and let dough rise at room temperature until it doubles in bulk, about 1 to 1½ hours.
VIII. Divide dough into 24 parts. Shape each into a rectangular bun and let rise once more.

COOKING:

1. Steam in steamer 20 minutes. Serve with Chinese red-cooked pork or use as bread spread with peanut butter or jam.

CHICKEN WITH SIMPLE SAVORY NOODLES
Gee Si La Hu Jiang Mein: Shanghai   雞　絲　辣　糊　醬　麵

A. 2 tablespoons peanut oil
B. 1 scallion, chopped
C. 1 cup diced chicken (or pork or beef)
D. 1 tablespoon light soy sauce

E. ½ cup water
F. 14-oz. can braised mixed vegetables in chili sauce
G. ½ lb. noodles or spaghetti, cooked

COOKING:

1. Heat A, add B, stir-fry a few seconds.
2. Add C, stir-fry 2 minutes.
3. Add D, E, F, mix well.

4. Add G, stir until thoroughly mixed. Cover, cook 5 to 10 minutes over low heat, stirring occasionally.

EGG NOODLES
Gee Don Mein: General   雞　蛋　麵

A. 4 eggs
B. 2 cups flour

C. cornstarch

PREPARATION:

I. Beat A slightly with fork. Add B gradually, mix well.
II. Knead mixture into a soft dough. Cover with damp dish towel, let stand 10 to 12 minutes. Knead again several minutes.

III. Sprinkle board and rolling pin with C. Roll dough out as thin as possible.
IV. Fold thin dough over several times. Cut across folds, slicing noodles as narrow (or as broad) as desired.

COOKING:

1. Bring 2 to 3 quarts water to boil.
2. Add prepared A–C, cook 2 minutes. Drain,

run under cold water until cold. Can be used for any noodle dish.

NOODLES WITH PORK AND SALTED BROWN BEAN SAUCE
Jiang Bao Tsu Ro Mein: Shanghai   醬 爆 豬 肉 麵

A. 1 lb. fresh noodles

B. 2 tablespoons peanut oil

C. 2 tablespoons brown (or yellow) bean sauce

D. 1 clove garlic, minced

E. ½ teaspoon salt

F. 1 slice ginger, minced

G. 1 lb. ground pork

H. 1½ tablespoons hoisin sauce

I. ½ teaspoon sugar

J. 1 tablespoon heavy soy sauce

K. 5 dried black mushrooms

L. ¾ cup water

PREPARATION:

I. Soak K in warm water 15 minutes, drain. Slice thin.

II. Mash C to a paste.

III. Mix C, D, E, F. Set aside.

IV. Mix G, H, I, J. Set aside 15 minutes.

COOKING:

1. Boil A 3 to 4 minutes. Drain.

2. Put B in very hot skillet and bring to high heat.

3. Add C–F and stir-fry rapidly 15 seconds to brown D slightly.

4. Add G–J and K. Stir-fry well until G is fully done.

5. Add L. Cover and cook 5 minutes over medium heat.

6. Pour very hot tap water over A to heat. Drain well.

7. Place A in serving dish and pour B–L over.

SHREDDED HAM NOODLES
Yuin Twei Si Mein: General   雲 腿 絲 麵

A. 1 cup water

B. 1 pkg. yee fu mein noodles

C. ¼ cup shredded baked Virginia ham

D. ½ teaspoon sesame oil

COOKING:

1. Bring A to boil in saucepan.

2. Add B, stir with chopsticks; cook about 2 or 3 minutes or until water is absorbed.

3. Add C, D, mix well and serve.

FRIED CELLOPHANE NOODLES
Tza Fun See: General   炸 粉 絲

A. 1 qt. vegetable oil

B. 1 oz. cellophane noodles

PREPARATION:

I. Separate B into four portions.

COOKING:

1. Heat A in skillet to 375°.

2. Add B, a portion at a time. As soon as each expands, remove and place on paper towel.

B is ready to serve as base for meat and vegetable dishes.

NOODLES IN CHICKEN SOUP
Gee Tong Mein: General   雞 湯 麵

A. 1 tablespoon peanut oil
B. ¼ lb. boned breast meat of chicken
C. 2 teaspoons light soy sauce
D. ¾ teaspoon salt
E. ¼ teaspoon sugar

F. ½ cup bamboo shoots, diced
G. 3 to 4 Chinese mushrooms
H. 1½ qts. chicken broth
I. 1 lb. fresh noodles
J. 2 scallions, sliced

PREPARATION:

I. Parboil I 4 minutes. Set aside in bowl.
II. Soak G 15 minutes. Slice into thin slivers. Discard water.

III. Dice B into ½-inch-square pieces.
IV. Dice F into ½-inch-square pieces.
V. Mix C, D, E. Add C–E to B and stir well.

COOKING:

1. Put A in very hot skillet and bring to high heat.
2. Add B–E mixture and stir-fry 15 seconds.
3. Add F, G. Stir-fry 45 seconds.

4. Add H; bring to boil; simmer 10 minutes.
5. Reheat I under running hot tap water.
6. Place I in deep bowl. Pour soup mixture over I. Serve with garnish of J.

BEAN CURD

Soy bean has been used for centuries to supplement the Chinese diet with vegetable protein. Bean curd is rich in calcium and a very digestible form of soy bean protein. Although originally designed as a dairy substitute, it has long since become a very popular Chinese food. Although some United States leading food companies have begun to manufacture foods from soy bean, they have yet to come up with an equivalent of the Chinese soy bean curd.

FLUFFY BEAN CURD
Fong Wo Do Fu: Peking

蜂 窩 豆 腐

A. 2 tablespoons peanut oil
B. ¼ lb. pork, shredded
C. 6 cakes bean curd
D. 6 Chinese black mushrooms

E. 10 dried shrimp
F. ½ cup chopped bamboo shoots
G. ¼ cup finely chopped preserved tea melon
H. 1 teaspoon salt

PREPARATION:

I. Cook C in boiling water until fluffy (about 25 minutes). Drain well, squeeze out water; shred.
II. Wash D and soak in warm water 15 minutes. Drain.

III. Wash E well, soak in water 15 minutes. Drain.
IV. Chop D, E fine.

COOKING:

1. Heat A. Add B, stir-fry 2 minutes.

2. Add C, D, E, F, G, H, stir-fry until gravy is almost absorbed.

159

BEAN CURD TOSSED WITH PEANUT BUTTER
Liang Ban Do Fu: Shanghai　　涼 拌 豆 腐

A. 4 cakes bean curd
B. 1 tablespoon peanut butter
C. 1 tablespoon light soy sauce
D. 1 tablespoon vinegar
E. few drops sesame oil

F. ½ to 1 teaspoon sugar
G. ½ to 1 teaspoon salt (to taste)
H. 4 slices ginger, chopped
I. 2 tablespoons chopped Chinese parsley
J. ¼ teaspoon MSG (optional)

PREPARATION:

I. Rinse A, cut each into 6 pieces.
II. Mix B, C, D, E, F, G thoroughly.

III. Mix A with B-G and J.
IV. Garnish with H, I.

STIR-FRIED FROZEN BEAN CURD
Tsao Dung Do Fu: Peking　　炒 凍 豆 腐

A. 2 tablespoons vegetable oil
B. 6 cakes frozen bean curd*
C. 2 slices ginger, shredded

D. 2 tablespoons mashed fermented bean cake
E. 1 tablespoon light soy sauce
F. few drops sesame oil

PREPARATION:

I. Cover B with warm water several hours ahead of cooking until defrosted. Squeeze out water; shred.

COOKING:

1. Heat A. Add B, C, stir-fry over high heat 1 to 2 minutes.

2. Add D, E, stir, mix well.
3. Remove to serving dish, add F; serve.

* Wrap 2 to 3 pieces fresh bean curd together in waxed paper, freeze until hard.

STIR-FRIED PRESSED BEAN CURD WITH PORK
Do Fu Gahn Tsao Ro Si: Shanghai　　豆 腐 乾 炒 肉 絲

A. 2 tablespoons peanut oil
B. ½ lb. pork, shredded
C. 1 tablespoon light soy sauce
D. 1 teaspoon cornstarch
E. ½ teaspoon sugar
F. 1 scallion, chopped

G. 4 cakes pressed bean curd
H. 6 stalks celery
I. 1 teaspoon sherry
J. ½ teaspoon salt
K. 3 tablespoons water

PREPARATION:

I. Wash G; cut each into long, thin strips.
II. Cut H diagonally into long, thin strips.

III. Mix B, C, D, E, F.

COOKING:

1. Heat A. Stir-fry B–F over high heat 1 to 2 minutes.
2. Add G, H. Continue stirring until well mixed.

3. Add I, J, K, mix well. Cover, cook over low heat 5 minutes.

STIR-FRIED PRESSED BEAN CURD WITH CHICKEN
Do Fu Gahn Tsao Gee Si: Shanghai   豆 腐 乾 炒 雞 絲

Substitute 1 boned chicken breast for B and in Step 2 add 6 Chinese black mushrooms which have been washed and soaked in water 15 minutes, drained, and cut into strips. Use mushroom water instead of K in Step 3.

STEAMED BEAN CURD WITH PORK
Do Fu Tsen Tsu Ro: Peking   豆 腐 蒸 豬 肉

A. 6 cakes bean curd
B. ¼ lb. ground pork, shredded
C. 1 tablespoon chopped scallion
D. 2 slices ginger, chopped
E. 2 teaspoons sherry

F. ½ teaspoon sugar
G. 2 tablespoons light soy sauce
H. 1 teaspoon sesame oil
I. ½ teaspoon salt

PREPARATION:

I. Cover A with boiling water 1 to 2 minutes. Remove from water, arrange in large bowl.

II. Mix B, C, D, E, F, G, H, I thoroughly.
III. Spread over A.

COOKING:

1. Place bowl in steamer, cover. Steam over boiling water 20 minutes.

STEAMED BEAN CURD WITH BEEF
Do Fu Tsen Niu Ro: Peking   豆 腐 蒸 牛 肉

Substitute beef for B. Steam over boiling water 15 minutes.

SHREDDED BEAN CURD WITH MIXED MEATS I
Shih Jing Do Fu: Shanghai   什 錦 豆 腐

A. 3 tablespoons peanut oil
B. ¼ cup shredded Smithfield ham
C. 4 Chinese black mushrooms
D. ½ cup shredded bamboo shoots
E. 1 cup chicken broth
F. 2 cakes bean curd, shredded
G. ¼ cup peas

H. ¼ cup diced shrimp
I. ¼ cup diced crab meat
J. ¼ cup shredded chicken white meat
K. 1 teaspoon sherry
L. 1 teaspoon light soy sauce
M. 1 teaspoon salt
N. 1 tablespoon cornstarch

PREPARATION:

I. Wash C, soak 15 minutes in warm water. Drain (saving water to mix with N), and cut each C into 4 or 5 pieces.

II. Mix K, L, M.
III. Mix 2 tablespoons C water with N.

COOKING:

1. Heat A, stir-fry B, C, D 1 minute.
2. Add E, bring to boil.
3. Add F, G, cover, and cook 1 minute.

4. Add H, I, J and K–M, bring back to boil; boil several seconds.
5. Thicken with N mixture. Serve hot with rice.

SHREDDED BEAN CURD WITH MIXED MEATS II
Sih Gin Gahn Si: Shanghai

什 錦 乾 絲

A. 3 tablespoons peanut oil
B. ¼ lb. pork, shredded, or
    ½ cup shredded ham
C. ½ cup diced frozen shrimp
D. 4 Chinese black mushrooms
E. ¼ cup shredded preserved kohlrabi

F. 1 teaspoon sugar
G. 1 tablespoon light soy sauce
H. 1 cup chicken broth
I. 3 cakes pressed bean curd
J. ½ cup shredded bamboo shoots
K. salt, pepper to taste

PREPARATION:

I. Slice I very thin, then shred.
II. Wash D and soak in warm water 15 minutes or until soft. Drain, save mushroom water and add to H. Discard stems, shred very fine.

COOKING:

1. Heat A, add B, C, stir-fry 1 to 2 minutes, remove from pan.
2. In same pan add D, E, F, G, stir-fry 1 to 2 minutes, add H, bring to boil.
3. Add I, J, lower heat, cook 3 minutes.
4. Add K and garnish with B–C mixture.

BLACK AND WHITE BEAN CURD
Heh Bai Do Fu: Shanghai

黑 白 豆 腐

A. 2 cups chicken broth
B. 1 cup water
C. 8 to 10 pieces dried sea cucumber
D. 3 cakes bean curd
E. 2 teaspoons cornstarch mixed with
    ¼ cup water

F. 1 egg
G. 1 tablespoon sherry
H. salt to taste
I. ¼ teaspoon MSG (optional)

PREPARATION:

I. Place C in bowl, cover with cold water, soak 4 to 6 days changing water 3 to 4 times a day. Drain and cut into cubes.
II. Cut D same size as C.
III. Beat F well.

COOKING:

1. Place A in cooking pot, add B; bring to boil, add C and cook over medium heat 30 minutes.
2. Add D, bring to boil. Remove from heat.
3. Stir in E slowly.
4. Return to heat, stirring constantly until it boils again. Remove from heat.
5. Stir in F gradually and add G. Mix well.
6. Add H, I.

BEAN CURD WITH BLACK MUSHROOMS
Dung Gu Do Fu: General

冬 菇 豆 腐

A. 2 tablespoons peanut oil
B. 8 Chinese black mushrooms
C. ½ cup mushroom water
D. 6 cakes bean curd
E. ½ teaspoon salt

F. ½ teaspoon sugar
G. 1 tablespoon sherry
H. ⅛ teaspoon sesame oil
I. 1 tablespoon light soy sauce
J. 2 teaspoons cornstarch

PREPARATION:

I. Wash B and soak 15 minutes in warm water. Drain, cut each into 5 to 6 pieces.
II. Cut each D into 8 pieces.
III. Mix I, J.

COOKING:

1. Heat A. Add B, stir-fry a few seconds. Add C, bring to boil.
2. Add D. Continue cooking 2 minutes.
3. Add E, F, G, H and I–J to thicken.

BEAN CURD WITH CRAB MEAT
Sha Ro Do Fu: Shanghai　　蟹 肉 豆 腐

A. 3 tablespoons peanut oil
B. 1 scallion, chopped
C. 2 slices ginger, shredded
D. 1 clove garlic, chopped
E. 1 cup chicken broth
F. 3 cakes bean curd, diced

G. ¼ cup peas
H. 7½-oz. can crab meat
I. 4-oz. can mushrooms
J. 1 teaspoon sherry
K. 1 teaspoon salt
L. 1 tablespoon cornstarch

PREPARATION:

I. Drain I, saving liquid.

II. Mix 2 tablespoons I liquid with L.

COOKING:

1. Heat A, stir-fry B, C, D several seconds.
2. Add E, bring to boil.
3. Add F, G, reduce heat, cover, and cook 2 minutes.

4. Add H, I, J, K, bring back to boil, and cook 1 minute.
5. Thicken with L. Serve with rice.

FRECKLED MA PO BEAN CURD
Ma Po Do Fu: Szechuan　　麻 婆 豆 腐

A. 3 tablespoons peanut oil
B. 2 cloves garlic, chopped
C. 2 teaspoons fermented salted black beans
D. ¼ lb. ground pork
E. 4 cakes bean curd
F. 2 tablespoons light soy sauce
G. 1 cup chicken broth
H. ½ teaspoon sugar

I. 1 scallion, chopped
J. 2 teaspoons yellow bean sauce
K. 1 teaspoon crushed red pepper
L. 3 slices ginger, chopped
M. 2 teaspoons cornstarch mixed with ¼ cup water
N. ½ to 1 teaspoon sesame oil
O. anise ground pepper to taste

PREPARATION:

I. Cut each E into 16 cubes.　　II. Mix F, G, H.　　III. Mix I, J, K, L.

COOKING:

1. Heat A in large frying pan. Add B, C, stir-fry a few seconds. Add D and stir-fry 2 minutes.
2. Add E and F–H mixture; cook 1 minute.

3. Add I–L mixture, mix well. Thicken with M, cook a few seconds.
4. Add N, stir.
5. Sprinkle with O to taste before serving.

BEAN CURD WITH SHRIMP
Sha Ren Do Fu: General　　蝦 仁 豆 腐

A. 3 tablespoons peanut oil
B. ½ lb. shrimp
C. 2 teaspoons sherry
D. 1 teaspoon light soy sauce

E. 1 teaspoon cornstarch
F. 1 teaspoon sugar
G. 1 scallion, chopped
H. 2 slices ginger, chopped

I. 6 cakes bean curd
J. 2 tablespoons brown bean sauce
K. ¼ cup water

PREPARATION:

I. Shell, devein, wash, and drain B. Cut each into 2 or 3 pieces.
II. Cut each I into 16 cubes.

III. Mix B, C, D, E, F, G, H thoroughly.
IV. Mix J, K.

COOKING:

1. Heat A. Add B–H, stir-fry over high heat 1 to 2 minutes.
2. Add I, mix well.

3. Add J, K, stir well, cover, and cook over low heat 5 minutes. Serve hot.

BEAN CURD WITH BEEF
Do Fu Niu Ro: General

豆 腐 牛 肉

A. 3 tablespoons peanut oil
B. ½ lb. flank steak
C. 2 slices ginger, chopped
D. 1 scallion, chopped
E. 2 tablespoons sherry
F. 4 cakes bean curd

G. 3 teaspoons light soy sauce
H. 2 teaspoons cornstarch
I. ½ teaspoon sugar
J. 1 teaspoon salt
K. ¼ cup water

PREPARATION:

I. Cut each F into 10 pieces.
II. Slice B into pieces ⅛ by 1½ inches.

III. Mix B, C, D, E, 1 teaspoon G, 1 teaspoon H.
IV. Mix remaining G and H with I, J, K.

COOKING:

1. Heat A, add B–E, stir-fry 1 minute.
2. Add F, mix well, stir 1 minute.

3. Thicken with G–K, and serve with rice.

RICE

There are two kinds of rice: long grain and short grain. Long grain rice is long and narrow, absorbs more water, is fluffier after cooking, and is the best kind to use for fried rice. Short grain rice is short and wide, absorbs less water, and is softer after cooking. Soft rice, which is easier to digest, is preferred by most Chinese. In this country, a dried, fluffier rice is preferred. Sweet rice, also known as glutinous rice, is used primarily in pastries and special festival dishes.

When properly cooked, a grain of rice is about twice its uncooked size, fluffy and white, and somewhat translucent. Each grain should be separated. If an insufficient amount of water has been used, the inside of the grain remains hard and white, whereas if too much water has been used, the outside of the rice becomes soft and mushy.

Rice goes particularly well with salty dishes or those cooked with large amounts of soy sauce. It may be cooked three ways. The first is a congee, a soup, essentially, in which a small amount of rice has been cooked in a large quantity of water for several hours. Congee prepared in advance is eaten for breakfast with salted eggs or other highly flavored foods, also as a late evening snack when bits of beef, chicken, pork, or sliced raw fish are added. The second method is to make a thicker, more chowderlike soup by boiling it in slightly less water and adding other ingredients. This method gives the greatest bulk of food for the least amount of rice. In the third technique, boiled or steamed rice is made with even less water, the amount being a matter of personal preference, until all the moisture has been evaporated. A general rule is for the water level to be approximately one inch above the rice level in the pot; also, a standard recipe cup of moistened rice will require 1½ cups of water and will serve three people. The pot should never be more than half filled with raw rice; if more is needed, a larger pot should be used. Once the proper technique for obtaining the desired consistency has been established, a little experience will readily produce the same kind of rice each time.

The cooking procedure should begin with the use of high heat and an uncovered pot. If foaming occurs, the heat should be adjusted so that the contents of the pot do not foam over the stove. Allow the rice to swell; when the liquid is almost completely absorbed, cover the pot and lower the heat. Allow to cook for 15 more minutes.

The type of pot used is important. It should have a snug lid and be made of aluminum so that if the rice is left on low heat for too long, it will not burn. Rice has a tendency to burn in copper-bottomed pots, and charred rice is difficult to remove. Always use the same pot for cooking rice since it will then be easier to judge how much water to add each time. Recently, automatic electric rice cookers have been introduced here and abroad which produce rice of just the desired consistency—uniformly and effortlessly, and ready to serve.

If cooked rice is not to be served immediately, it may be kept warm in a pot over the very lowest possible heat or in a warm oven at very low heat. If necessary, several tablespoons of water may be sprinkled around the edge of the pot.

It is better to cook too much rice, rather than too little, since it is served with almost every dish, and any that is left over may be reused. Leftover rice should be loosened with a lifting motion of a fork or chopstick and not stirred, to avoid breaking up the grains. It should be refrigerated in a covered container (it is preferable for fried rice to be hard), and thoroughly chilled before refrying, otherwise the rice grains will stick together in a gluey mess.

To warm cooked rice, add 2 tablespoons of hot water for each cup of cold cooked rice, then loosen the grains with a fork, cover the pot tightly, and warm over low heat for 8 to 10 minutes, allowing the rice to steam until it is hot. Cold cooked rice that is lumpy can best be separated with wet hands.

Leftover boiled or steamed rice that sticks to the bottom and sometimes the sides of the pan can be removed and refrigerated; it makes a delicious dish—sizzling rice.

RED-IN-SNOW WITH PORK RICE
Shieh Tsai Ro Si Fan: Shanghai

雪 荣 肉 絲 飯

A. 1 to 1½ cups cooked rice
B. ½ cup Red-in Snow with Pork (see Index)

C. ½ cup boiling water
D. salt to taste

COOKING:

1. Place A in a pot.
2. Add B, C, mix well, and bring to boil.

3. Lower heat, simmer 5 minutes.
4. Add D.

ROAST BEEF FRIED RICE
Niu Ro Tsao Fan: General

牛 肉 炒 飯

A. 2 eggs
B. 3 tablespoons peanut or vegetable oil
C. 1 clove garlic, diced
D. 1 small onion, diced
E. 1 cup diced roast beef

F. 1 cup frozen peas
G. 4 cups cold cooked rice
H. 2 tablespoons light soy sauce
I. 1 teaspoon salt

PREPARATION:

I. Pour hot water over F for 1 minute, drain.

COOKING:

1. Scramble A in 2 tablespoons B; set aside.
2. Heat remaining B in same pan, stir-fry C, D ½ minute.

3. Add E, stir-fry 1 minute.
4. Add F, G, H, I. Stir 2 minutes.
5. Add A and mix well, serve hot.

SIMPLE SCALLION EGG FRIED RICE
Chung Hwa Don Tsao Fan: General

葱 花 蛋 炒 飯

A. 3 tablespoons peanut oil
B. ¼ cup chopped scallion
C. 3 to 4 eggs

D. 2 to 2½ cups cold cooked rice
E. 1 tablespoon light soy sauce
F. salt and pepper to taste

PREPARATION:

I. Beat C slightly.

COOKING:

1. Heat A, add B, stir-fry a few seconds.
2. Add C, stir like scrambled eggs. When egg is almost done, add D; stir well 1 to 2 minutes

over medium heat.
3. Add E, mix well.
4. Add F and serve.

FRIED RICE
Chao Fan: General 炒 飯

A. 2 eggs
B. 3 tablespoons peanut oil
C. 1 small onion, sliced
D. 1 clove garlic, minced
E. ¼ lb. shrimp
F. ½ cup frozen peas

G. ½ cup diced cooked ham (or pork)
H. 2 cups cold cooked rice
I. 1 tablespoon light soy sauce
J. salt and pepper to taste
K. 1 scallion

PREPARATION:

I. Beat A.
II. Shell and clean E; cut into small pieces.

III. Chop K thin.

COOKING:

1. Scramble A in 1 tablespoon B. Set aside.
2. Put remaining B into very hot skillet and heat. Fry C, D until golden brown.
3. Add E; cook ½ minute.
4. Add F, G; stir continuously and cook until F is heated through.

5. Add A; stir well.
6. Add H, I, J. Mix well; cook until H is heated through.
7. Garnish with K.
8. Serve hot.

YANGCHOW FRIED RICE
Chao Fan: Yangchow 楊 州 炒 飯

A. 5 tablespoons peanut oil
B. ½ cup diced medium frozen shrimp
C. ½ cup diced cooked chicken
D. ½ cup diced cooked ham or Cantonese roast pork
E. ½ cup frozen peas
F. ½ cup diced bamboo shoots

G. 4 Chinese mushrooms
H. 2 eggs
I. 4 cups cold cooked rice
J. 1 tablespoon sherry
K. 2 tablespoons light soy sauce
L. salt, pepper to taste

PREPARATION:

I. Add dash of L and 1 teaspoon J to B.
II. Wash G, soak in warm water 15 minutes; drain and dice.

III. Mix C, D, E, F, G.
IV. Beat H.
V. Mix remaining J, K.

COOKING:

1. Heat 3 tablespoons A in frying pan. When hot, stir-fry B 30 seconds.
2. Add C–G, stir-fry 2 to 3 minutes; put aside.

3. Heat remaining A, add H, and scramble.
4. Add I, J, K and stir over low heat.
5. Add B–G, mix thoroughly. Add L. Serve hot.

SAUCES, ETC.

Chinese sauces are numerous and very exotic. Many sauces emanate directly from the dish being prepared. However, some are prepared in advance and are added to a dish either as a flavor enhancer or they are eaten in conjunction with particular foods.

HOT OIL SAUCE
Hung Yo: Szechuan　　　　　　　　　　紅 油

A. 1 to 2 red-hot peppers　　　　　　　B. ¼ cup salad oil

PREPARATION:

I. Wash A, dry with paper towels. Remove A stems and seeds, cut into 1-inch pieces.

COOKING:

1. Heat B to 375°, add A, cook 1 to 2 minutes.　The longer A remains, the hotter B will be. To
2. Remove from heat, leaving A in B until cold.　use, remove A.

HOT SESAME OIL SAUCE
La Ma Yo: Szechuan　　　　　　　　辣 麻 油

Substitute sesame oil for B and leave A in B 3 to 4 days.

HOT SAVORY SAUCE
La Fu Jiang: Shanghai

辣 糊 醬

A. 3 tablespoons vegetable oil
B. ¼ cup diced dried shrimp
C. 3 slices ginger, minced
D. 2 lbs. pork chops
E. 4 cakes pressed bean curd
F. 4- to 6-oz. can bamboo shoots
G. 8 Chinese black mushrooms

H. 3 tablespoons hoisin sauce
I. 1 tablespoon light soy sauce
J. 1 teaspoon hot red pepper, or to taste
K. 1 tablespoon sherry
L. 1 tablespoon cornstarch mixed with 2 tablespoons water
M. salt to taste

PREPARATION:

I. Bone D, cut D, E, F into ½-inch cubes.
II. Wash B, G, soak in hot water 15 minutes or until soft; drain, combine waters and save.

Cut B and G into ½-inch pieces.
III. Mix H, I, J, K, adding ¼ cup water from B, G.

COOKING:

1. Heat A in casserole or heavy pot; stir-fry B, C 1 to 2 minutes. Add D and stir-fry 1 minute.
2. Add E, F, G, and H–K; cover and simmer 30 minutes, adding more water if needed.
3. Add L to thicken; sauce should be like gravy but not soupy. Adjust with M and serve with noodles or rice.

RED HOT PEPPER OIL
Hung La Yo: Szechuan

紅 辣 油

A. ¼ cup peanut oil   B. 1 tablespoon ground cayenne (red pepper)   C. 2 teaspoons sesame oil

COOKING:

1. Heat A to 375°, remove from heat.
2. Add B, stir well; cool.
3. Add C, mix thoroughly.
4. Line funnel with a piece of tissue paper and place over a small jar. Pour A mixture in and let it drip into jar. It can be served with any dish that requires a hot sauce, or add few drops to a noodle dish or fried rice.

ANISE PEPPER SALT
Jiao Yen: Szechuan

椒 鹽

A. 1 teaspoon anise pepper

B. 1 tablespoon salt

PREPARATION:

I. Brown A in ungreased pan over medium heat until the fragrance is strong and the color is dark brown (3 to 5 minutes).
II. Grind A with pepper grinder.

III. Mix with B and serve with meat and poultry dishes. Anise pepper salt can be kept indefinitely.

RED OIL SAUCE
Hung Yo: Hunan

紅 油

A. 2 lbs. red-hot peppers   **B.** 1½ qts. water

PREPARATION:

I. Shred A, removing stems (do not discard seeds) ; chop A fine.

COOKING:

1. Combine A, B, bring to boil, simmer until A disintegrates. Strain mixture through fine strainer and boil down sauce by continuous simmering until only red oil remains.

GINGER JUICE
Jiang Tze: General

薑 汁

A. 6 chunks ginger, about thumb size in length and breadth

PREPARATION:

I. Peel skin from ginger and wash chunks.

II. Pound A in mortar with pestle (if available) until it turns mushy, or cut up and mince in blender.

III. Remove to a piece of gauze and squeeze out the juice into a cup.

This recipe will make about 1 tablespoonful Ginger Juice.

GINGER TEA
Jiang Tsa: Shanghai

薑 茶

A. 1 large ginger root   **B.** 3 to 4 tablespoons brown sugar

PREPARATION:

I. Peel and slice A into half-dollar-size pieces.

COOKING:

Place A, B, in pot and add 3 cups water. Bring to boil and allow to simmer 5 minutes. Serve hot. This is always served after eating crab or lobster.

SALADS

Salads are very common and popular in China. However, it is only within the last few years that they have been served at Chinese restaurants here. The dressing is mainly based on a proportionate amount of salt, vinegar, and sugar, with a small amount of sesame oil as flavoring agent.

SWEET AND SOUR COLD RADISHES
Lun Ban Shiao Lo Bo: Peking

冷 拌 蘿 蔔

A. 30 radishes
B. 3 tablespoons vinegar
C. 3 tablespoons light soy sauce

D. 1 tablespoon sugar
E. sesame oil to taste
F. ¼ teaspoon MSG (optional)

PREPARATION:

I. Remove tops and tails of A.
II. Crush each A with blow from the side of a cleaver.
III. Mix B, C, D.
IV. Place A in deep serving bowl.

V. Add B–D. Mix well.
VI. Refrigerate 1 to 2 hours.
VII. Add E, F to taste and serve.

172

PEKING SALAD
Ban San Si: Peking　　　　　拌 三 絲

A. 1 large kohlrabi
B. 1 carrot
C. ½ cup shredded celery cabbage
D. 1½ teaspoons salt

E. ½ teaspoon anise pepper
F. ½ teaspoon sesame oil
G. ½ cup chopped Chinese parsley
H. ¼ teaspoon MSG (optional)

PREPARATION:

I. Peel A, B, slice very thin, then shred.
II. Wash G.
III. Mix A, B, C, D, E thoroughly, marinate

vegetables 30 to 45 minutes.
IV. Pour off excess water, add F, G, H. Mix well and serve.

KOHLRABI SALAD
Pieh La (Liang Ban Da To Tsai) : Peking　　涼 拌 大 頭 荣

A. 1 lb. kohlrabi
B. ¼ cup vinegar
C. 3 tablespoons sugar

D. 1 teaspoon salt
E. 1 teaspoon sesame oil
F. ½ teaspoon MSG (optional)

PREPARATION:

I. Peel A and shred.
II. Mix B, C, D, E thoroughly.

III. Add A to B–F, mix again, let stand a few minutes and serve.

AGAR AGAR SALAD
Lun Ban Liang Tsai: Peking　　　冷 拌 涼 荣

A. 2 tablespoons peanut oil
B. 1 chicken breast
C. 2 oz. agar agar
D. 1 to 2 small tender cucumbers
E. 2 tablespoons light soy sauce
F. 1 to 1½ tablespoons vinegar

G. 1 to 2 teaspoons sesame oil
H. dash mustard
I. ½ egg white
J. 1 teaspoon cornstarch
K. ¼ teaspoon salt
L. ¼ teaspoon MSG (optional)

PREPARATION:

I. Bone B, discard skin and shred, mix with I, J, K.
II. Wash D, cut diagonally in ⅛-inch slices, then shred.

III. Cut C into pieces 1 to 2 inches long, wash in cold water. When strips are separated from each other, rinse and drain.
IV. Mix E, F, G, H.

COOKING:

1. Heat A, add B, stir-fry 1 to 2 minutes. Drain and cool.
2. Place C in dish, top with A–B.

3. Place D on top of A–B.
4. Pour E–H over all; add L and serve.

KIDNEY SALAD
Liang Ban Yao Pien: Peking

涼 拌 腰 花

A. 1 tablespoon sherry
B. 1 scallion
C. 1 to 2 slices ginger
D. 4 pork kidneys
E. 1 tablespoon light soy sauce
F. 1 tablespoon peanut butter
G. 1 teaspoon sesame seed paste

from Chinese grocery
H. 1 teaspoon sugar
I. ½ to 1 teaspoon sesame oil
J. 2 teaspoons vinegar
K. salt, pepper to taste
L. 1 cucumber
M. ½ teaspoon MSG (optional)

PREPARATION:

I. Wash D and remove any outer membrane; split lengthwise; use sharp scissors to remove all white veins. Rub with salt and squeeze out any blood, rinse with water. Cover with cold water and soak 1 to 2 hours.

II. Drain, slice into thin pieces, rub again with salt, and rinse.

III. Split L, remove seeds, dip in boiling water mixed with 1 teaspoon salt for a few seconds. Cut into thin slices, drain.

IV. Arrange L in dish. (Pour off any excess water before serving.)

V. Mix E, F, G, H, I, J, K, M thoroughly.

COOKING:

1. To 1 qt. water add A, B, C, bring to boil.
2. Add D when water comes to boil again, turn off heat, keep stirring 20 seconds, drain.

3. Mix A–D with E–K, M, and marinate 5 to 10 minutes.
4. Pour on top of L and serve.

CELERY TOSSED SHRIMP SALAD I
Sha Mi Ban Ching Tsai: Peking

蝦 米 拌 芹 菜

A. 10 to 12 large dried shrimp
B. 1 tablespoon sherry
C. 1 small celery heart
D. 2 teaspoons sesame oil

E. ½ teaspoon anise pepper
F. 1 teaspoon salt
G. ¼ teaspoon MSG (optional)

PREPARATION AND COOKING:

I. Clean and wash A, soak in B 20 to 30 minutes, drain.

II. Wash C, cut into 1-inch diagonal pieces, dip into boiling water for a minute; drain and cool.

III. Heat D very hot, fry E until dark brown, discard E; mix in F, G.

IV. Mix all ingredients and serve.

CELERY TOSSED SHRIMP SALAD II
Sha Tze Ban Ching Tsai: Peking

蝦 子 拌 芹 菜

A. 4 teaspoons sesame oil
B. ½ cup diced shelled shrimp
C. 1 celery heart

D. 2 tablespoons light soy sauce
E. 1 tablespoon vinegar
F. ¼ teaspoon MSG (optional)

PREPARATION AND COOKING:

I. Wash C and cut diagonally into 1-inch pieces. Parboil 1 minute, drain, cool.

II. Heat A and stir-fry B 1 to 2 minutes.

III. Add B to C.

IV. Add D–F, mix well and serve.

DRAGON WHISKERS SALAD
Lun Ban Lung Shu Tsai: Shanghai 冷 拌 龍 鬚 菜

A. 1 lb. asparagus
B. 1 tablespoon vinegar
C. 1 tablespoon sugar

D. 1 teaspoon salt
E. 1 teaspoon sesame oil
F. ¼ teaspoon MSG (optional)

PREPARATION AND COOKING:

I. Break each green and tender (edible) part of A into 2-inch pieces. Wash.
II. Pour 1 qt. boiling water over A and cook 4 minutes, uncovered.

III. Drain, run under cold water a few seconds.
IV. Mix B–F well, add to A. Let stand a few minutes before serving.

BEAN SPROUT SALAD
Lun Ban Nying Ya: Shanghai 冷 拌 銀 芽

A. ½ lb. bean sprouts
B. 3 scallions, chopped
C. 1 teaspoon salt
D. 2 teaspoons light soy sauce

E. ¼ cup vinegar
F. ¼ cup sugar
G. 1 teaspoon sesame oil
H. ½ teaspoon MSG (optional)

PREPARATION:

I. Wash A thoroughly.

II. Combine C, D, E, F, G, H; mix well.

COOKING:

1. Put A into 1 qt. boiling water. Let stand 30 seconds. Drain.
2. Rinse A under running cold water until thoroughly cold. Drain well.

3. Mix A, B. Just before serving, add C–H; mix well.

LITCHI ROAST DUCK SALAD
Lun Ban La-ee-tzee Ya: Shanghai 冷 拌 荔 枝 鴨

A. ½ Cantonese roasted duck
B. 1 teaspoon sesame oil
C. 2 teaspoons light soy sauce

D. 20 fresh litchis
E. few leaves Chinese parsley
F. ¼ teaspoon MSG (optional)

PREPARATION:

I. Bone A, shred, mix with B, C, place on a platter.
II. Discard skin and pits of D and cut in quar-

ters; spread on top of A.
III. Garnish with E, F.

PEANUT AND PRESSED BEAN CURD SALAD
Hwa Sun Mi Do Fu Gahn: Shanghai 花 生 米 豆 腐 乾

A. 8 ozs. roasted peanuts (in shell)
B. 2 cakes pressed bean curd, diced
C. 2 stalks celery, diced

D. 1 tablespoon light soy sauce
E. ½ to 1 teaspoon sesame oil
F. ½ teaspoon MSG (optional)

PREPARATION:

I. Shell and skin A.

II. Combine all ingredients, mix well, serve.

PRESSED BEAN CURD SALAD
Ching Tsai Ban Gahn Si: Shanghai

芹 荣 乾 絲

A. 6 cakes pressed bean curd
B. 1 celery heart
C. 2 tablespoons vinegar
D. 2 tablespoons sugar

E. 1 tablespoon light soy sauce
F. 1 teaspoon sesame oil
G. ½ teaspoon salt
H. ½ teaspoon MSG (optional)

PREPARATION:

I. Wash A, dry; cut into long, thin strips.
II. Wash B, cut diagonally into long, thin strips.
III. Mix A, B.

IV. Mix C, D, E, F, G, H.
V. Pour C–H over A–B. Combine well; serve.

TOSSED HOT SALAD
La Bai Tsai: Szechuan

辣 白 菜

A. 1 lb. celery cabbage
B. ½ to 1 teaspoon hot pepper flakes (to taste)
C. ¼ to ½ teaspoon anise pepper salt (see Index)
D. 2 teaspoons sugar

E. 1½ tablespoons vinegar
F. ½ to 1 teaspoon sesame oil (to taste)
G. 4 slices ginger
H. ¼ teaspoon MSG (optional)

PREPARATION:

I. Split A into half lengthwise; use only half cut crosswise into 1-inch pieces.
II. Bring 1 qt. water with ½ teaspoon salt to boil; add A stir in boiling water 2 minutes.

Turn off heat and drain.
III. Shred G very thin.
IV. Mix B, C, D, E, F, G, H.
V. Mix A, B–H, and serve.

DESSERT

The Chinese generally do not serve dessert at the end of a meal but rather in the middle or sometimes as late as the second to the last dish. It is usually followed by a major dish, such as steamed duck or pork. The Chinese find that a sweet dish between courses serves as a change of pace from the salty and highly seasoned main dishes. However, this custom varies from region to region. In Szechuan, for example, dessert is sometimes served after a meal.

Few Chinese restaurants in America offer much in the way of authentic Chinese desserts. For this reason many Americans are unfamiliar with sweet Chinese dishes, and comparatively few such recipes are found in American-Chinese cookbooks.

During the Chinese New Year festival, it is customary to offer a guest tea with mixed, sweet preserved fruits, or with such other delicacies as kumquats, melon, lotus seeds, lotus roots, and dates— to wish him a year filled with sweetness.

STEAMED FRUIT NUT MIX
Ba Bao Yang Ping Go: Peking

八 寶 蘋 果

A. 5 cooking apples
B. ¼ teaspoon salt
C. ¼ cup sugar
D. ¼ cup canned sliced peaches

E. 3 tablespoons raisins
F. 2 tablespoons shelled walnuts
G. 2 tablespoons sugared winter melon
H. 2 tablespoons blanched, shelled almonds

PREPARATION:

I. Core and peel A, place in large shallow bowl.
II. Sprinkle B on A. Then sprinkle on half of C.
III. Mix D, remaining C and E, F, G, H.

IV. Pour all over A.
V. Cover bowl with aluminum foil.

COOKING:

1. Steam dish in steamer 30 minutes.

FRIED FRUIT PUFFS
Ruan Dza Go Jiu: Peking   軟 炸 果 球

A.   1 cup pitted dates
B.   ½ cup raisins
C.   ¼ cup dried apricots
D.   ¼ cup peanut butter
E.   ¼ teaspoon salt
F.   1 teaspoon sugar

G.   2 teaspoons sesame seeds
H.   2 egg whites
I.   ½ cup cornstarch
J.   red food coloring (few drops)
K.   vegetable oil for deep frying

PREPARATION:
I. Chop or grind A, B, C.
II. Mix with D, E, F, G.

III. Mix H, I, J.
IV. Roll A–G into 30 to 40 balls; roll balls in H–J until coated.

COOKING:
1. Heat K to 375° and deep fry A–J.

APPLE FRITTERS
Ba Se Pin Goh: Peking   拔 絲 蘋 果

A.   2 cups peanut oil
B.   1 lb. apples (about 3)
C.   ½ cup sugar
D.   2 tablespoons water
E.   1 tablespoon peanut oil

F.   3 tablespoons flour
G.   2 egg whites
H.   1 tablespoon cornstarch
I.   3 tablespoons flour

PREPARATION:
I. Peel B, discard seeds and cores, cut each into 8 pieces.
II. Place F in a paper bag, put in B and shake until B pieces are coated.

III. Mix G, H, I into a smooth batter.
IV. Coat each B with G–I.

COOKING:
1. Heat A to 375°, deep fry B until golden brown (about 2 to 3 minutes); remove to paper towel and drain.
2. Mix C, D, E in a saucepan, cook over medium heat until it forms long threads when dropped from spoon.
3. Add B, mix well, and spread out on platter.
4. Dip each piece in ice-cold water prior to eating.

DRAGON EYE AND LITCHI DESSERT
Mi Tong Lung Yien: Shanghai   米 湯 龍 眼

A.   ¼ cup rock sugar
B.   12 to 15 fresh (or canned) litchis

C.   24 fresh (or canned) longans
D.   1 cup rice

PREPARATION:
I. Wash and drain D. Cover with 1 qt. water, bring to boil, lower heat and cook 10 minutes. Pour about 2 cups rice water out and set aside. (Save rice for congee or serve with other dishes as is.)
II. Peel skins of fresh B, discard seeds, cut each in half. If canned litchis are used, simply cut each in half.

COOKING:
1. Bring rice water to boil, add A, stir until sugar dissolves.
2. Place A in bowl, add B, C, and serve.

SWEET CONGEE
Tien Shi Fan: Shanghai   甜 稀 飯

A. 20 dried lotus seeds
B. ½ cup glutinous rice
C. ½ cup dried longans or raisins

D. 10 Chinese or American dates
E. 2 tablespoons brown sugar

PREPARATION:

I. Cover A with hot water and soak for 30 to 45 minutes.
II. Place A, B in 3-qt. saucepan.

III. Add 2 qts. water.
IV. Add C, D.

COOKING:

1. Simmer 1 hour. Add 1½ to 2 cups water if needed.

2. When consistency is mushy, it is done. Add E.

SWEET CONGEE
Tien Tso: General   甜 粥

A. ½ cup glutinous rice
B. ½ cup raisins
C. ½ cup American dates

D. 2 tablespoons brown sugar
E. 6 Bing cherries

COOKING:

1. Put A, B, C in 3-qt. saucepan. Add 2 qts. water, simmer 1 hour.

2. Add 1½ to 2 cups water and D (optional). When congee is mushy and soft, serve in bowl, adding E on top for color.

HONEY WALNUTS
Mi Tze Hu Tao: Suchow   蜜 汁 核 桃

A. ½ lb. shelled walnut halves
B. ½ teaspoon salt
C. 2 tablespoons vegetable oil
D. 2 tablespoons honey

E. 2 teaspoons sugar
F. 1 teaspoon cornstarch mixed with 1 teaspoon water

PREPARATION AND COOKING:

1. Soak A in water with B until membrane peels easily; drain and air dry.
2. Heat C in frying pan; brown A in pan 2 minutes; drain oil from pan.

3. Mix D, E with A over medium heat. When well mixed, add F to thicken; serve hot or cold.

SILVER EARS WITH TANGERINES
Jing Jiu Ning Erh: Szechuan   金 橘 銀 耳

A. 15-oz. can white jelly fungus (silver ears) from Chinese grocery

B. 2 large fresh tangerines or oranges

PREPARATION:

I. Skin B, remove inside membrane and seeds; cut each segment into 2 to 3 pieces.

II. Open A and transfer to greaseless saucepan.

COOKING:

1. Bring A to boil.

2. Add B, bring to boil and serve.

STEAMED CHINESE CAKE
Tsen Don Gow: General

蒸 蛋 糕

A. 7 eggs
B. 1½ cups sugar
C. ¾ cup peanut oil
D. 3 cups self-rising flour
E. 1 cup milk
F. 1 teaspoon vanilla extract

PREPARATION:

I. Separate A whites from yolks.
II. Beat yolks and add B gradually.
III. Add C and mix well.
IV. Mix in D alternately with E; beat well.
V. Add F.
VI. Beat A whites until very stiff peaks are formed.

VII. Slowly pour B yolk mixture over whites, folding in mixture gently with rubber spatula until yolk mixture is just blended.
VIII. Line bottom of steam basket with cheesecloth, pour cake mixture in.

COOKING:

1. Steam over boiling water 45 minutes. Cake may be served hot or cold, and may be frozen.

ALMOND COOKIES
Shing Ren Bing: General

杏 仁 餅

A. ¼ cup lard
B. 1 cup sugar
C. 2 tablespoons vegetable oil
D. ¼ teaspoon sesame oil
E. 1 egg
F. 1 cup rice flour
G. 1 teaspoon baking powder
H. ½ teaspoon salt
I. ⅓ cup finely chopped almonds
J. 1 teaspoon almond extract

PREPARATION:

I. Cream A, B together thoroughly. Add C, D, E, beat until fluffy.
II. Sift together F, G, H, add to A–E, mix well.

III. Add I, J (reserving half of I for topping); mix well.
IV. Form dough into balls 1 inch in diameter. Top each with a bit of I.

COOKING:

1. Place balls 2 inches apart on greased cooky sheet.

2. Bake 20 minutes in 350° oven. Makes 2 dozen cookies.

ALMOND BEAN CURD WITH PINEAPPLE, CHERRIES, AND LITCHIS
Han Yen Do Fu Bo Lo: General

杏 仁 豆 腐

A. 1 envelope unflavored gelatin
B. 3 tablespoons cold water
C. ½ cup evaporated milk
D. 1¼ cups water
E. 3 tablespoons sugar
F. 2 teaspoons almond extract
G. 1 can litchis with juice
H. ⅓ cup maraschino cherries
I. ½ cup pineapple chunks

PREPARATION AND COOKING:

I. Mix A, B well in a saucepan.
II. Place over low heat, stir until A is dissolved.
III. Add C, D, E, stir until E is completely dissolved.

IV. Add F, mix well.
V. Pour into 9- by 5- by 2½-inch dish and refrigerate.
VI. When set, cut into cubes, mix with G, H, I.

EIGHT PRECIOUS RICE PUDDING
Ba Bao Fan: General

八　寶　飯

A. 1½ cups glutinous rice
B. 2 tablespoons mixed candied
    fruit
C. 2 tablespoons raisins
D. 2 tablespoons chopped pitted
    dates
E. 12 maraschino cherries
F. 1 cup sweet bean filling
    (do sa)

G. ¼ cup sugar
H. 1 cup water
I. ¼ cup milk
J. 1 tablespoon cornstarch
K. 1 teaspoon almond extract
L. butter or margarine for
    greasing bowl

PREPARATON:

I. Cover A with water and soak overnight. Drain. Cover steamer with cheesecloth, spread A on top, and steam over boiling water 10 minutes.

II. Grease a 7-inch bowl with L. Place B in a small circle at the bottom of the bowl. Then arrange C, D, E, F, in a flower pattern.

III. Place half of A over B–F. Add G.

IV. Cover G with rest of A, spreading it evenly.

COOKING:

1. Place bowl in steamer over boiling water and steam for 45 minutes.

2. Turn pudding upside down on platter.

3. Mix H, I, J, K in pot and bring to a boil, stirring constantly until it thickens. Add L, stir well. Pour over hot pudding and serve.

Index